EASY GUITAR
WITH NOTES & TAB

THE CONTEMPORARY
CHRISTIAN
COLLECTION

ISBN 978-1-4234-9436-2

HAL•LEONARD®
CORPORATION

7777 W. BLUEMOUND RD. P.O. BOX 13819 MILWAUKEE, WI 53213

Visit Hal Leonard Online at
www.halleonard.com

CONTENTS

STRUM AND PICK PATTERNS

This chart contains the suggested strum and pick patterns that are referred to by number at the beginning of each song in this book. The symbols ⊓ and ∨ in the strum patterns refer to down and up strokes, respectively. The letters in the pick patterns indicate which right-hand fingers play which strings.

p = thumb
i = index finger
m = middle finger
a = ring finger

For example; Pick Pattern 2
is played: thumb - index - middle - ring

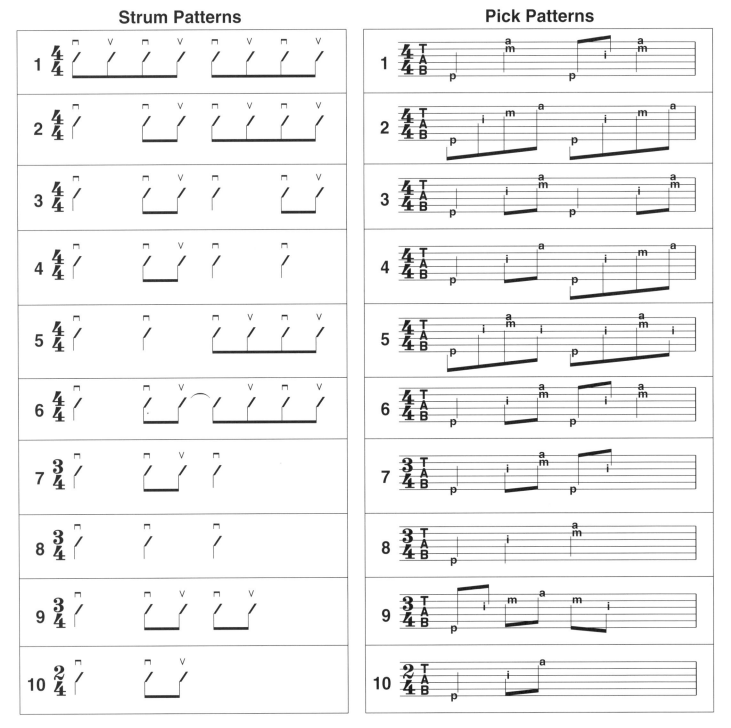

You can use the 3/4 Strum and Pick Patterns in songs written in compound meter (6/8, 9/8, 12/8, etc.).
For example, you can accompany a song in 6/8 by playing the 3/4 pattern twice in each measure.
The 4/4 Strum and Pick Patterns can be used for songs written in cut time (¢) by doubling the note time values in the patterns. Each pattern would therefore last two measures in cut time.

Alive Again

Words and Music by Matt Maher and Jason Ingram

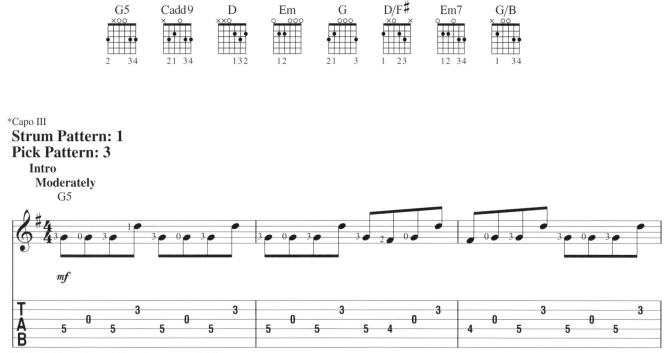

*Capo III

Strum Pattern: 1
Pick Pattern: 3

Intro
Moderately

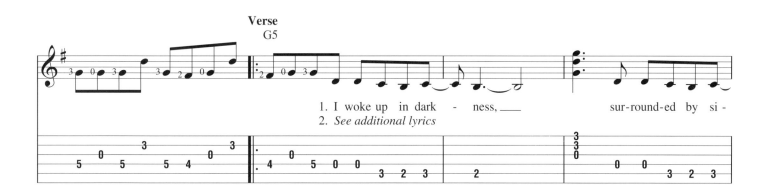

*Optional: To match recording, place capo at 3rd fret.

1. I woke up in dark - ness, ___ sur-round-ed by si -
2. *See additional lyrics*

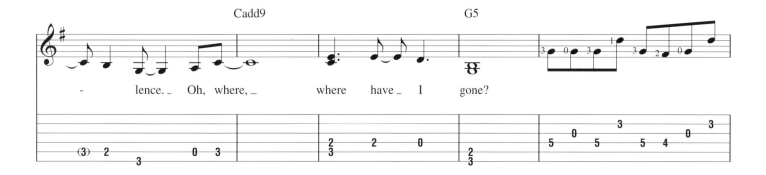

- lence. ___ Oh, where, ___ where have ___ I gone?

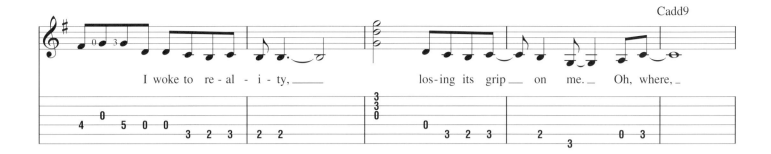

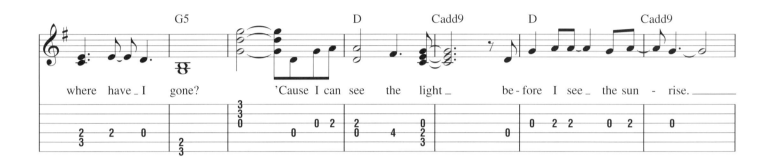

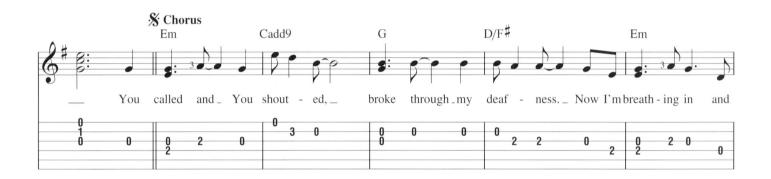

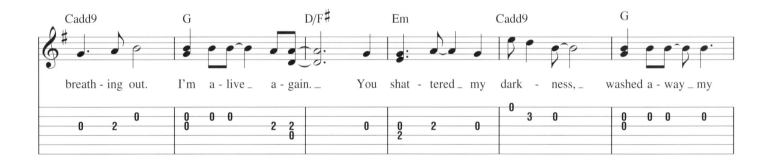

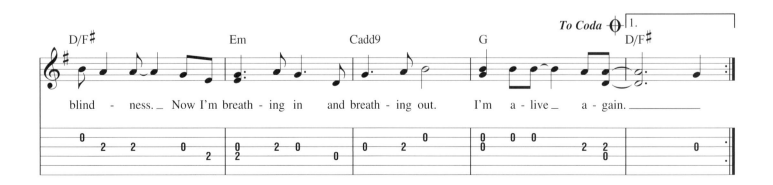

I'm a-live __ a-gain. __

Bridge

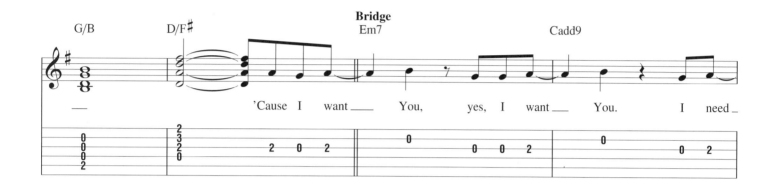

'Cause I want __ You, yes, I want __ You. I need __

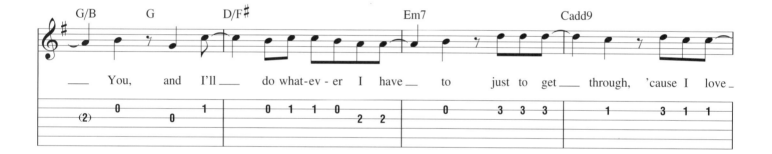

__ You, and I'll __ do what-ev-er I have __ to just to get __ through, 'cause I love __

D.S. al Coda

Coda

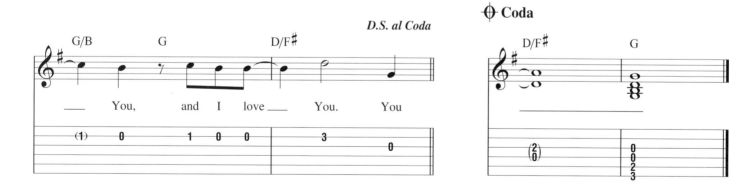

__ You, and I love __ You. You

Additional Lyrics

2. Late have I loved You.
   You waited for me, I searched for You.
   What took me so long?
   I was looking outside,
   As if love would ever want to hide.
   I'm finding I was wrong.
   'Cause I can feel the wind before it hits my skin.

All Around Me

Words and Music by Sameer Bhattacharya, Jared Hartmann,
Kirkpatrick Seals, James Culpepper and Lacey Mosley

*Let chord ring.

1. My hands are search - ing for ___ You. My arms are out - stretched towards _ You. I

feel You on __ my fin - ger - tips. __ My tongue danc - es __ be - hind __ my lips __ for You. __

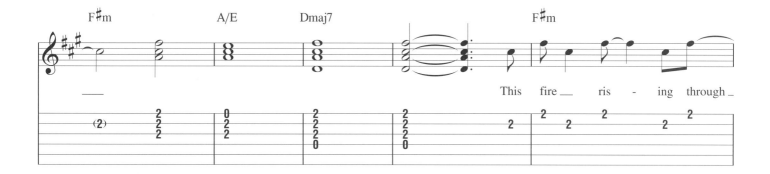

__ This fire __ ris - ing through __

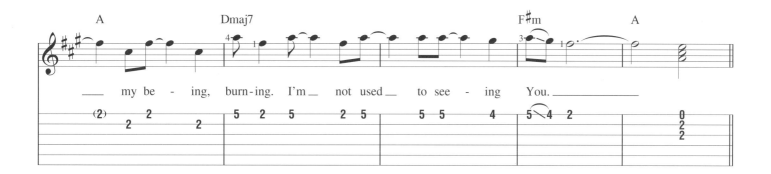

__ my be - ing, burn-ing. I'm __ not used __ to see - ing You.

Pre-Chorus

I'm a - live. __ I'm a - live. __

*Sung one octave higher, next 5 meas.

𝄋 Chorus

__ I can feel You all a - round me thick - en - ing the

**As before, next 8 meas.

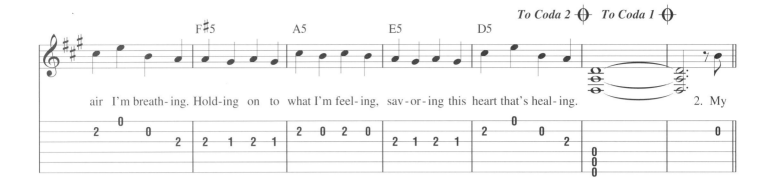

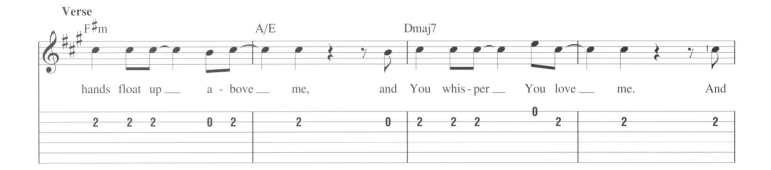

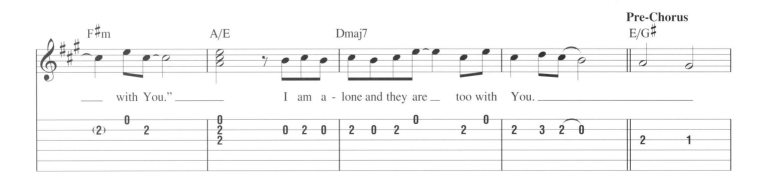

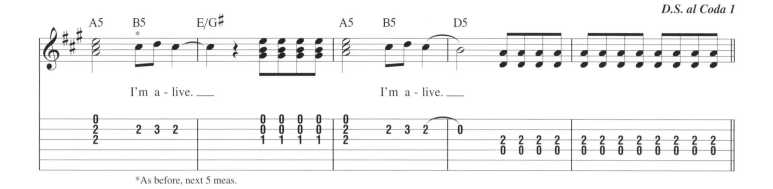

*As before, next 5 meas.

Coda 1

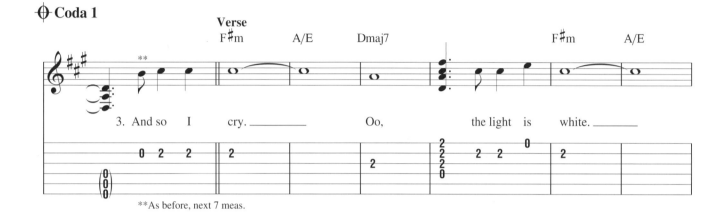

**As before, next 7 meas.

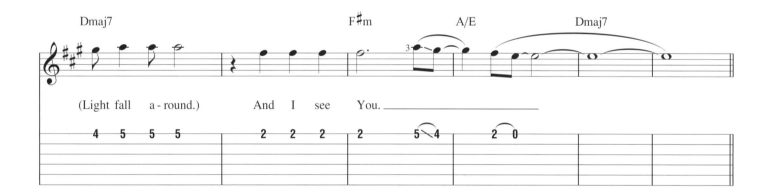

***As before, next 7 meas.

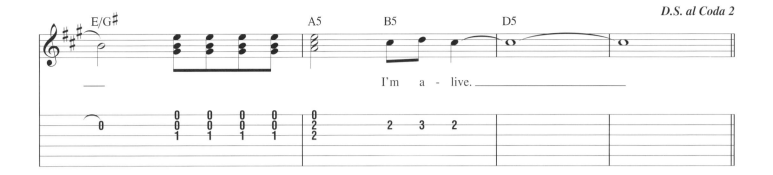

Coda 2

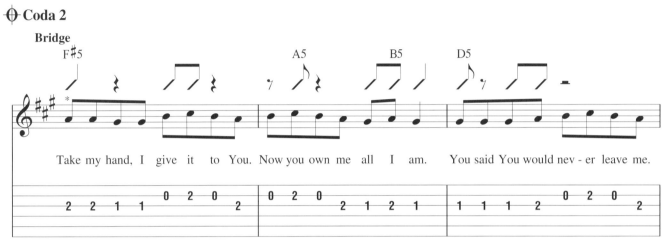

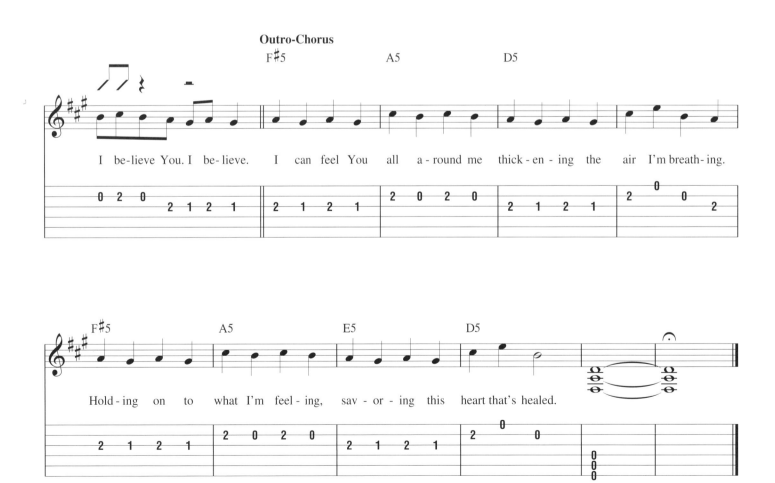

City on Our Knees

Words and Music by Toby McKeehan, James Moore and Cary Barlowe

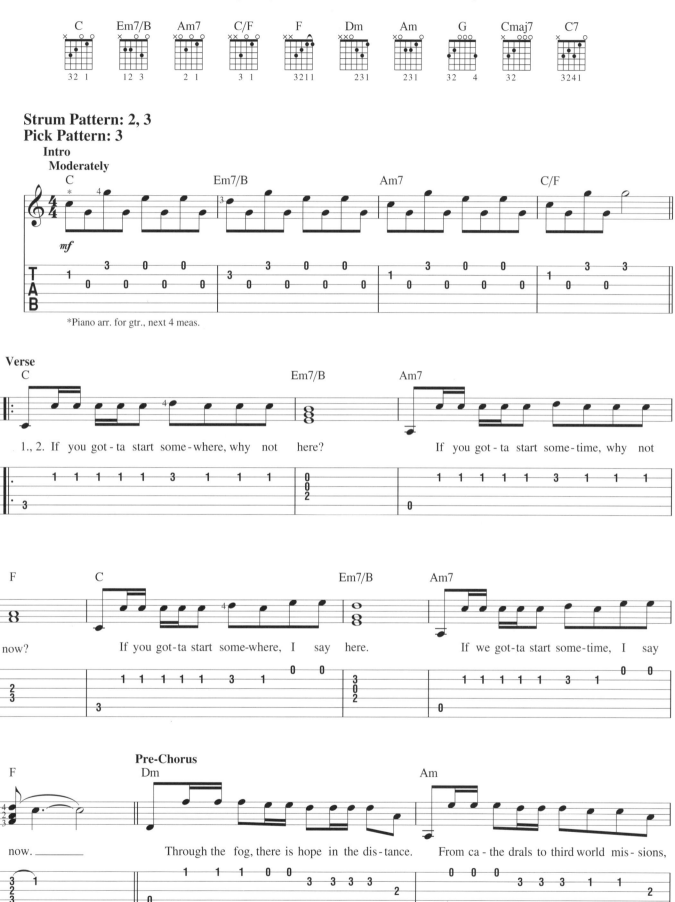

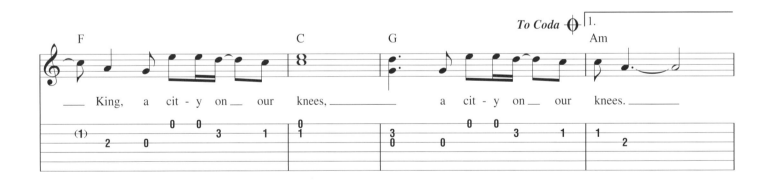

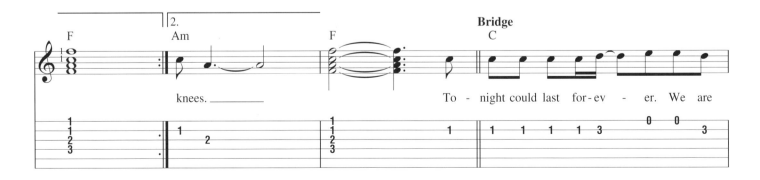

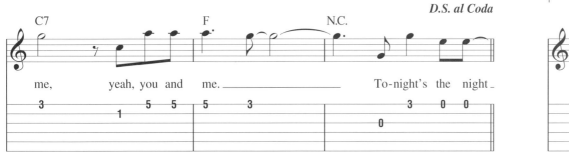

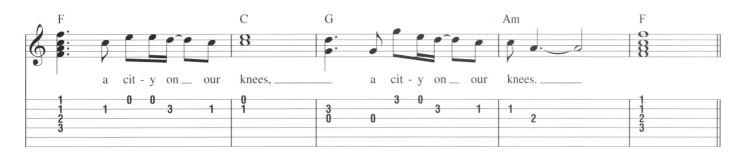

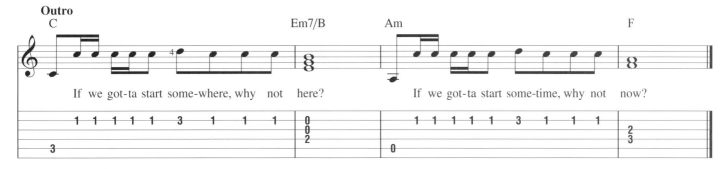

All Because of Jesus

Words and Music by Steve Fee

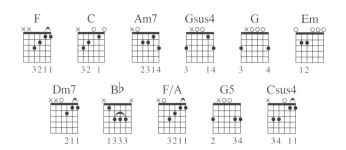

Strum Pattern: 2
Pick Pattern: 3

Verse

Moderately

1. Giv - er of ev - (2.) 'ry breath _ I breathe, _ au - thor of all ___ e - ter - ni - ty, _

___ giv - er of ev - 'ry per - fect thing, _ to You be the glo - ry.

Mak - er of heav - en and _ of earth, _ no one can com - pre - hend _ Your worth. _

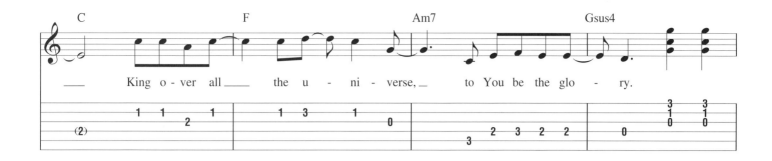

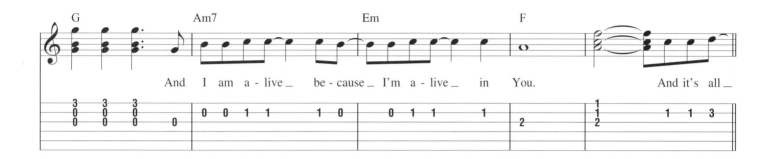

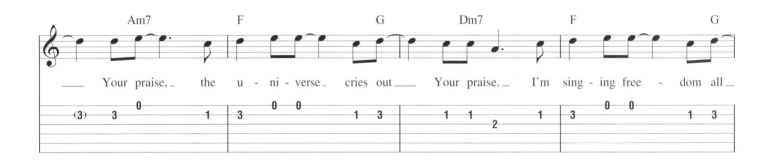

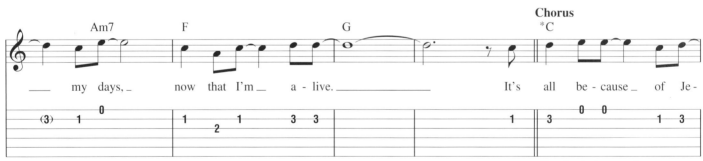

*Let chords ring, next 8 meas.

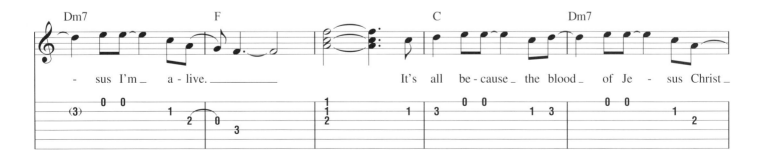

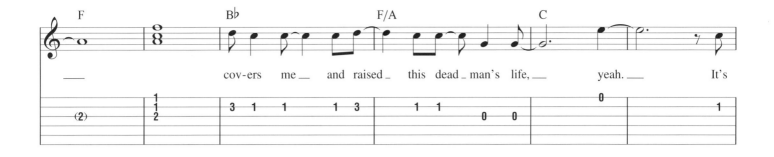

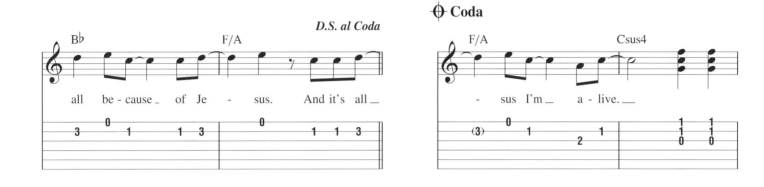

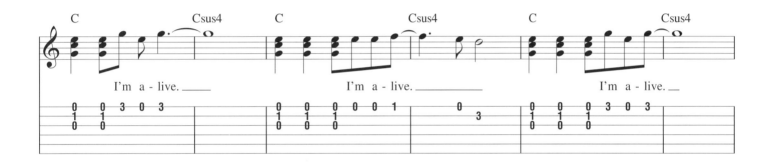

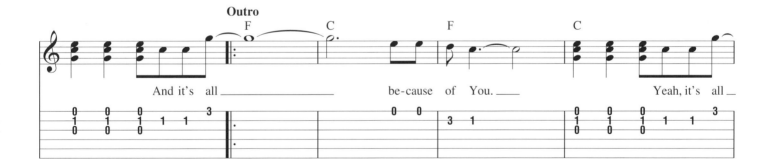

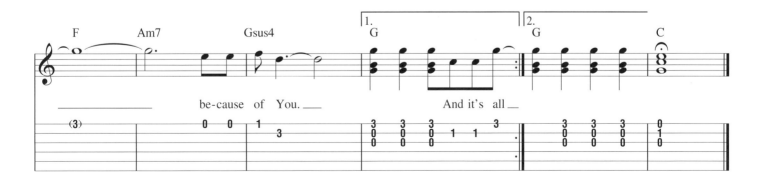

19

All to You

Words and Music by Lincoln Brewster and Reid McNulty

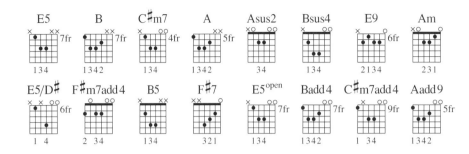

Strum Pattern: 1
Pick Pattern: 3

Intro
Moderately

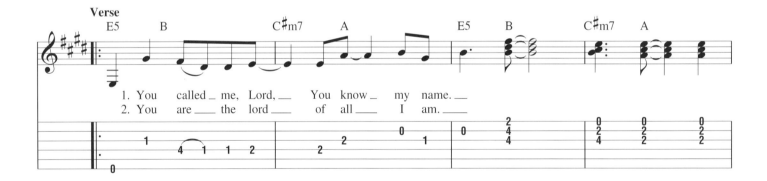

Verse

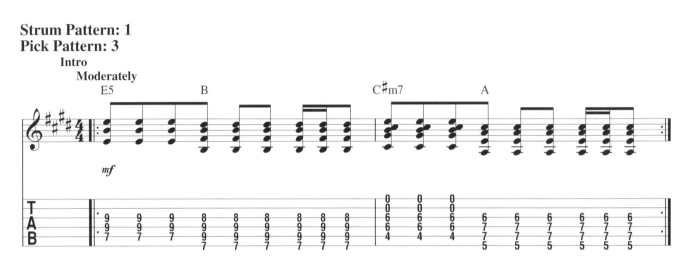

1. You called me, Lord, You know my name.
2. You are the lord of all I am.

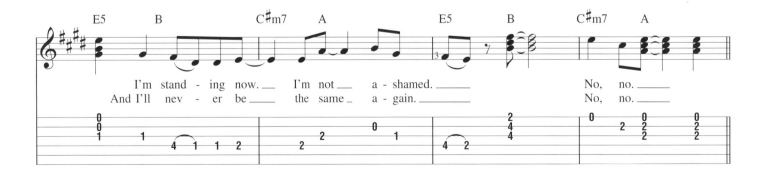

I'm stand-ing now. I'm not a-shamed. No, no.
And I'll nev-er be the same a-gain. No, no.

Pre-Chorus

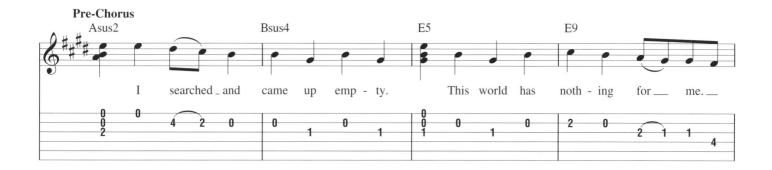

I searched and came up emp - ty. This world has noth - ing for me.

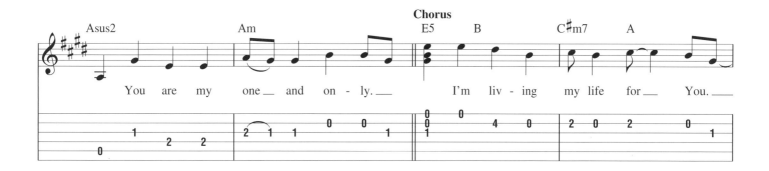

You are my one and on - ly. **Chorus** I'm liv - ing my life for You.

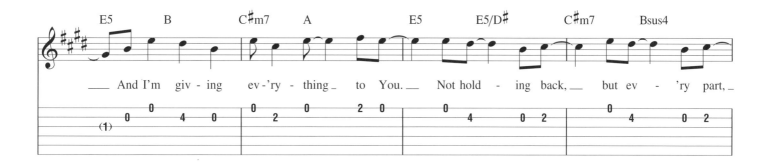

And I'm giv - ing ev - 'ry - thing to You. Not hold - ing back, but ev - 'ry part,

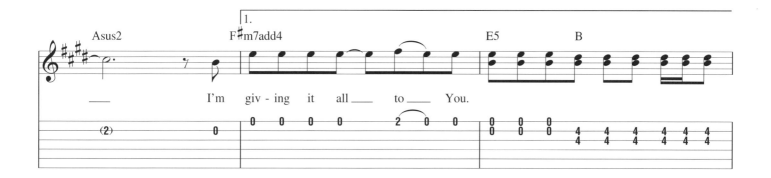

I'm giv - ing it all to You.

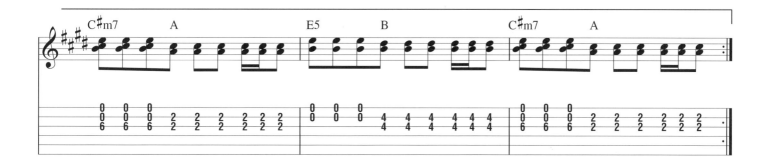

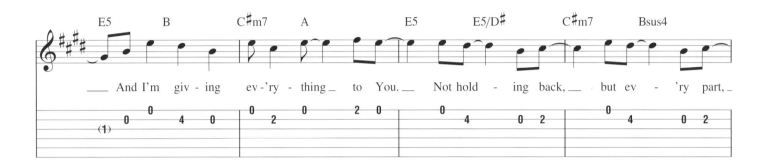

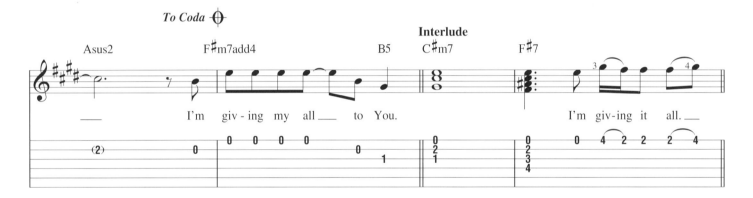

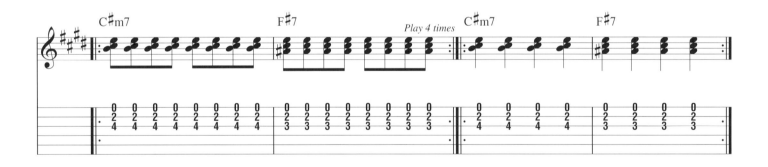

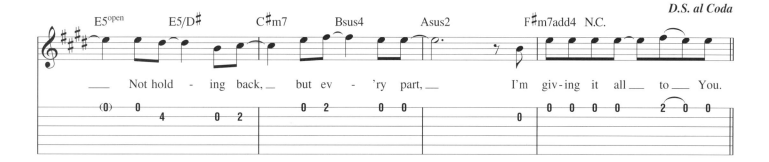

Coda

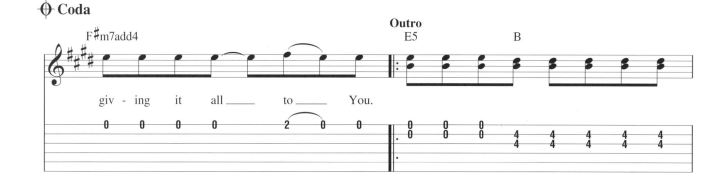

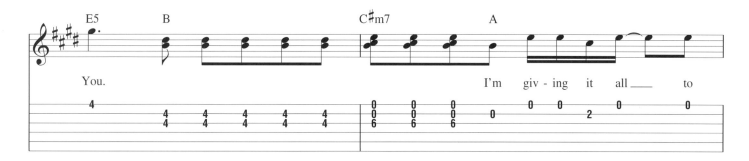

Beautiful

Words and Music by Mark Stuart, Will McGinniss, Bob Herdman, Tyler Burkum and Ben Cissell

Strum Pattern: 2, 5
Pick Pattern: 1

Intro
Moderately

*Muffled strings: lay the fret hand across the strings without
depressing, and strike them w/ the pick hand.

Ooh, beau-ti-ful. Ooh, You're beau-ti-ful. 1. We got

Verse

mu-sic to soothe your soul. We're gon-na get down with a lit-tle bit of rock and roll.
2. *See additional lyrics*

We got rhy-thm to move your feet. We're gon-na

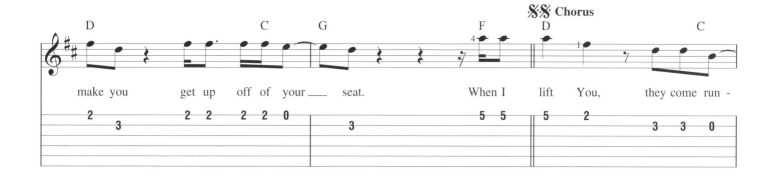

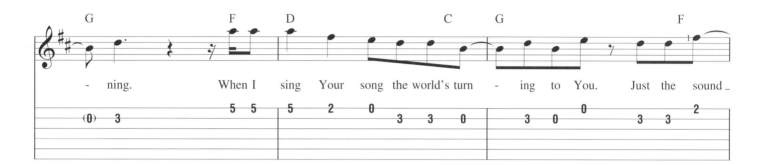

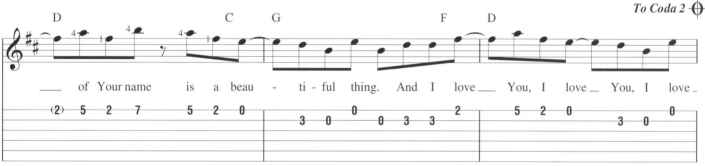

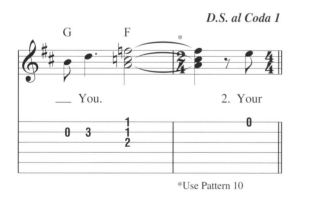

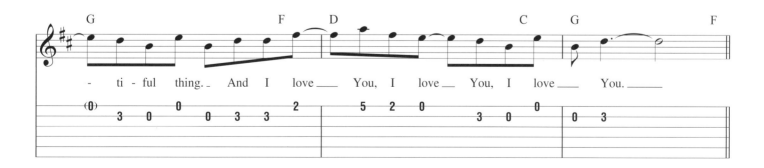

Interlude

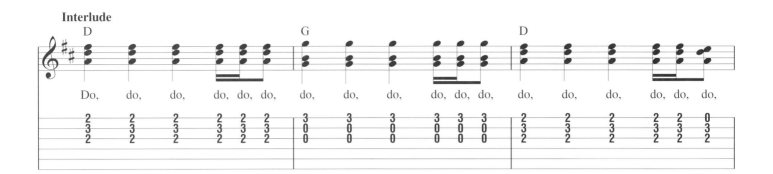

Do, do, do, do, do, do, do, do, do, do, do, do, do, do, do, do, do, do,

Bridge

do. When I lift You up, they come run - nin'. When I

sing Your song the world's turn - ing. Just the sound ___ of Your name is a beau -

D.S.S. al Coda 2

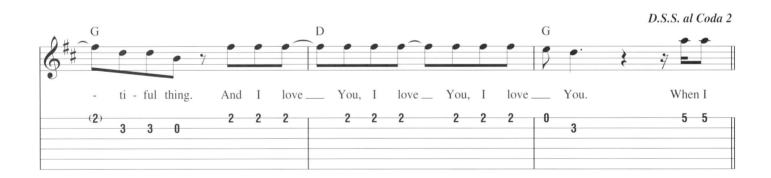

- ti - ful thing. And I love ___ You, I love ___ You, I love ___ You. When I

 Coda 2

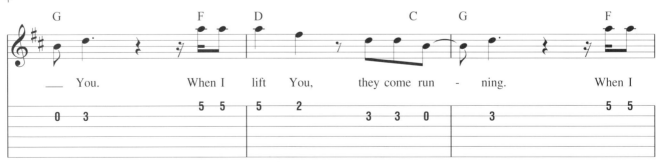

___ You. When I lift You, they come run - ning. When I

26

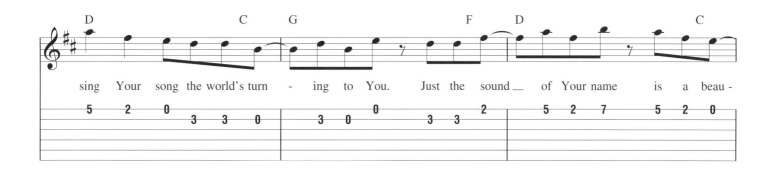

sing Your song the world's turn - ing to You. Just the sound __ of Your name is a beau -

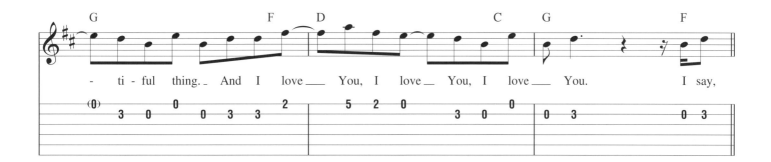

- ti - ful thing. __ And I love __ You, I love __ You, I love __ You. I say,

Outro

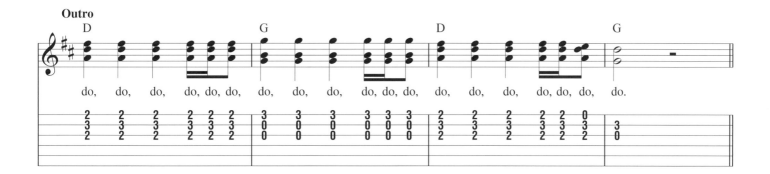

do, do, do, do, do, do, do, do, do, do, do, do, do, do, do, do, do, do, do.

Repeat and fade

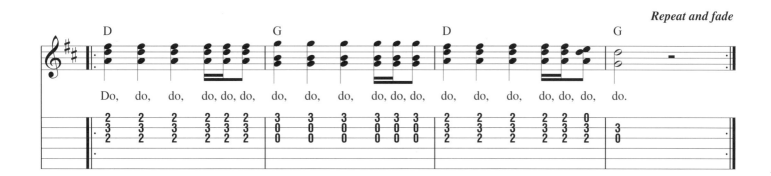

Do, do, do, do, do, do, do, do, do, do, do, do, do, do, do, do, do, do, do.

Additional Lyrics

2. Your name is beautiful
It drips off of my lips like drops of gold.
It makes me want to dance.
You're my treasure, my deliverance.

Big House

Words and Music by Mark Stuart, Barry Blair, Will McGinniss and Bob Herdman

D   E   D   A   E

ham-mock in the shade.

2.   **Chorus**

D   E   D   A   D

bet you wish you had.   Come   and go with me   to   my fath-er's house.

A   D   A

Come   and go with me   to   my fath-er's   house.   It's a big,   big

E   A   E

house   with lots and lots of   room.   A big, big   ta-ble   with lots and lots of

A   E   A   *To Coda 1*   *To Coda 2*   E   *To Coda 3*

food.   A big, big   yard   where we can play foot-ball.   A big, big   house.   It's my fath-er's

29

Guitar Solo

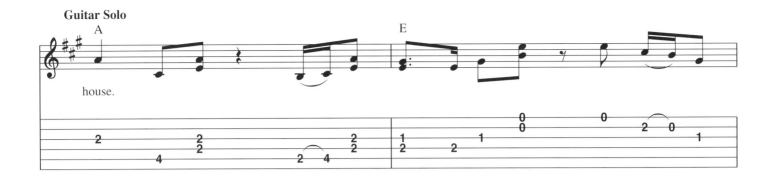

house.

D.S. al Coda 1
(take 2nd ending)

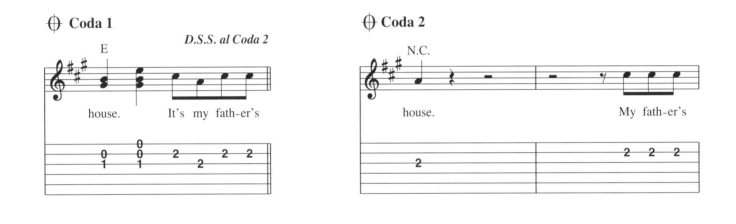

🎵 **Coda 1**

D.S.S. al Coda 2

🎵 **Coda 2**

house.   It's my fath-er's

house.   My fath-er's

house.   Come   and go with me __ to   my fath-er's house. __

Come   and go with me __ to my fath - er's house.   It's a big, big

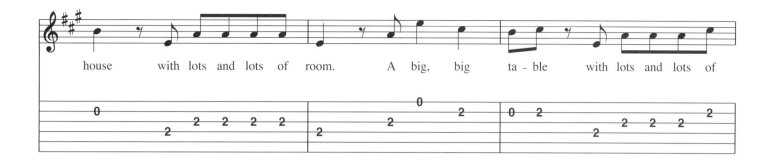

house   with lots and lots of room.   A   big,   big   ta - ble   with lots and lots of

D.S.S. al Coda 3

food.   A   big,   big   yard   where we can play foot - ball.   A   big,   big   house.   It's my fath - er's

Coda 3

house.

Additional Lyrics

2. I don't know if you got some shelter,
Say a place to hide.
I don't know if you live with friends
In whom you can confide.
I don't know if you got a fam'ly,
Say a mom or dad.
I don't know if you feel love at all
But I bet you wish you had.

3. All I know is a big ol' house
With rooms for ev'ryone.
All I know is alots of land
Where we can play and run.
All I know is that you need love
And I've got a family.
All I know is you're all alone,
So why not come with me?

Bring the Rain

Words and Music by Bart Millard, Barry Graul, Jim Bryson,
Nathan Cochran, Mike Scheuchzer and Robby Shaffer

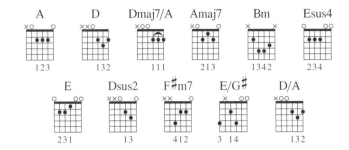

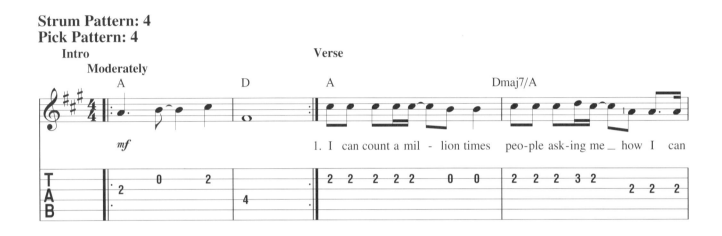

Strum Pattern: 4
Pick Pattern: 4

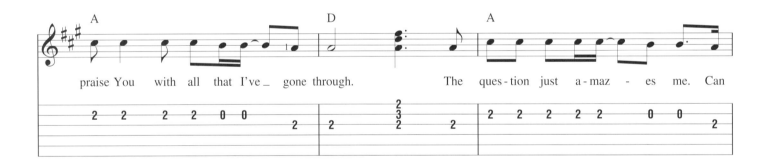

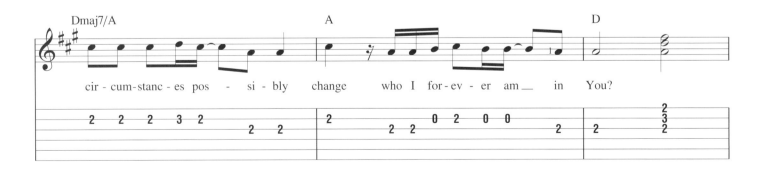

Verse

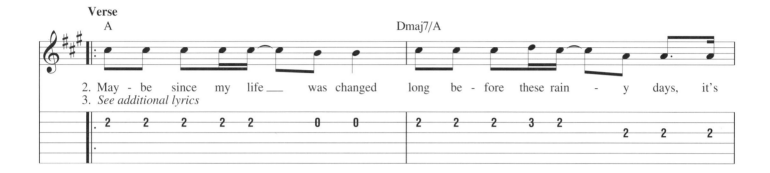

2. May - be since my life ___ was changed long be - fore these rain - y days, it's
3. *See additional lyrics*

nev - er real - ly ev - er crossed my mind to turn my back on You, _ oh Lord, my

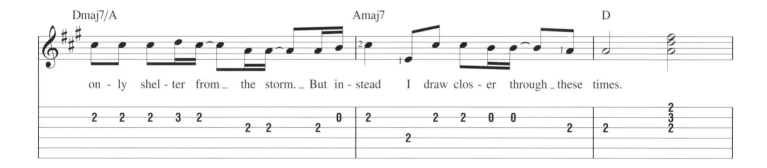

on - ly shel - ter from _ the storm. _ But in - stead I draw clos - er through _ these times.

Chorus

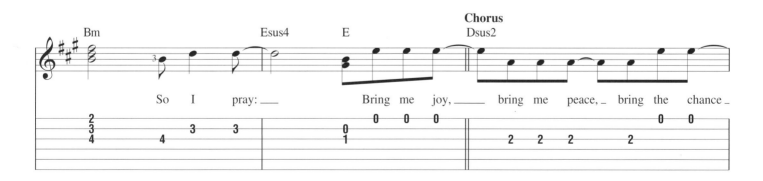

So I pray: ___ Bring me joy, _____ bring me peace, _ bring the chance _

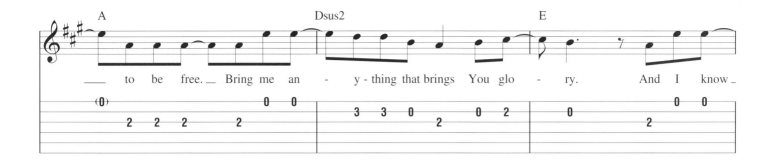

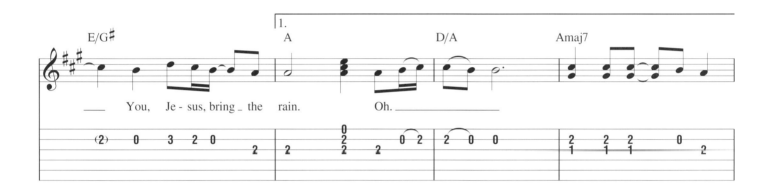

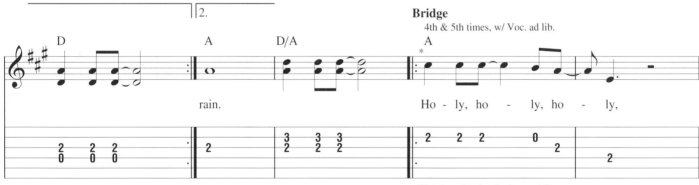

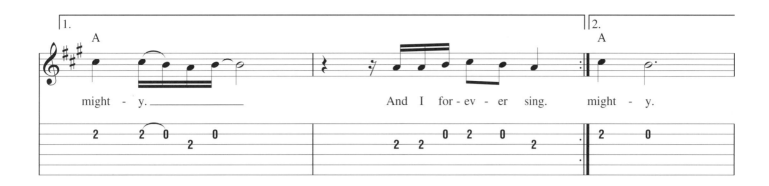

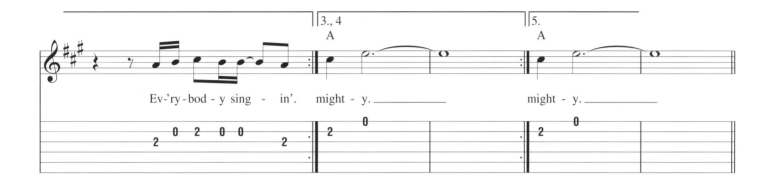

*Let chords ring till end.

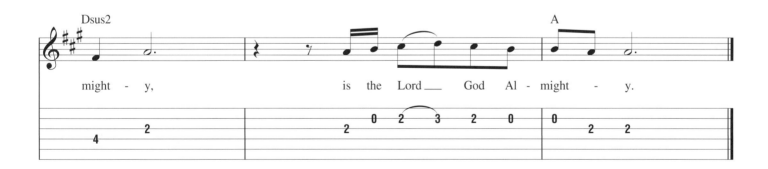

Additional Lyrics

3. I am Yours regardless of the clouds that may loom above,
   Because You are much greater than my pain.
   You who made a way for me by suffering Your destiny.
   So tell me, what's a little rain?
   So I pray:

By Your Side

Words and Music by Jason Ingram, Phillip LaRue and Mike Donehey

Strum Pattern: 2
Pick Pattern: 2

Intro
Slowly, in 2

*Chord symbols in parentheses reflect implied harmony.

Verse

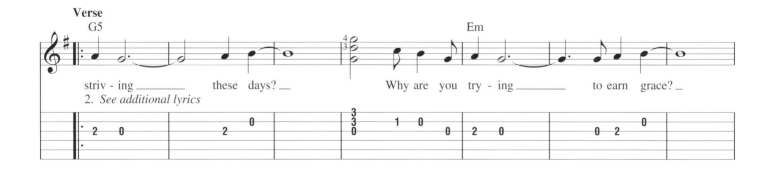

striv - ing _____ these days? _ Why are you try - ing _____ to earn grace? _
2. *See additional lyrics*

Additional Lyrics

2. Why are you looking for love?
   Why are you still searching as if I'm not enough?
   Where will you go, child?
   Tell Me, where will you run? To where will you run?

Come on Back to Me

Words by Mac Powell
Music by Tai Anderson, Brad Avery, David Carr, Mark Lee and Mac Powell

*Tune down 1/2 step:
(low to high) Eb-Ab-Db-Gb-Bb-Eb

Strum Pattern: 2
Pick Pattern: 4

Intro
Moderately

*Optional: To match recording, tune down 1/2 step.

Verse

1. Well, you've been hid - ing now for so ____ long, ____

and nev - er un - der - stand - ing why. ____

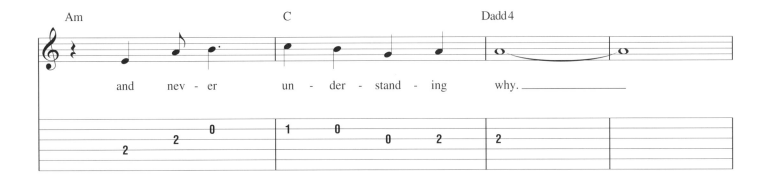

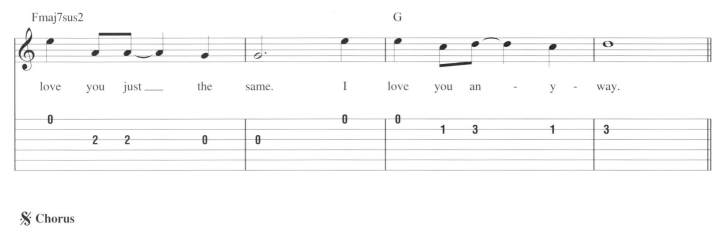

Chorus

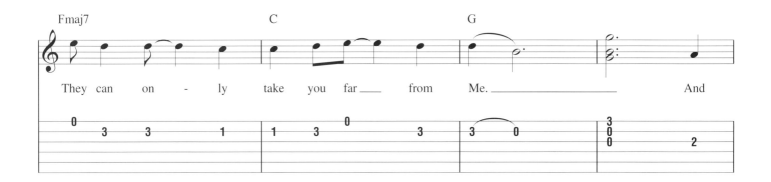

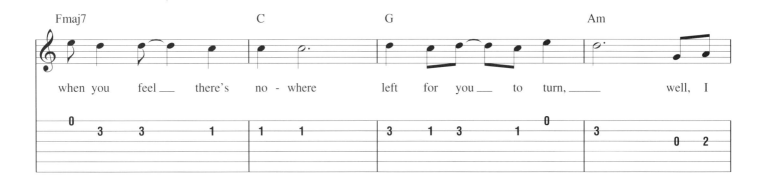

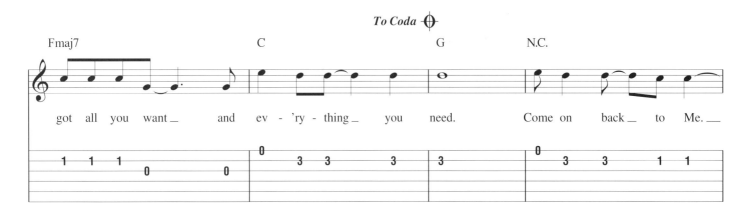

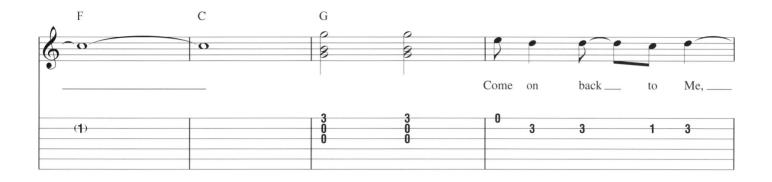

Come on back ___ to Me, ___

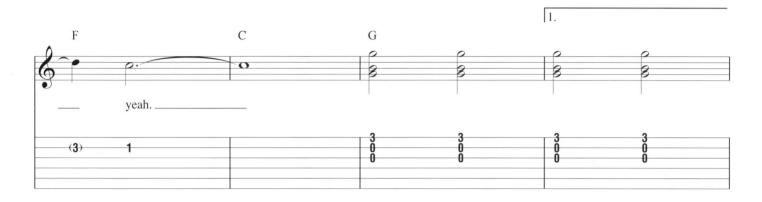

___ yeah. _____

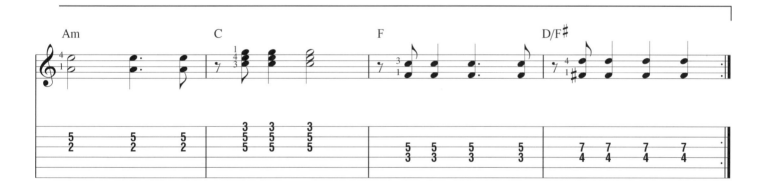

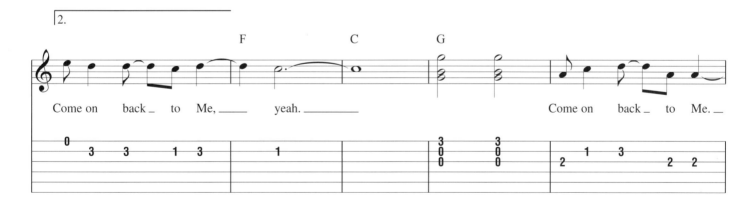

Come on back ___ to Me, ___ yeah. _____ Come on back ___ to Me. ___

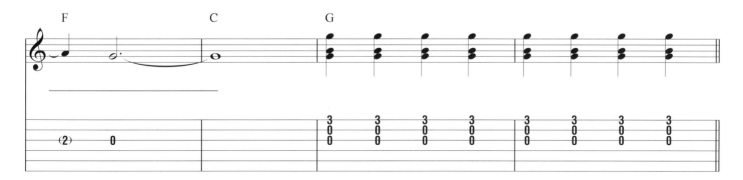

Interlude

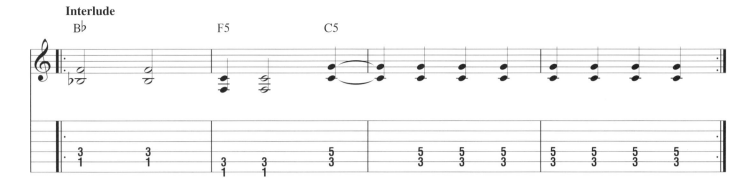

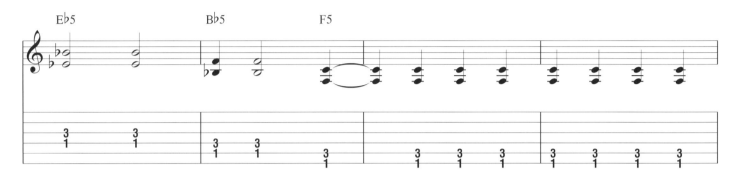

D.S. al Coda

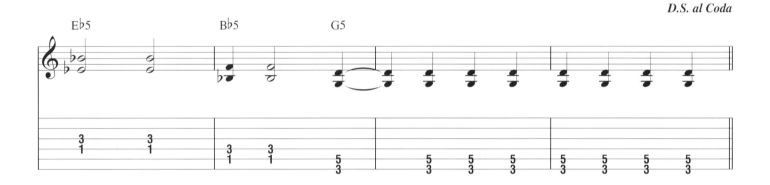

Coda

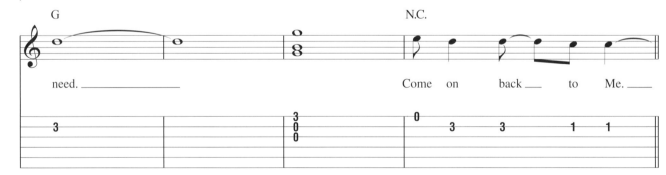

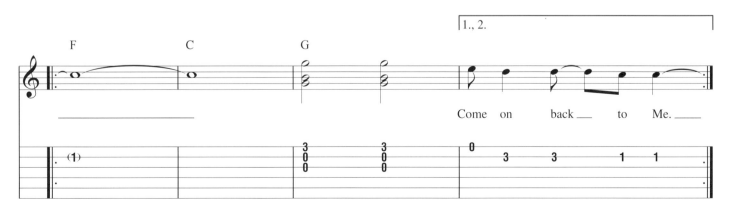

Additional Lyrics

3. Do you believe in second chances,
   Or a love that never fades?
   Put your faith in what you can't see.
   Just put your hand in Mine.
   I'll show you the way.

Dare You to Move

Words and Music by Jonathan Foreman

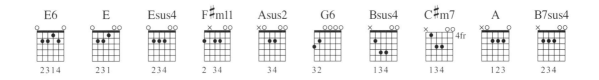

Strum Pattern: 1
Pick Pattern: 3

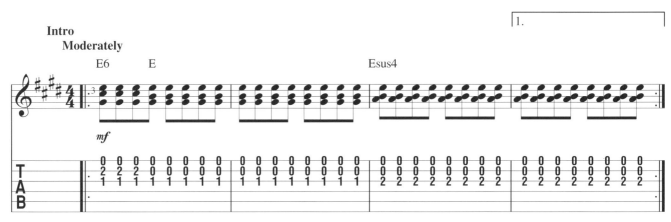

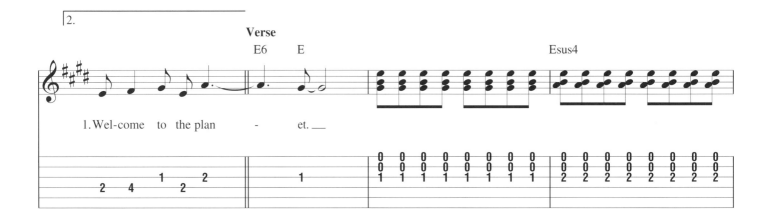

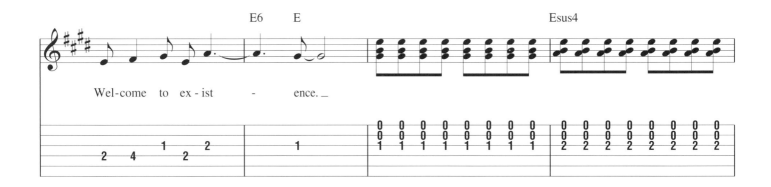

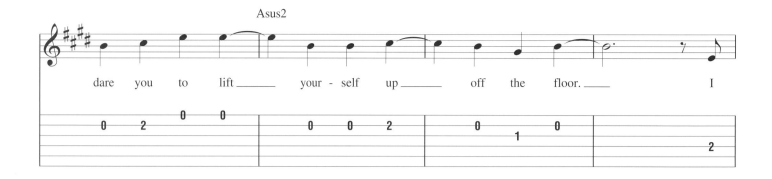

dare you to lift ____ your - self up ____ off the floor. ____ I

dare you to move. _____ I dare you to move _____ like to - day _

To Coda ⊕

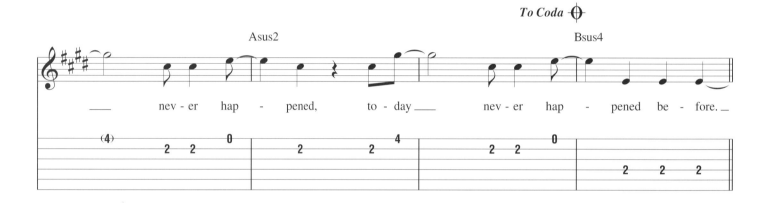

___ nev - er hap - pened, to - day ____ nev - er hap - pened be - fore. _

Interlude

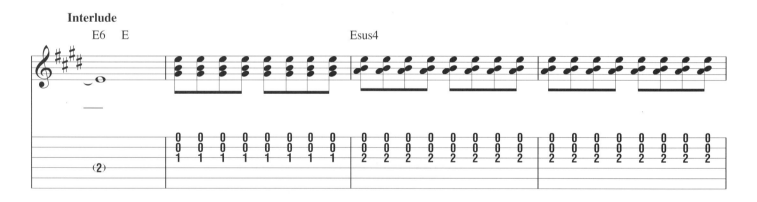

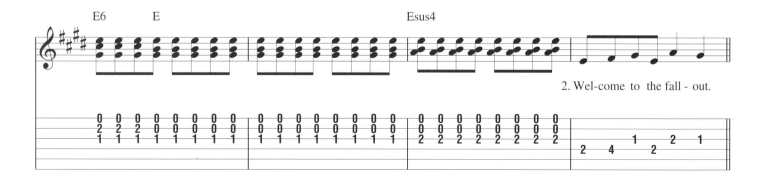

2. Wel - come to the fall - out.

Verse

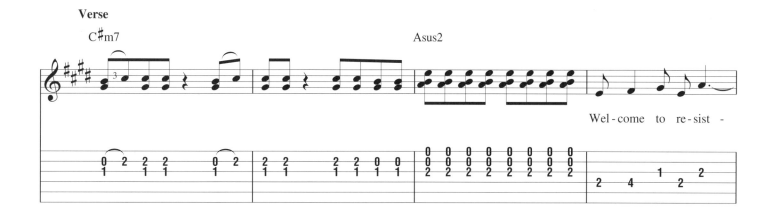

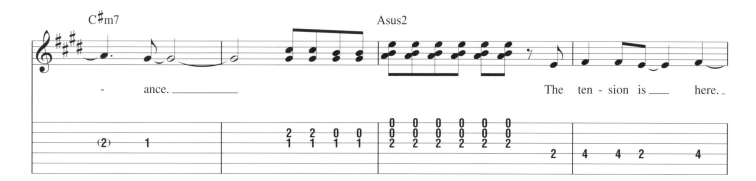

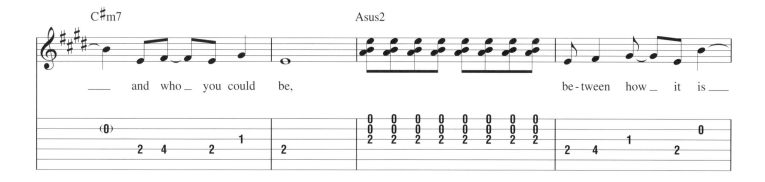

Coda

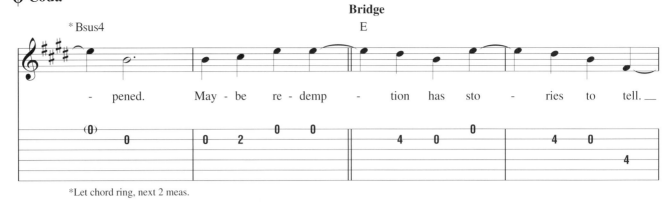

*Let chord ring, next 2 meas.

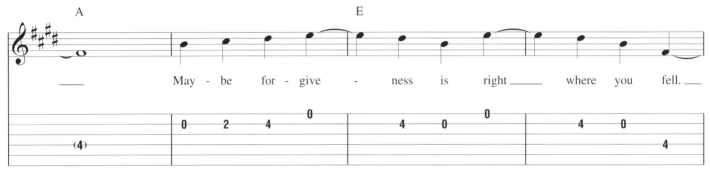

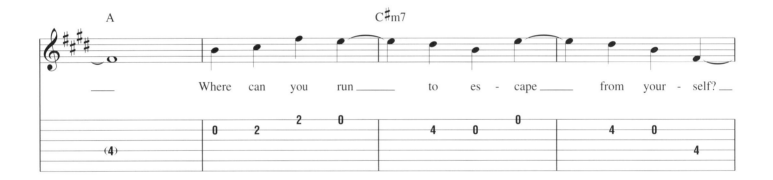

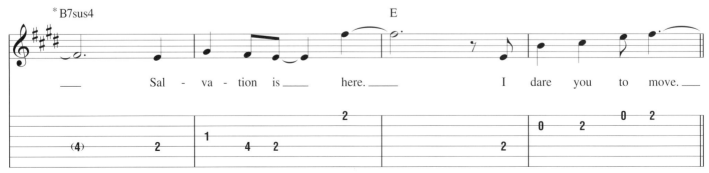

*Let chord ring, next 2 meas.

Chorus

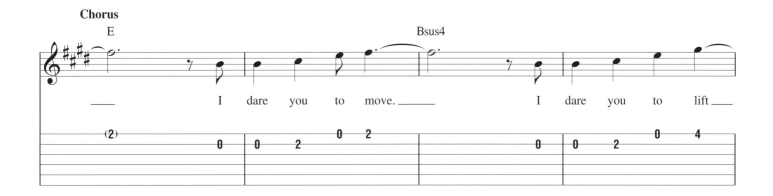

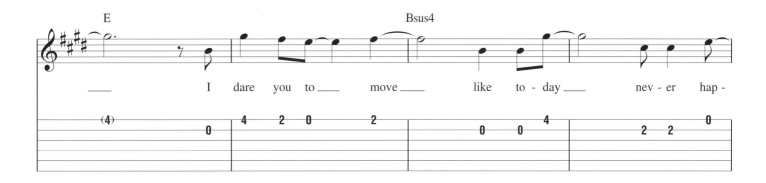

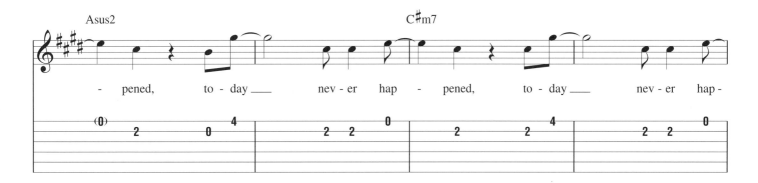

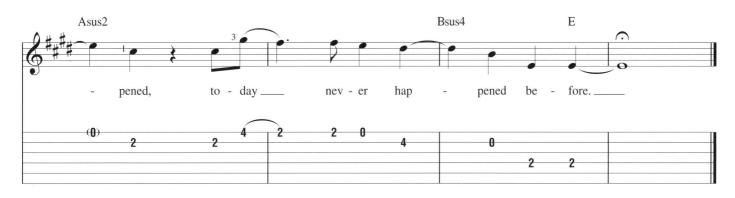

Dive

Words and Music by Steven Curtis Chapman

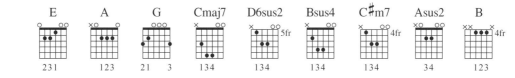

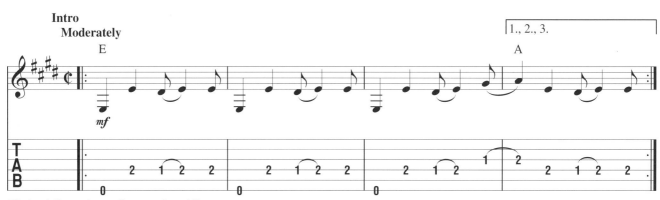

*Tune down 1/2 step:
(low to high) E♭-A♭-D♭-G♭-B♭-E♭

Strum Pattern: 2
Pick Pattern: 4

Intro
Moderately

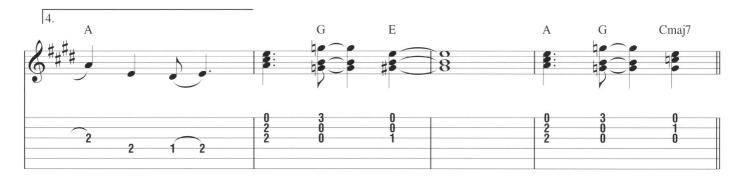

*Optional: To match recording, tune down 1/2 step.

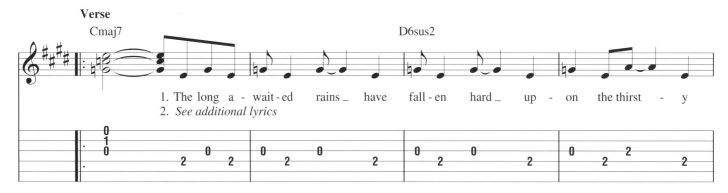

Verse

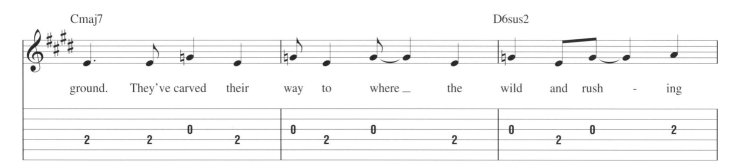

1. The long a-wait-ed rains _ have fall-en hard _ up-on the thirst-y
2. *See additional lyrics*

ground. They've carved their way to where _ the wild and rush-ing

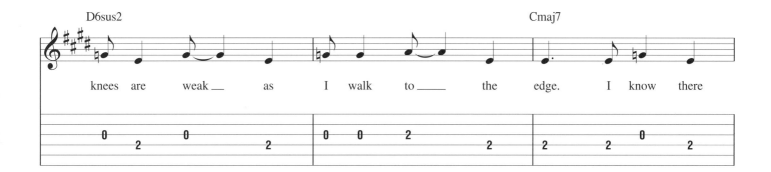

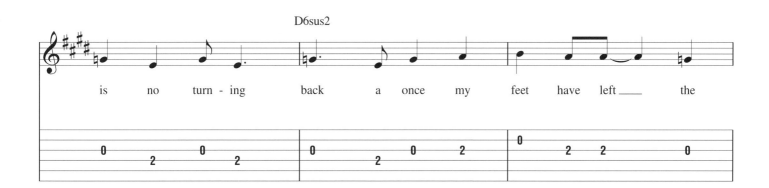

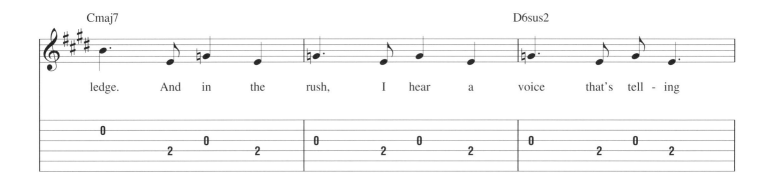

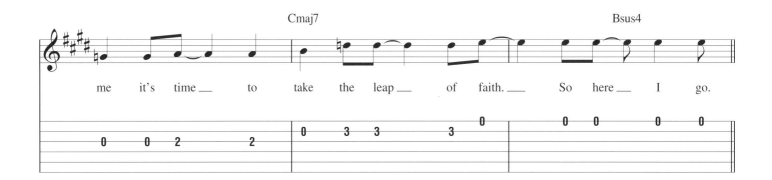

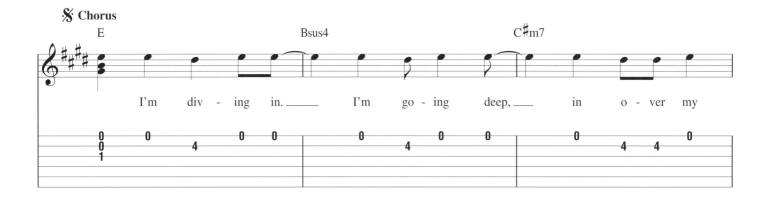

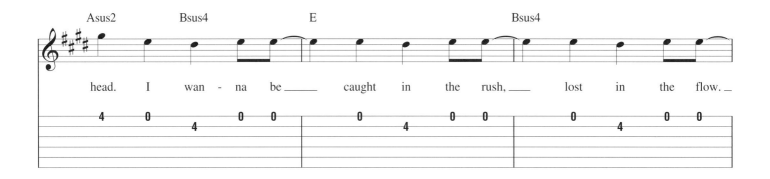

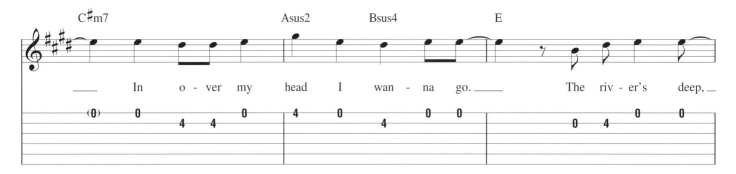

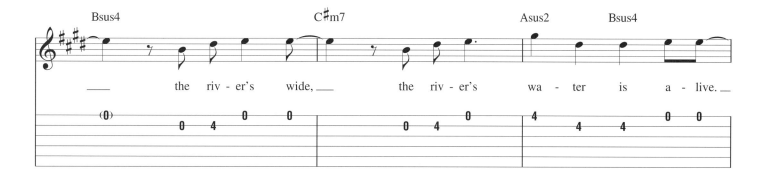

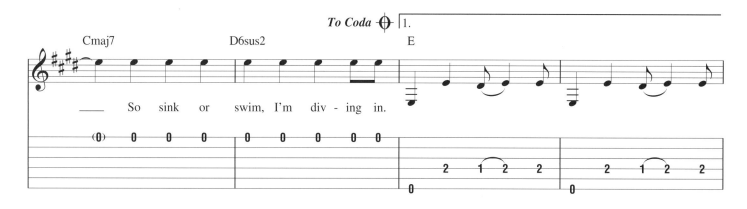

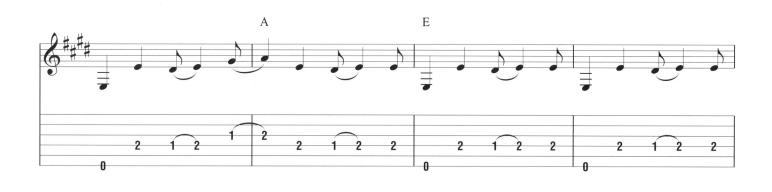

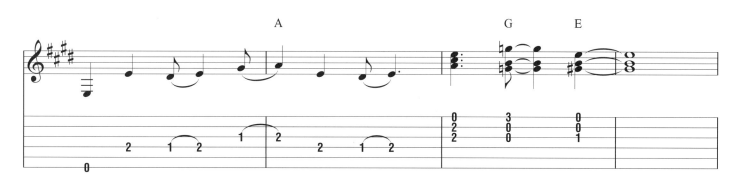

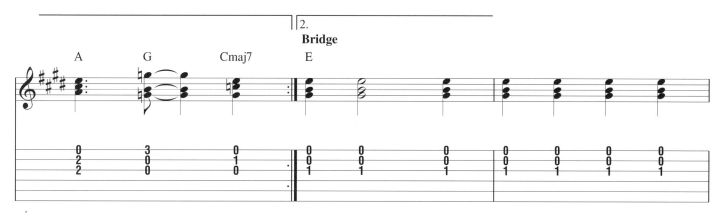

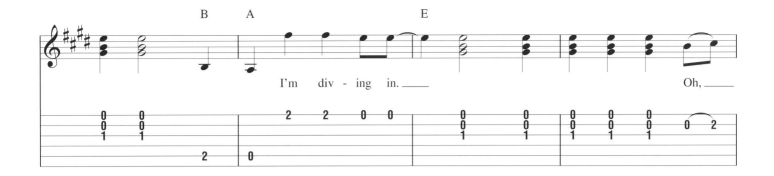

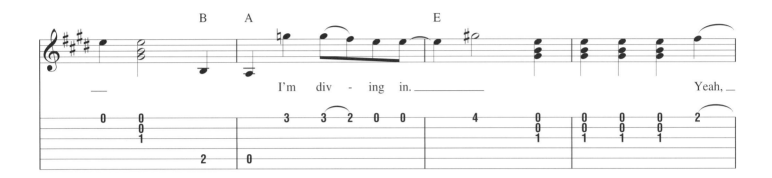

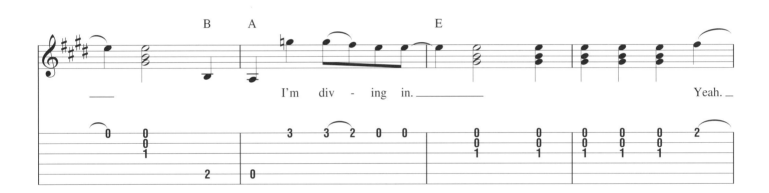

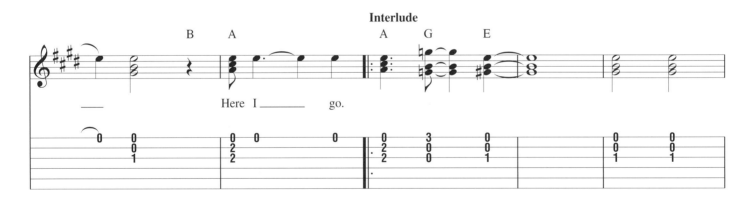

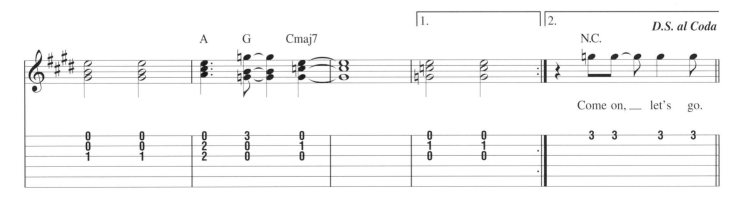

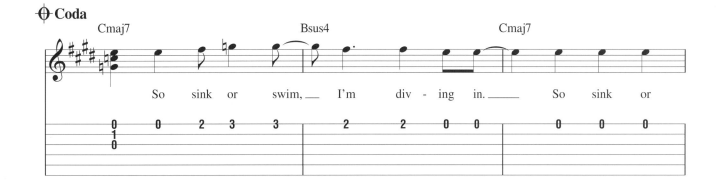

So sink or swim, __ I'm div - ing in. __ So sink or

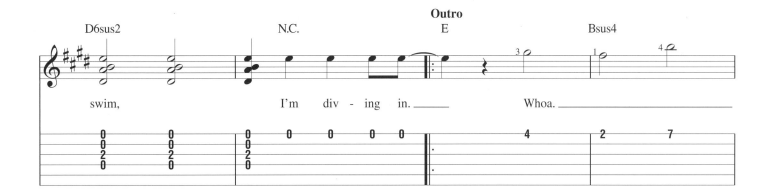

Outro

swim, I'm div - ing in. __ Whoa. ___

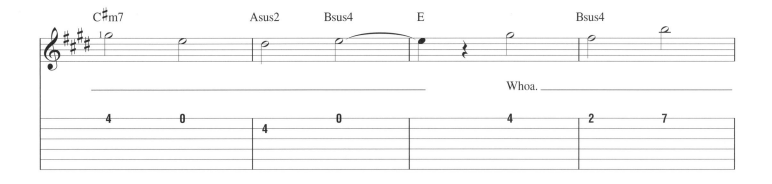

Whoa. ___

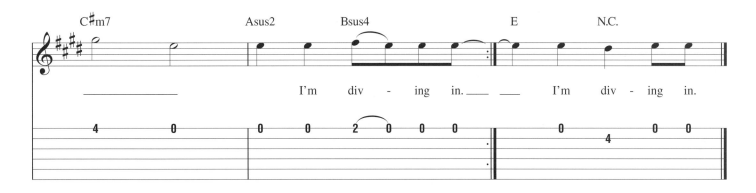

I'm div - ing in. __ __ I'm div - ing in.

Additional Lyrics

2. There is a supernatural power in this mighty river's flow.
   It can bring the dead to life and it can fill an empty soul,
   And give our heart the only thing worth living and worth dying for, yeah.
   But we will never know the awesome power of the grace of God
   Until we let ourselves get swept away into this holy flood.
   So if you take my hand, we'll close our eyes and count to three,
   And take the leap of faith. Come on let's go.

East to West

Words and Music by Mark Hall and Bernie Herms

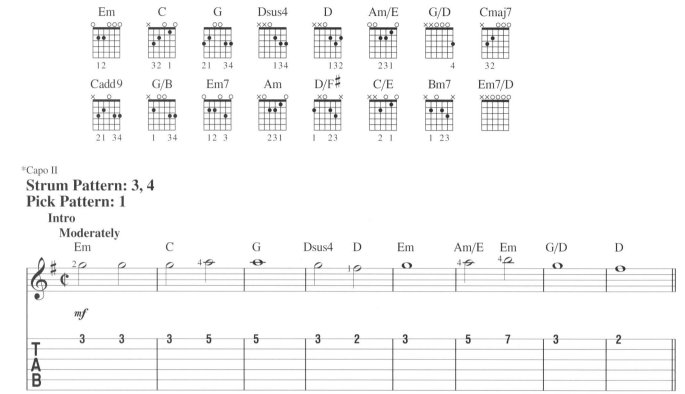

*Capo II

Strum Pattern: 3, 4
Pick Pattern: 1

Intro
Moderately

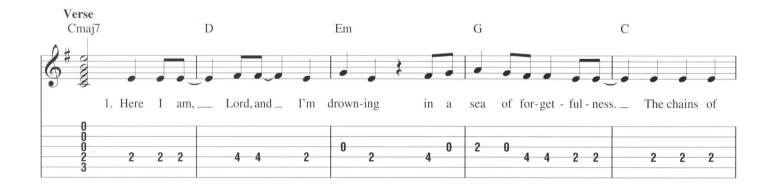

*Optional: To match recording, place capo at 2nd fret.

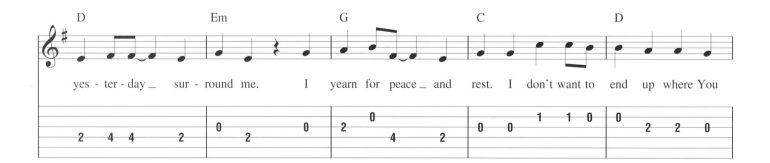

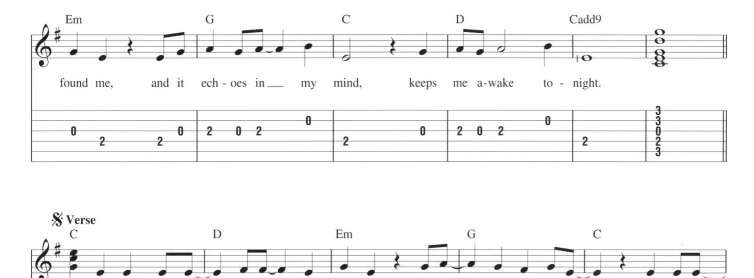

found me,   and it ech - oes in ___ my mind,   keeps me a-wake   to - night.

% Verse

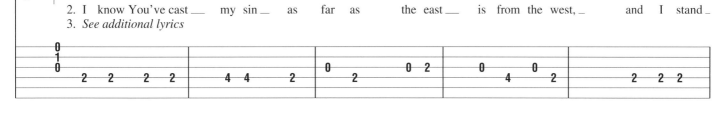

2. I know You've cast ___ my sin ___ as far as   the east ___ is from the west, ___   and I stand ___
3. *See additional lyrics*

___ be - fore ___ You   now as,   as though I've nev-er sinned.   But to-day I   feel like I'm just

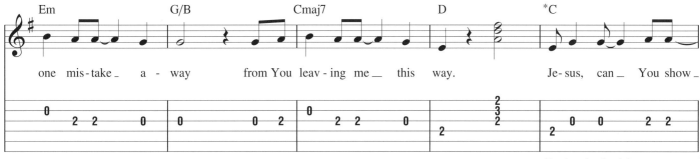

one mis-take ___ a - way   from You leav - ing me ___ this way.   Je - sus, can ___ You show ___

*1st time, let chord ring.

Chorus

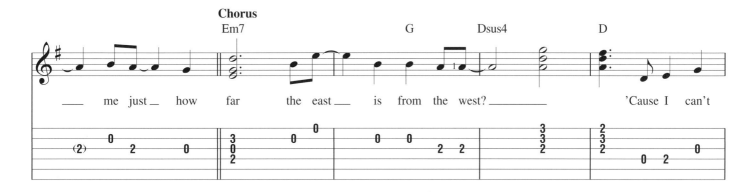

___ me just ___ how   far   the east ___ is from the west? _____   'Cause I   can't

*Let chord ring.

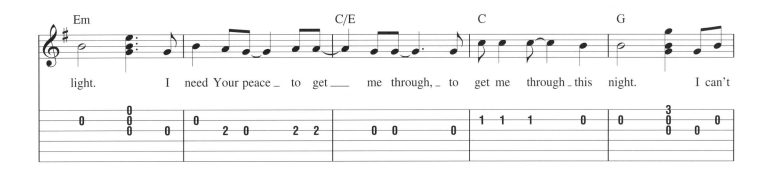

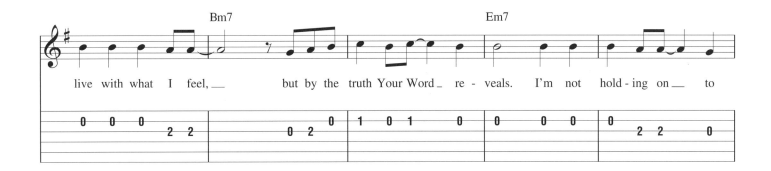

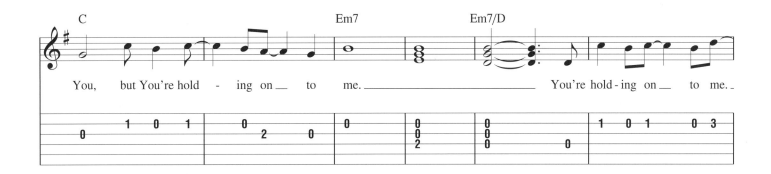

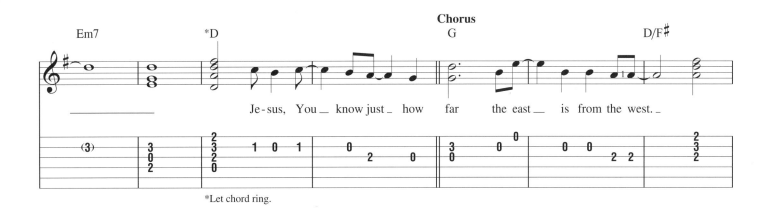

*Let chord ring.

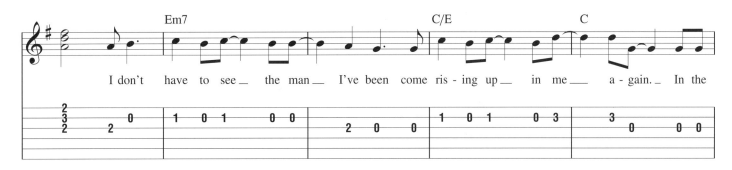

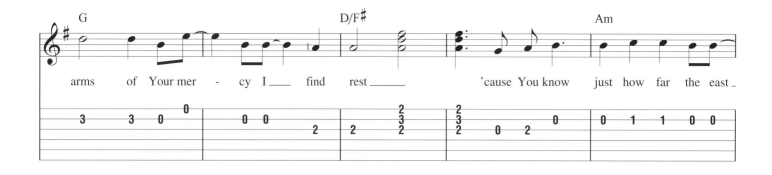

arms of Your mer - cy I ___ find rest _____ 'cause You know just how far the east _

___ is from the west, _ from one scarred hand to the oth - er. _____

*Let chord ring.

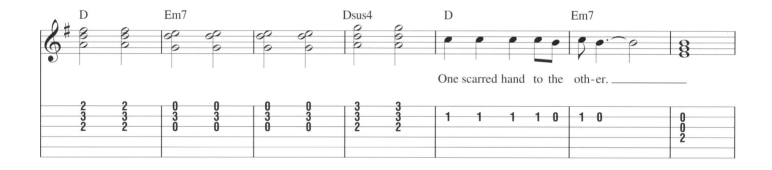

One scarred hand to the oth-er. _____

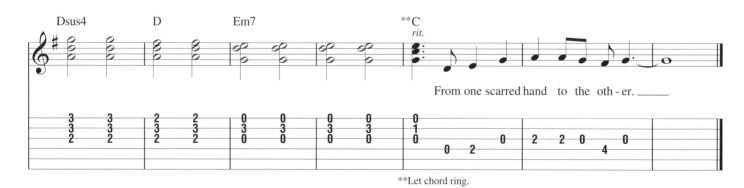

From one scarred hand to the oth - er. _____

**Let chord ring.

Additional Lyrics

2. I start the day, the war begins, endless reminding of my sin.
   Time and time again Your truth is drowned out by the storm I'm in.
   Today I feel like I'm just one mistake away
   From You leaving me this way.

Everything Glorious

Words and Music by David Crowder

*Optional: To match recording, place capo at 1st fret.

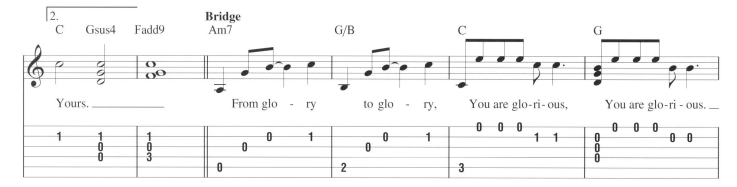

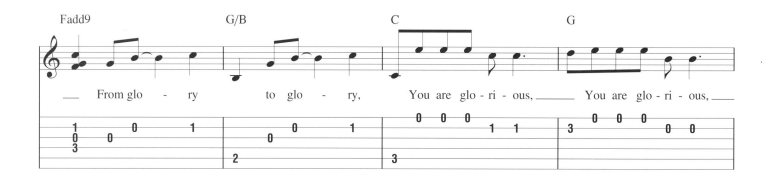

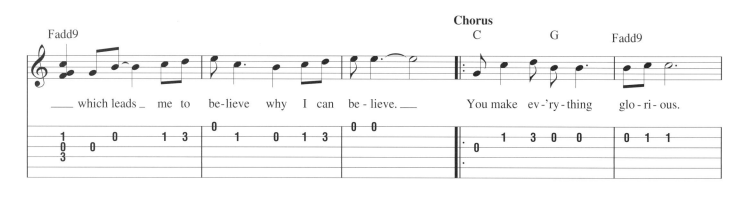

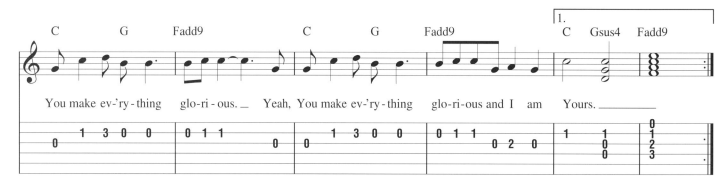

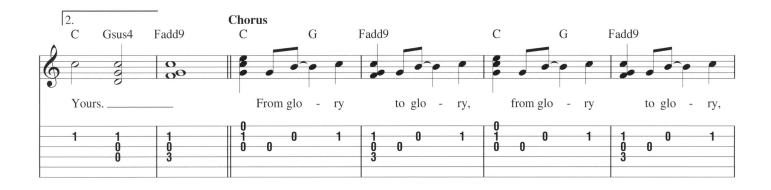

Yours. _____ From glo - ry to glo - ry, from glo - ry to glo - ry,

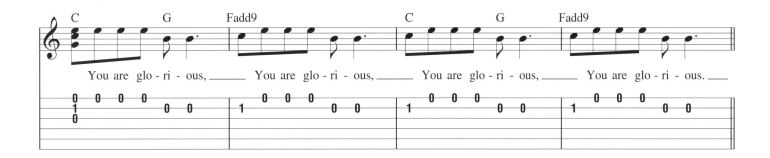

You are glo - ri - ous, _____ You are glo - ri - ous, _____ You are glo - ri - ous, _____ You are glo - ri - ous. _____

Outro

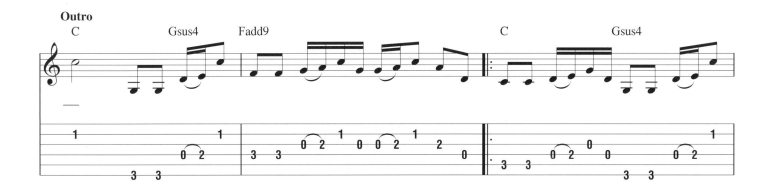

Additional Lyrics

2. My eyes are small, but they have seen
   The beauty of enormous things,
   Which leads me to believe there's light enough to see,
   Oh, that...

Enough

Words and Music by Chris Tomlin and Louie Giglio

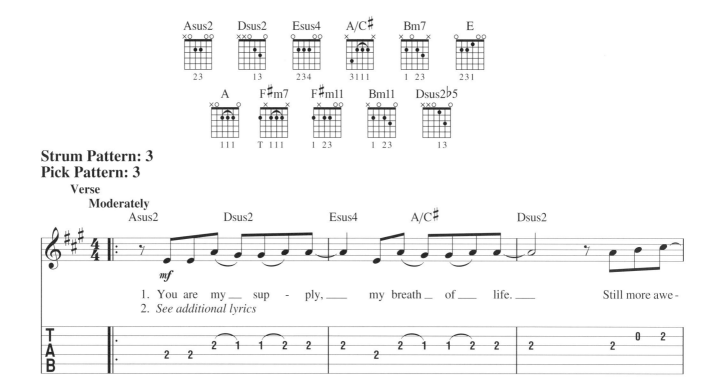

Strum Pattern: 3
Pick Pattern: 3

Verse
Moderately

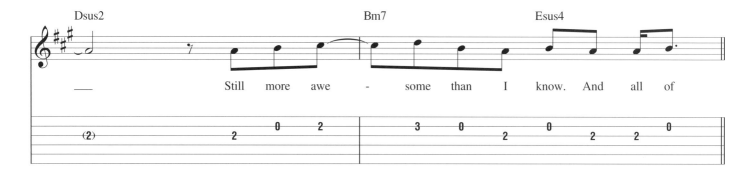

1. You are my __ sup - ply, __ my breath __ of __ life. __ Still more awe-

2. *See additional lyrics*

- some than I know. You are my __ re - ward, __ worth liv - ing __ for.

__ Still more awe - some than I know. And all of

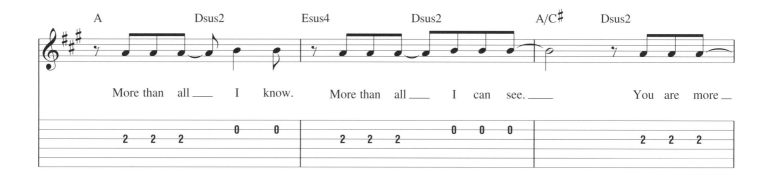

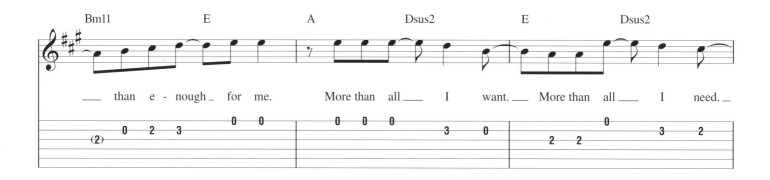

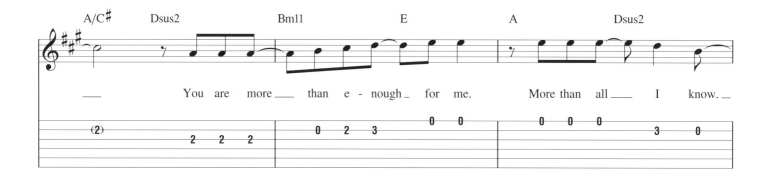

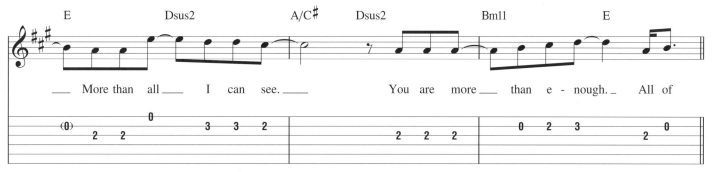

More than all ___ I can see. ___ You are more ___ than e - nough. ___ All of

Coda

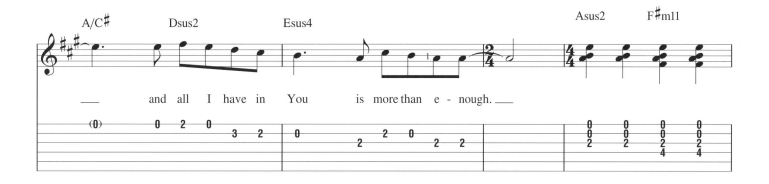

You, oh, yeah. ___ And all I have in You, Je - sus, ___

___ and all I have in You is more than e - nough. ___

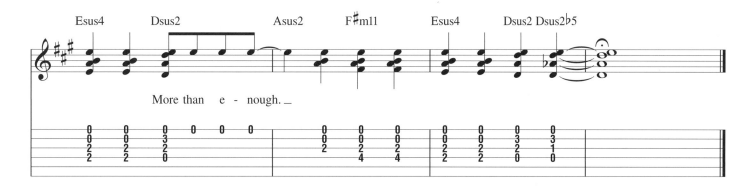

More than e - nough. ___

Additional Lyrics

2. You're my sacrifice of greatest price.
   Still more awesome than I know.
   You're my coming king.
   You're my ev'rything.
   Still more awesome than I know.

For the Sake of the Call

Words and Music by Steven Curtis Chapman

plaud - ed them, _ so they knew from the start this road would not lead to

fame. _____ All they real - ly knew for sure was Je - sus had

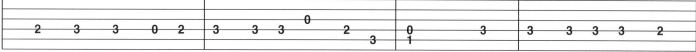

called to them. He said, "Come fol - low me," and they came. With reck - less a - ban - don ___

1.

2.

___ they came. 2. Emp - ty ___ by name. And they ans - wered,

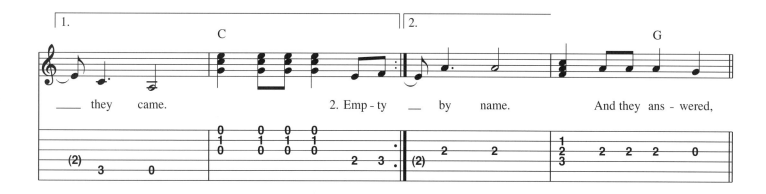

Chorus

We will a - ban - don it all for the sake of the call. _____

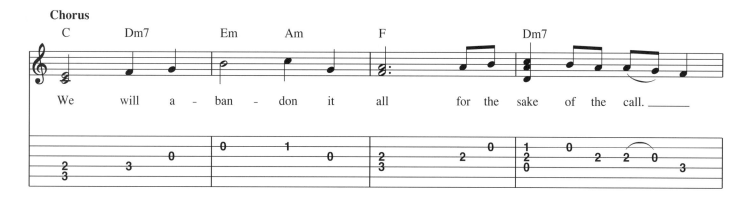

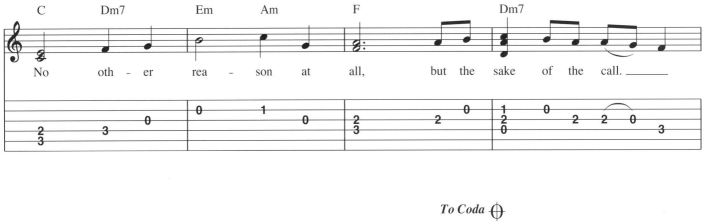

No oth-er rea-son at all, but the sake of the call. _____

To Coda ⊕

Whol - ly de - vot - ed to live and to die for the sake of the

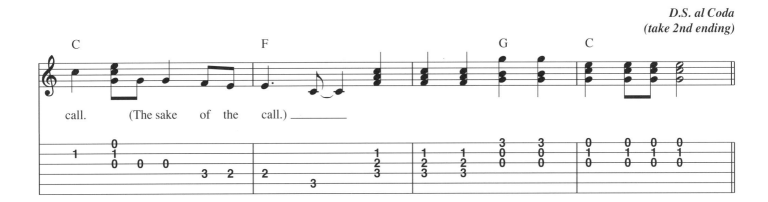

D.S. al Coda
(take 2nd ending)

call. (The sake of the call.) _____

⊕ **Coda**   **Bridge**

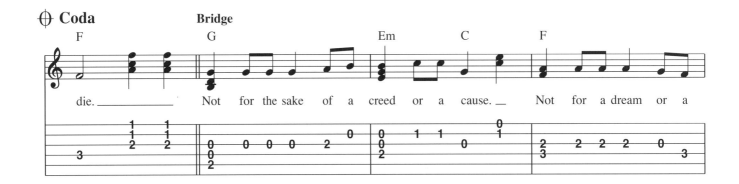

die. _____ Not for the sake of a creed or a cause. __ Not for a dream or a

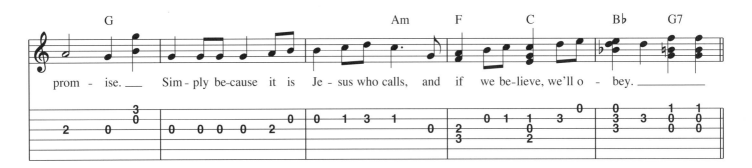

prom - ise. __ Sim - ply be-cause it is Je - sus who calls, and if we be-lieve, we'll o - bey. _____

Chorus

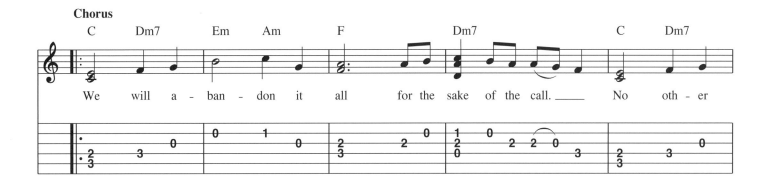

We will a - ban - don it all for the sake of the call. _____ No oth - er

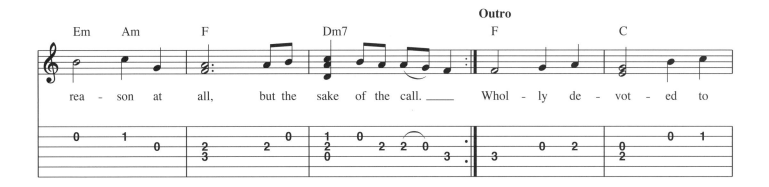

Outro

rea - son at all, but the sake of the call. _____ Whol - ly de - vot - ed to

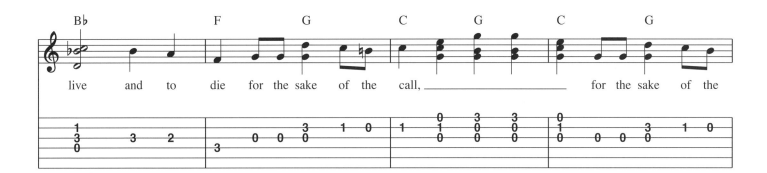

live and to die for the sake of the call, _____ for the sake of the

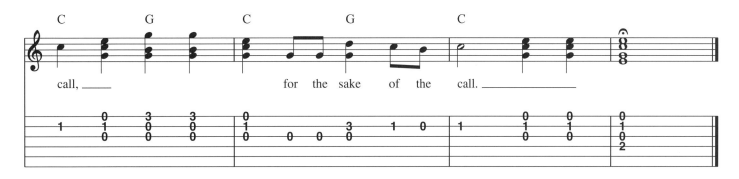

call, _____ for the sake of the call. _____

Additional Lyrics

2. Empty nets lying there at the water's edge
   Told a story that few could believe and none could explain.
   How some crazy fishermen agreed to go where Jesus led,
   With no thought of what they would gain,
   For Jesus had called them by name.

3. Drawn like the rivers are drawn to the sea,
   There's no turning back, for the water cannot help but flow.
   Once we hear the Savior's call, we'll follow wherever He leads
   Because of the love He has shown,
   Because He has called us to go.

Give Me Your Eyes

Words and Music by Jason Ingram and Brandon Heath

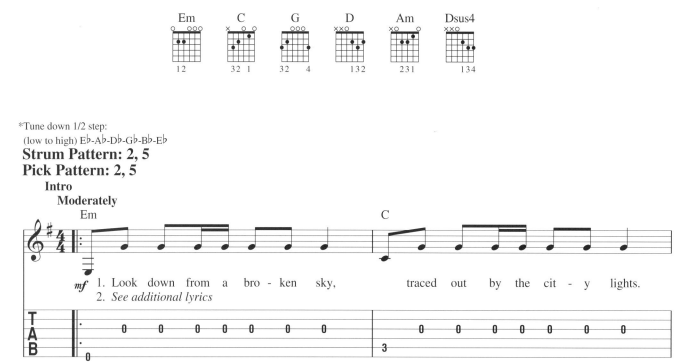

*Tune down 1/2 step:
(low to high) E♭-A♭-D♭-G♭-B♭-E♭

Strum Pattern: 2, 5

Pick Pattern: 2, 5

Intro
Moderately

1. Look down from a bro-ken sky, traced out by the cit-y lights.
2. *See additional lyrics*

My world from a mile high, best sent in the house to-night. Touch down on the cold black-top,

*Optional: To match recording, tune down 1/2 step.

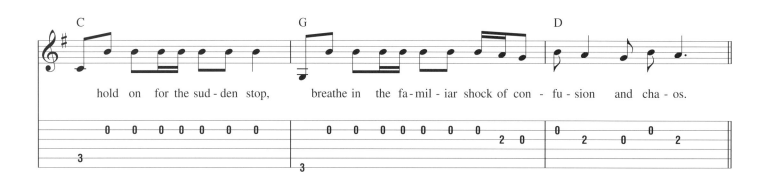

hold on for the sud-den stop, breathe in the fa-mil-iar shock of con-fu-sion and cha-os.

Pre-Chorus

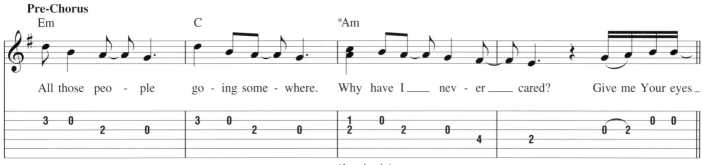

All those peo - ple go - ing some - where. Why have I ____ nev - er ____ cared? Give me Your eyes ____

*Let chord ring.

𝄋 Chorus

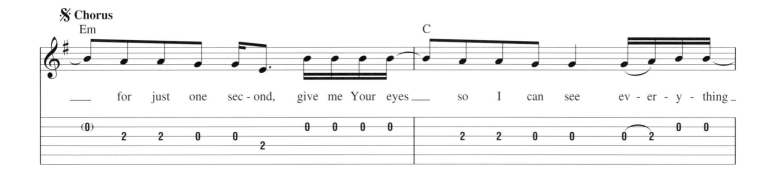

____ for just one sec - ond, give me Your eyes ____ so I can see ev - er - y - thing ____

____ that I keep miss - ing. Give me Your love ____ for hu - man - i - ty. Give me Your arms ____

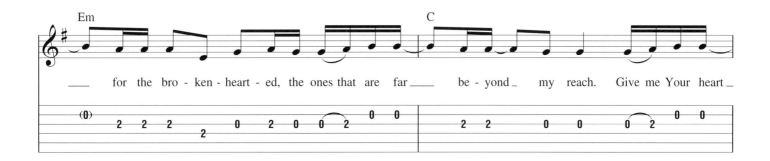

____ for the bro - ken - heart - ed, the ones that are far ____ be - yond ____ my reach. Give me Your heart ____

To Coda ⊕

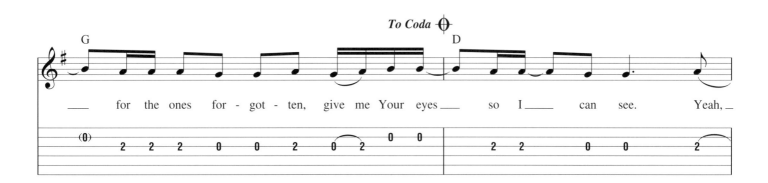

____ for the ones for - got - ten, give me Your eyes ____ so I ____ can see. Yeah, ____

yeah, _____ yeah, __ yeah. __ I've been here a mil - lion times,

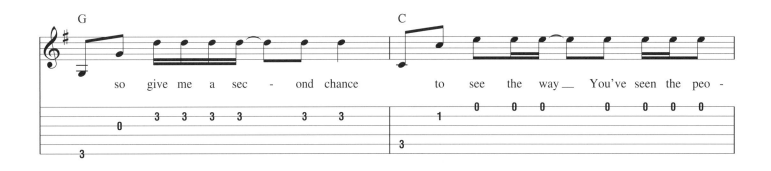

a cou - ple of mil - lion eyes just move and pass __ me by. I

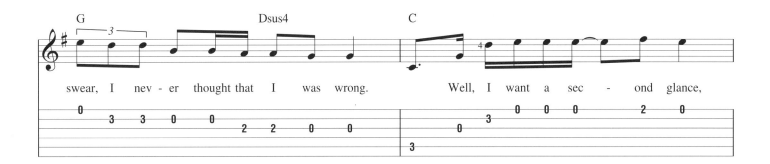

swear, I nev - er thought that I was wrong. Well, I want a sec - ond glance,

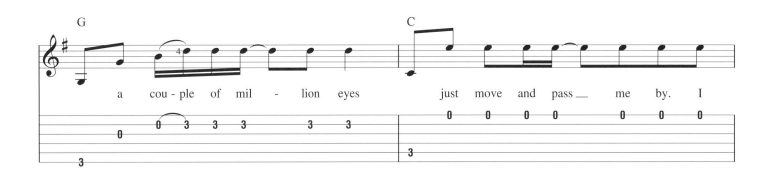

so give me a sec - ond chance to see the way __ You've seen the peo -

D.S. al Coda

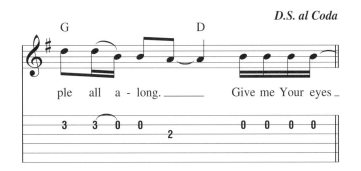

ple all a - long. _____ Give me Your eyes _

Coda

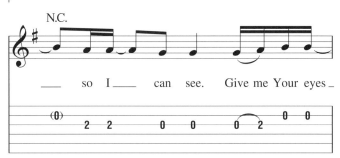

___ so I __ can see. Give me Your eyes _

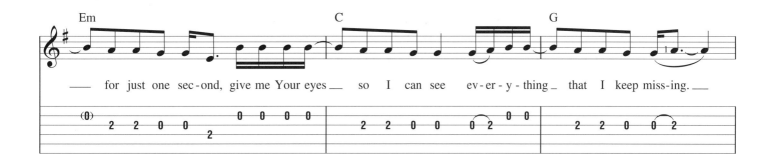

for just one sec-ond, give me Your eyes ___ so I can see ev-er-y-thing ___ that I keep miss-ing.

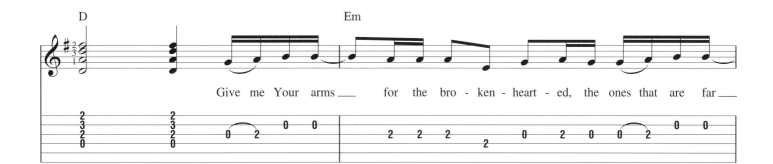

Give me Your arms ___ for the bro-ken-heart-ed, the ones that are far ___

___ be-yond ___ my reach. Give me Your heart ___ for the ones for-got-ten, give me Your eyes ___ so I ___ can see. Yeah, ___

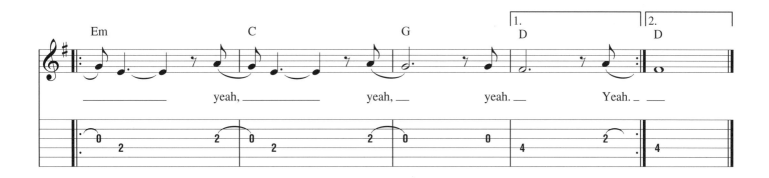

_____ yeah, _____ yeah, ___ yeah. ___ Yeah. ___

Additional Lyrics

2. Step out on a busy street,
See a girl and our eyes meet.
Does her best to smile at me to hide what's underneath.
There's a man just to her right,
Black suit and bright red tie,
Too ashamed to tell his wife he's out of work; he's buying time.

God You Reign

Words and Music by Lincoln Brewster and Mia Fieldes

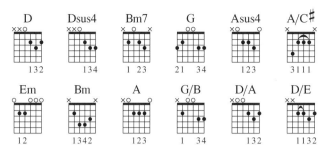

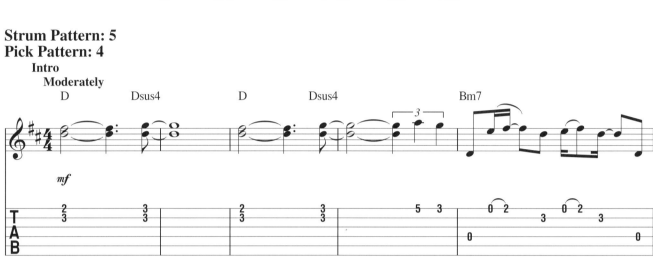

Strum Pattern: 5
Pick Pattern: 4

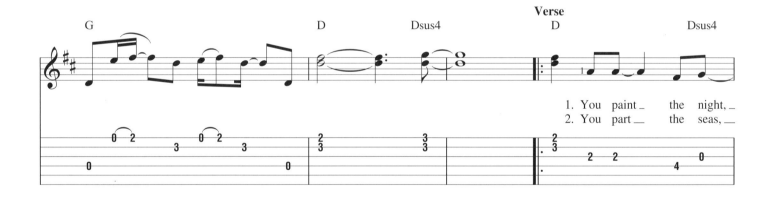

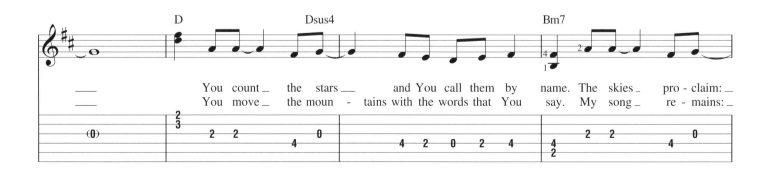

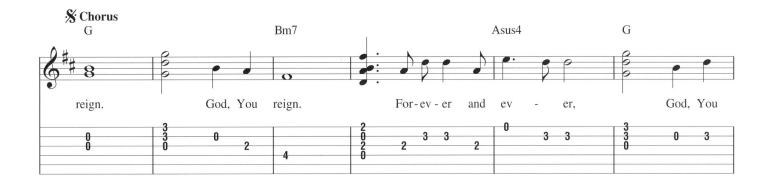

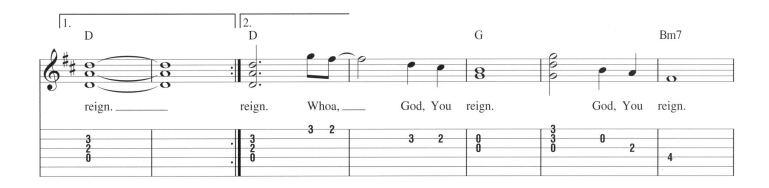

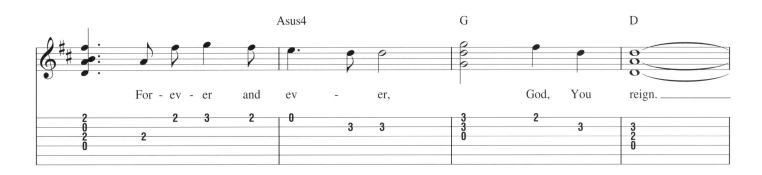

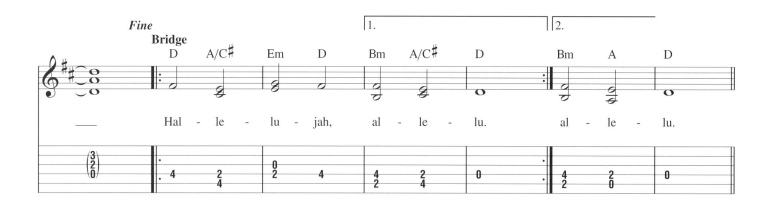

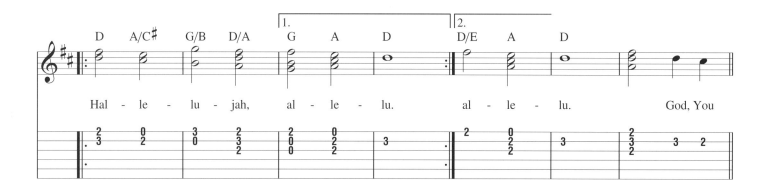

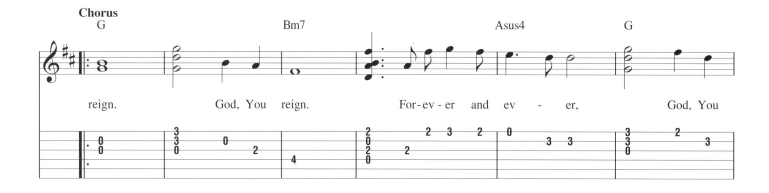

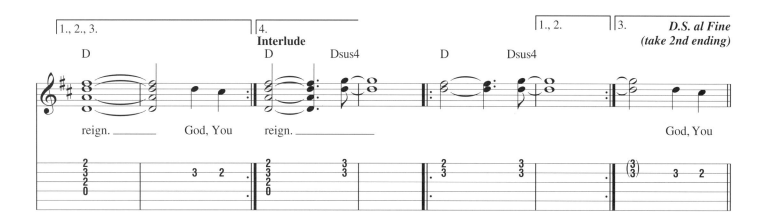

Hold My Heart

Words and Music by Jason Ingram, Phillip LaRue and Mike Donehey

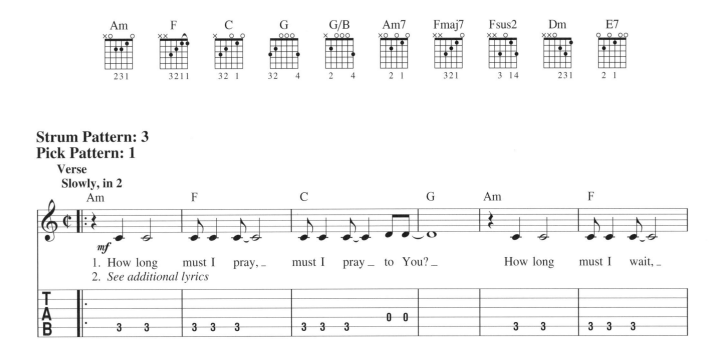

Strum Pattern: 3
Pick Pattern: 1

Verse
Slowly, in 2

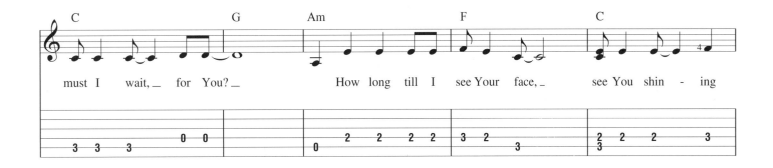

1. How long must I pray, must I pray to You? How long must I wait,

2. *See additional lyrics*

must I wait, for You? How long till I see Your face, see You shin - ing

through? I'm on my knees, beg-ging You to no - tice me. I'm on my knees.

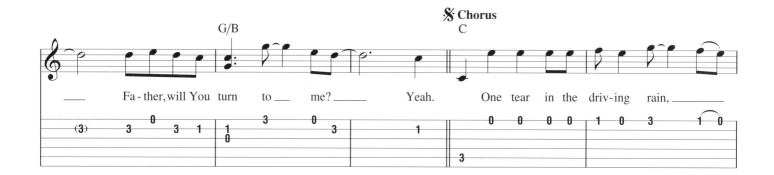

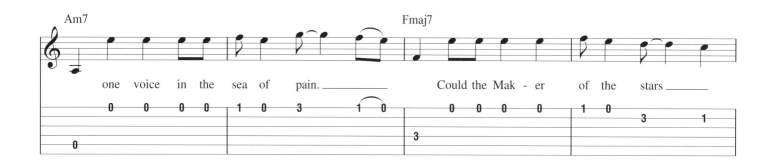

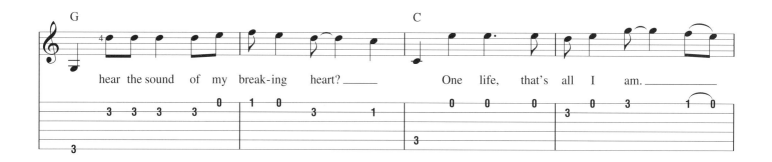

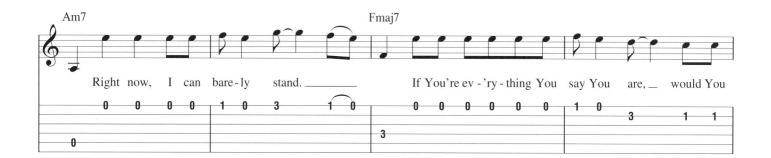

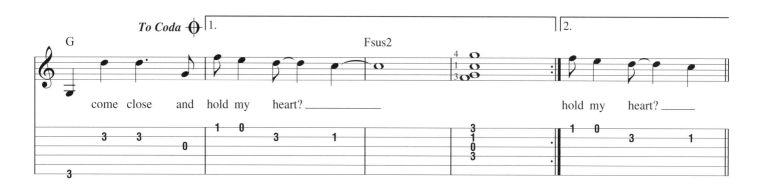

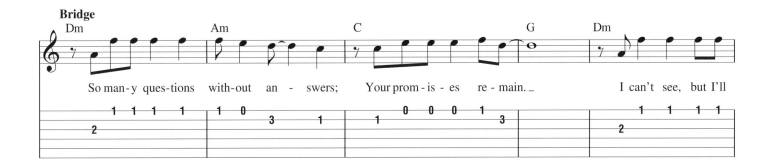

D.S. al Coda

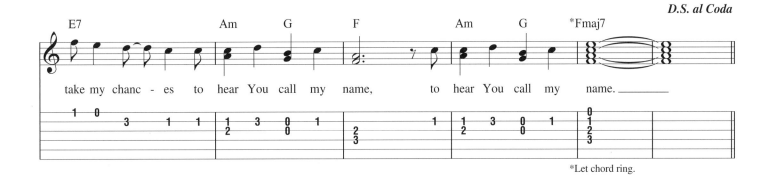

*Let chord ring.

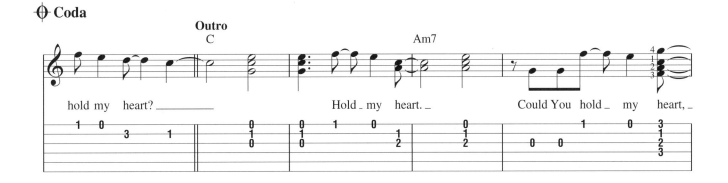

Additional Lyrics

2. I've been so afraid, afraid to close my eyes.
So much can slip away before I say good-bye.
But if there's no other way, I'm done asking why.
'Cause I'm on my knees, begging You to turn to me.
I'm on my knees. Father, will You run to me?
Yeah.

Hold Fast

Words and Music by Bart Millard, Barry Graul, Jim Bryson, Nathan Cochran, Mike Scheuchzer and Robby Shaffer

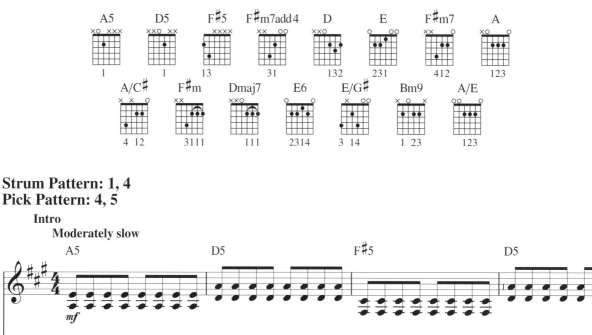

Strum Pattern: 1, 4
Pick Pattern: 4, 5

Intro
Moderately slow

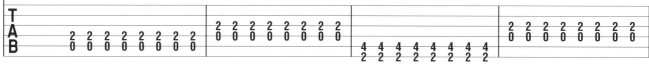

Verse

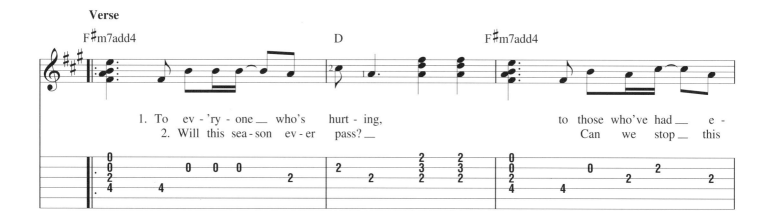

1. To ev-'ry-one __ who's hurt-ing, to those who've had __ e-
2. Will this sea-son ev-er pass? __ Can we stop __ this

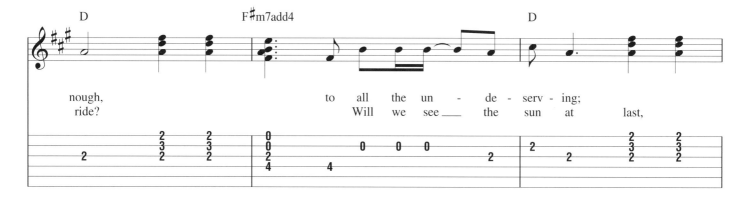

nough, to all the un- de- serv- ing;
ride? Will we see __ the sun at last,

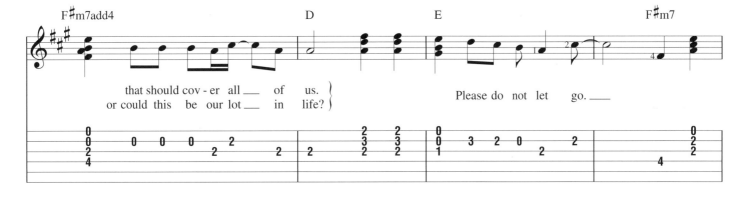

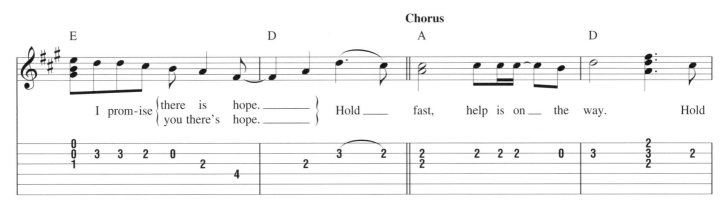

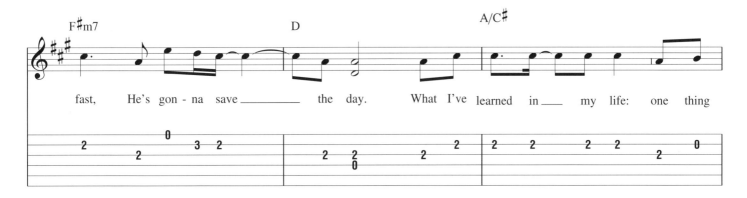

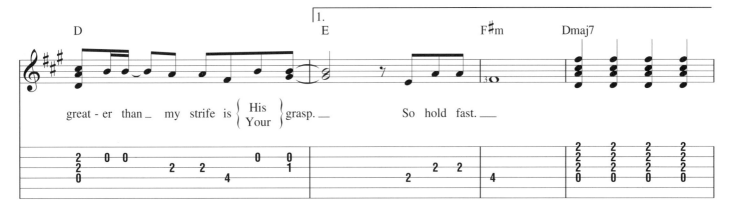

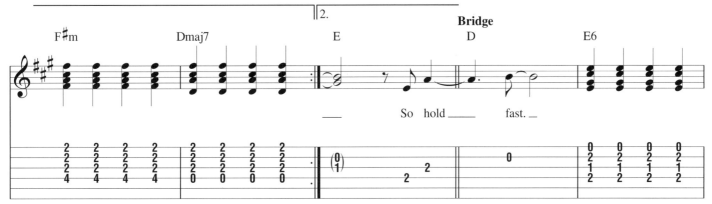

You may think you're all ___ a - lone and

there's no way that an - y - one could know what you're go - ing through. But

if you on - ly hear ___ one thing, just un - der - stand that we ___ are all the same, search - ing for the

truth, the truth of what we're soon ___ to face un - less some - one comes ___ to take our

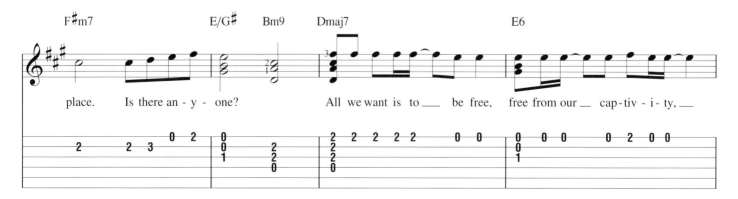

place. Is there an - y - one? All we want is to ___ be free, free from our ___ cap - tiv - i - ty, ___

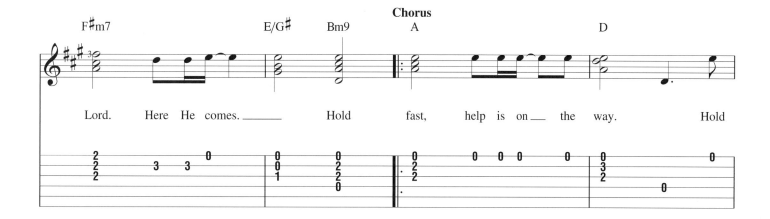

Lord. Here He comes. _____ Hold fast, help is on _ the way. Hold

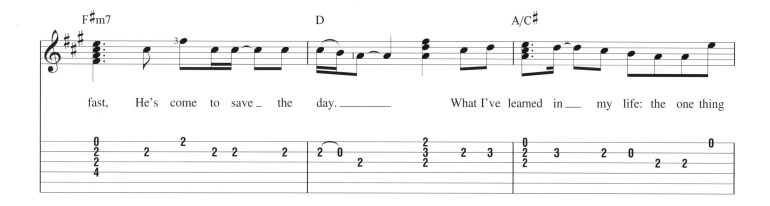

fast, He's come to save _ the day. _____ What I've learned in _ my life: the one thing

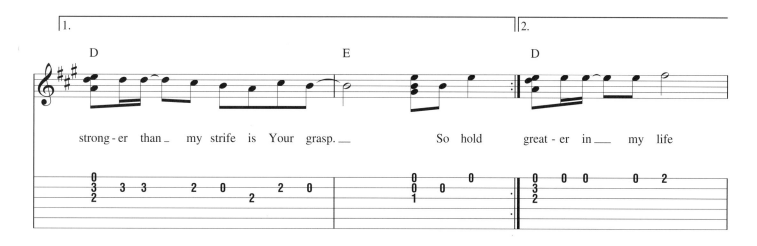

strong - er than _ my strife is Your grasp. _ So hold great - er in _ my life

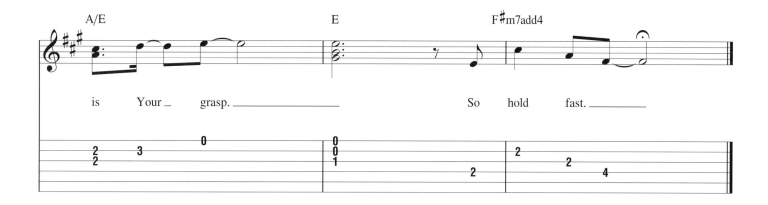

is Your _ grasp. _____ So hold fast. _____

I Still Believe

Words and Music by Jeremy Camp

*Capo I

Strum Pattern: 7. 8
Pick Pattern: 7, 8

Intro
Fast

*Optional: To match recording, place capo at 1st fret.   **T=Thumb on 6th string.

Verse

1. Scat-tered words   and   emp - ty thoughts   seem   to   pour from my   heart.
2. Though the ques-tions still   fog up my   mind with prom-is - es I   still seem to   bear,   or

I've nev-er felt   so   torn   be - fore.   Seems I don't know where to   start.
e - ven when   an - swers slow-ly un - wind,   it's   my heart I   see You pre - pare.

But it's

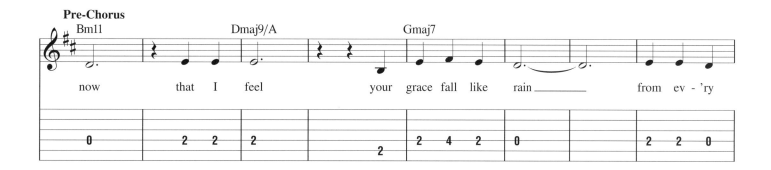

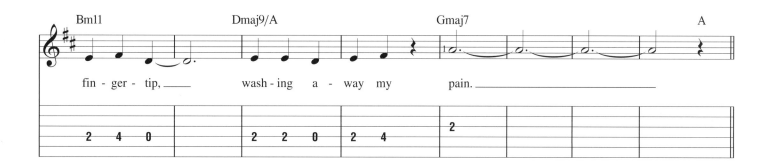

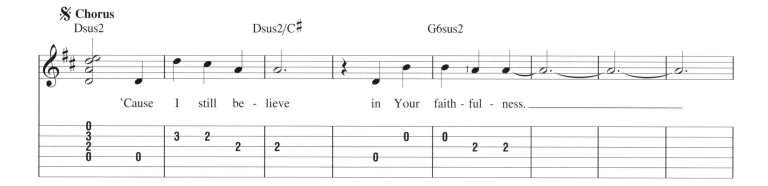

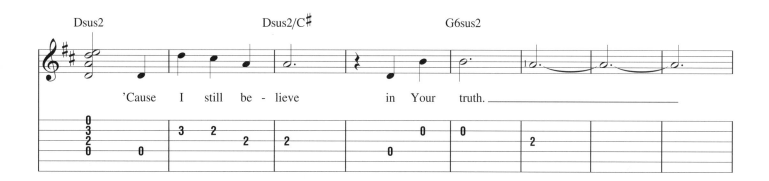

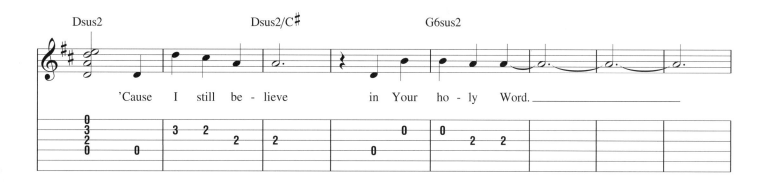

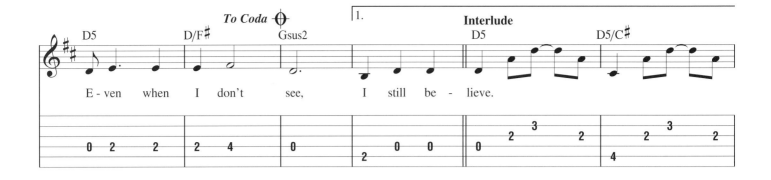

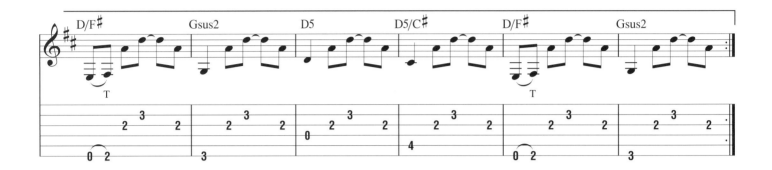

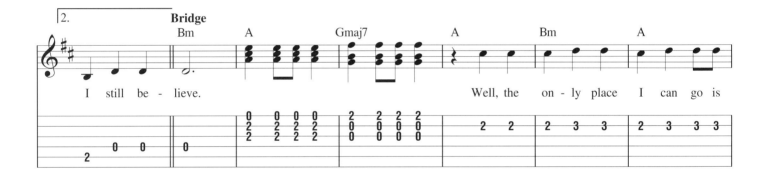

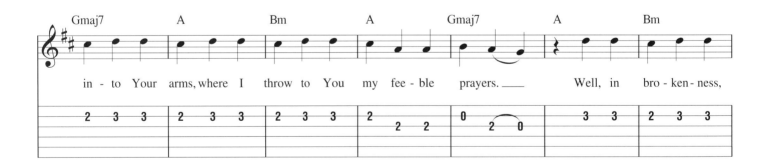

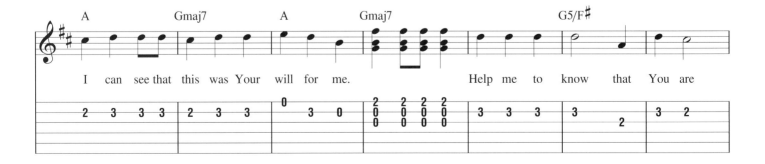

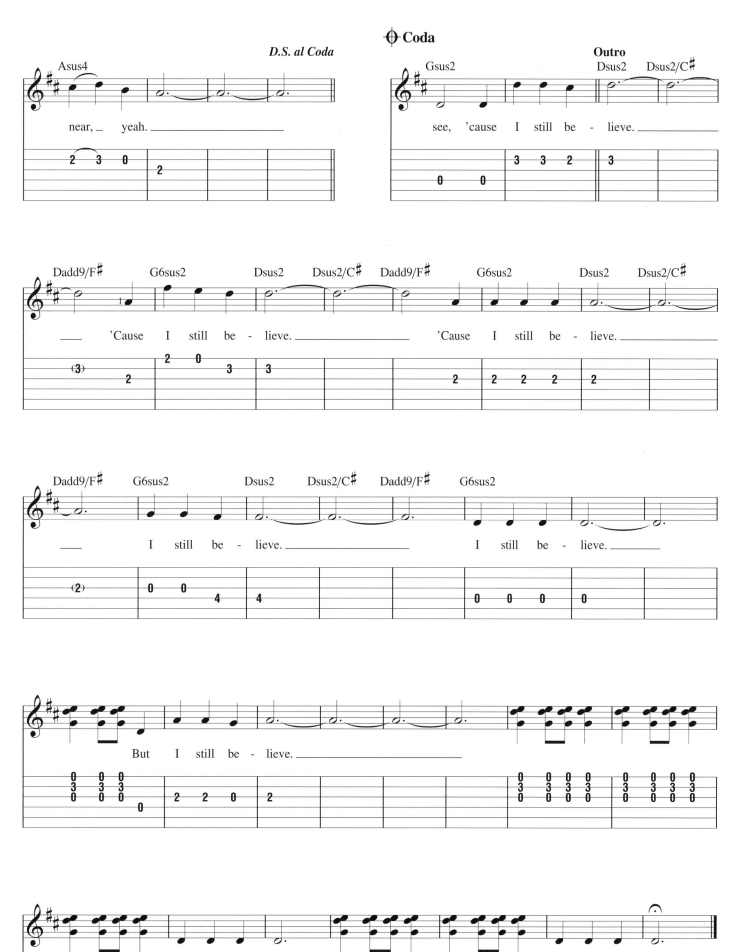

I Will Rise

Words and Music by Chris Tomlin, Jesse Reeves, Louie Giglio and Matt Maher

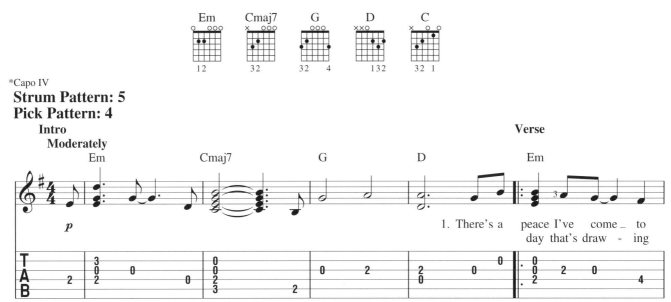

*Capo IV

Strum Pattern: 5
Pick Pattern: 4

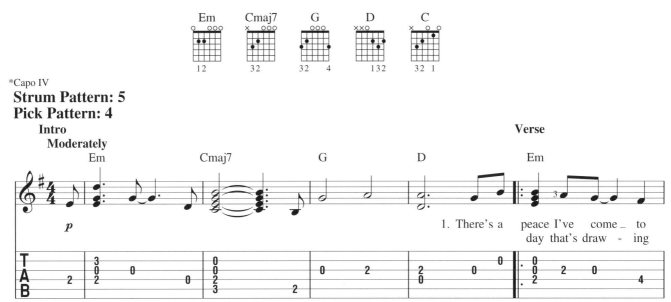

*Optional: To match recording, place capo at 4th fret.

Intro
Moderately

1. There's a peace I've come to day that's draw - ing

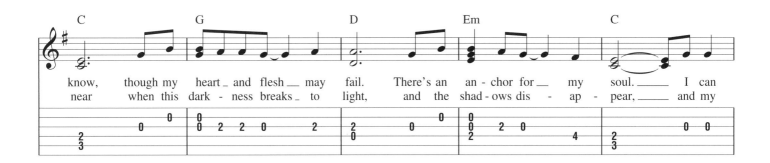

know, though my heart _ and flesh _ may fail. There's an an - chor for _ my soul. _____ I can
near when this dark - ness breaks _ to light, and the shad - ows dis - ap - pear, _____ and my

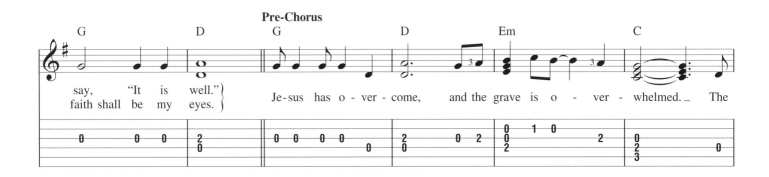

say, "It is well."
faith shall be my eyes. } Je - sus has o - ver - come, and the grave is o - ver - whelmed. _ The

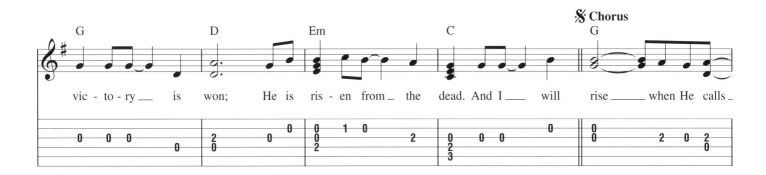

vic - to - ry _ is won; He is ris - en from _ the dead. And I _____ will rise _____ when He calls _

D Em C G D
my name; no more sor - row, no more pain. I will rise on ea - gles' wings; be -
To Coda
1. 2.
Em C G C G D D
fore my God fall on my knees, and rise I will rise. 2. There's a
Bridge
C G D C G
And I hear the voice of man - y an - gels sing, "Wor - thy is the Lamb!"
D C G D C G
And I hear the cry of ev - 'ry long - ing heart, "Wor - thy is the Lamb!"
1. 2.
Interlude
D D C G D G D
And I hear the voice "Wor - thy is the Lamb!"
D.S. al Coda
Em C
I will
Coda
G C G D G
rit.
rise. I will rise.

I'm Not Alright

**Words and Music by Douglas Caine McKelvey, Matt Hammitt,
Chris Rohman, Mark Graalman, Chris Stevens and Dan Gartley**

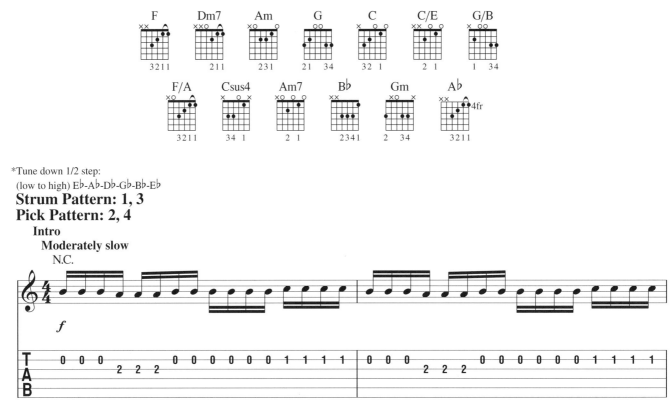

*Tune down 1/2 step:
(low to high) Eb-Ab-Db-Gb-Bb-Eb

Strum Pattern: 1, 3
Pick Pattern: 2, 4

Intro
Moderately slow

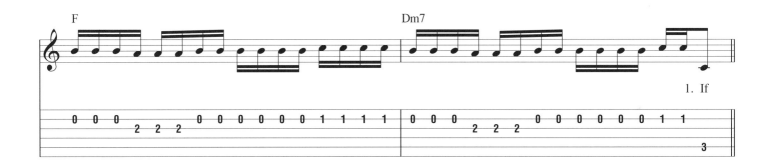

*Optional: To match recording, tune down 1/2 step.

Verse

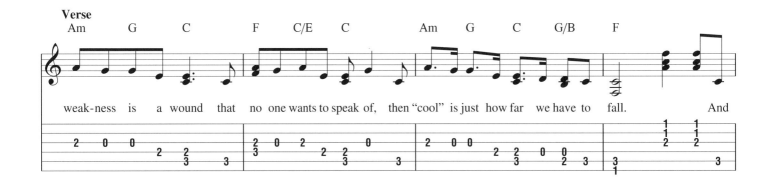

weak-ness is a wound that no one wants to speak of, then "cool" is just how far we have to fall. And

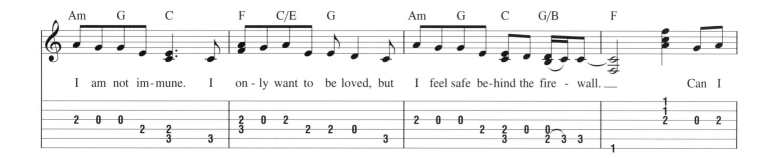

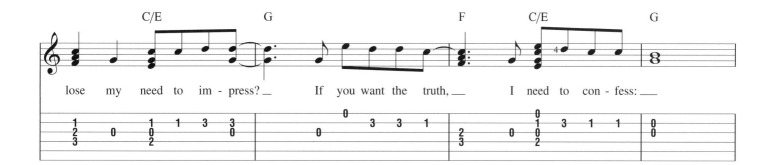

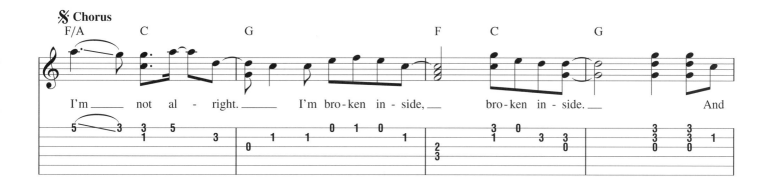

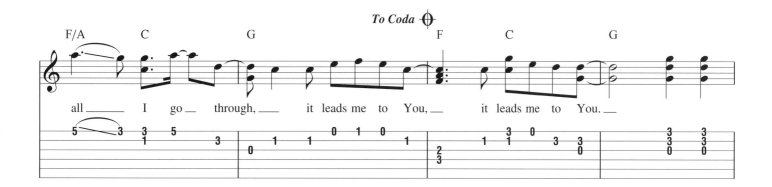

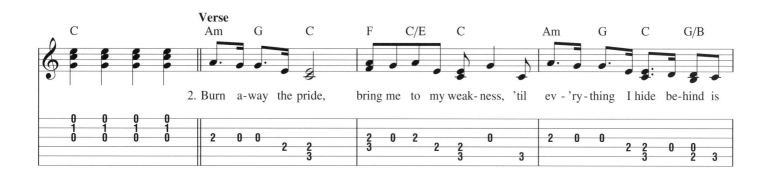

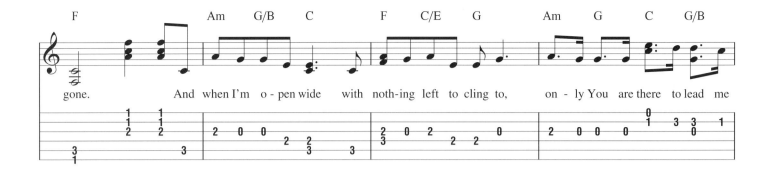

gone. And when I'm o-pen wide with noth-ing left to cling to, on-ly You are there to lead me

D.S. al Coda

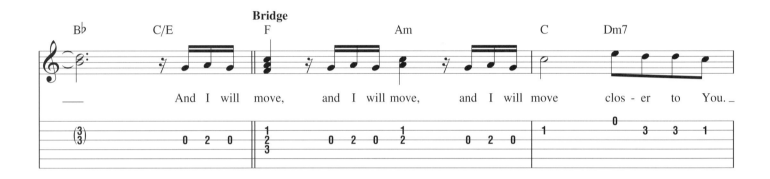

on. 'Cause hon-est-ly, I'm not that strong.

⊕ **Coda**

it leads me to You.

Bridge

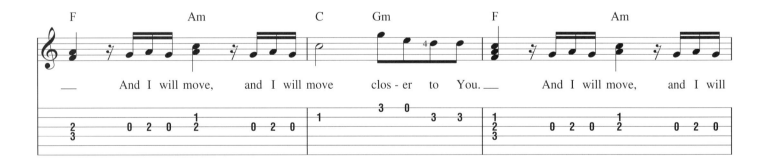

And I will move, and I will move, and I will move clos-er to You.

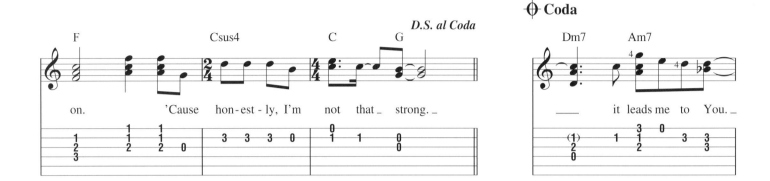

And I will move, and I will move clos-er to You. And I will move, and I will

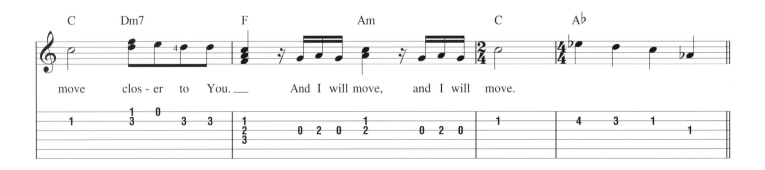

move clos-er to You. And I will move, and I will move.

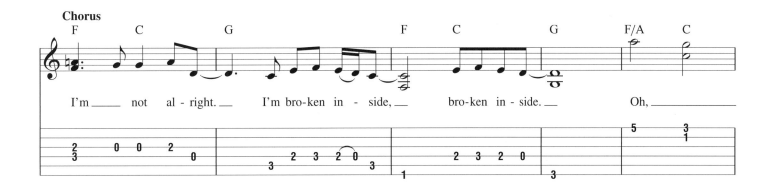

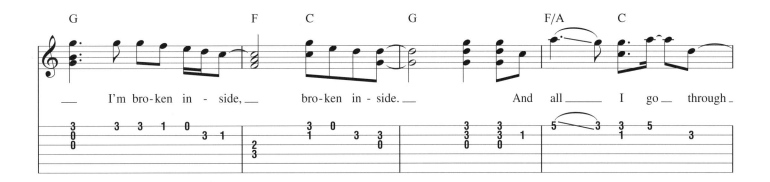

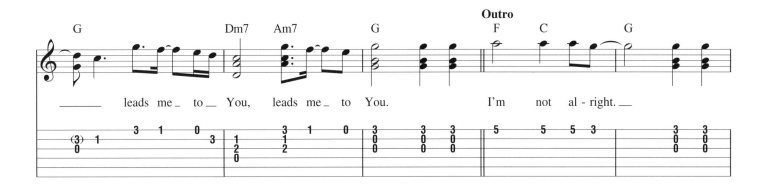

If We Are the Body

Words and Music by Mark Hall

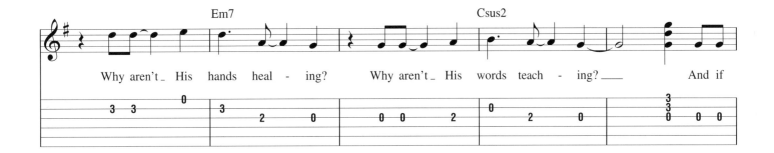

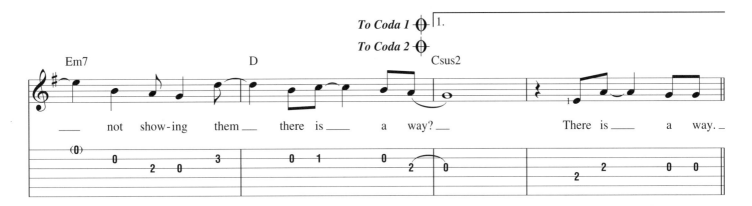

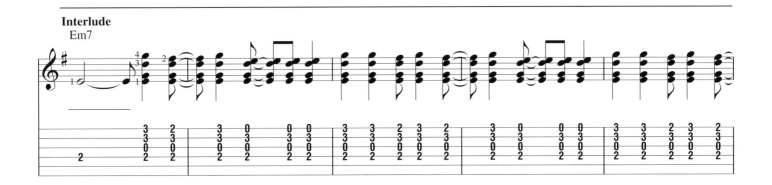

Interlude

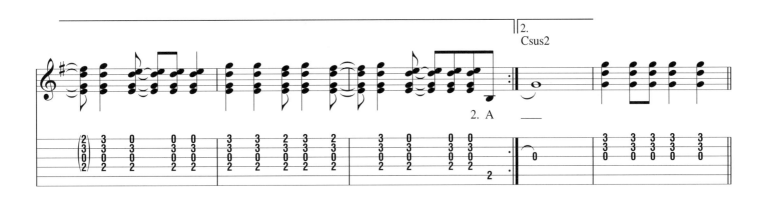

Bridge

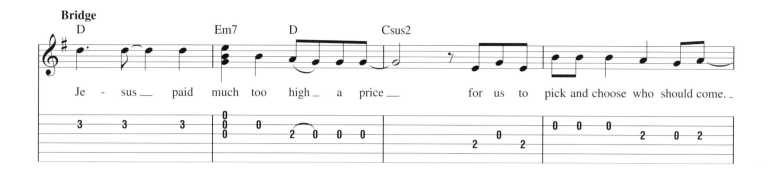

Je - sus ___ paid much too high ___ a price ___ for us to pick and choose who should come. ___

D.S. al Coda 1

Coda 1

D.S. al Coda 2

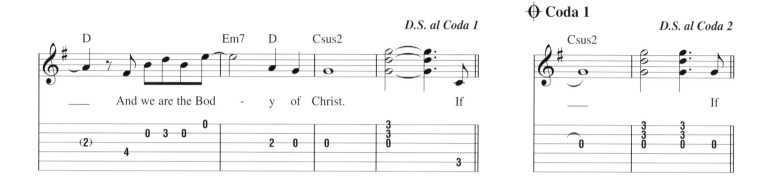

___ And we are the Bod - y of Christ. If

___ If

Coda 2

Outro

___ Je - sus is ___ the way. ___ You are ___ the One. ___

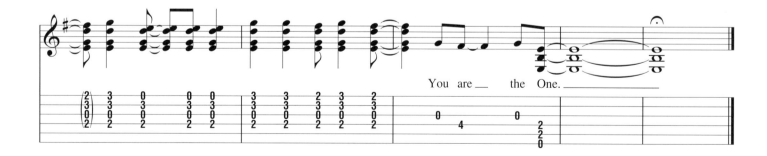

You are ___ the One. ___

Additional Lyrics

2. A trav'ler is far away from home.
   He sheds his coat and quietly sinks into the back row.
   The weight of their judgmental glance tells
   Him that his chances are better out on the road.

Joy

Words and Music by Peter Furler and Steve Taylor

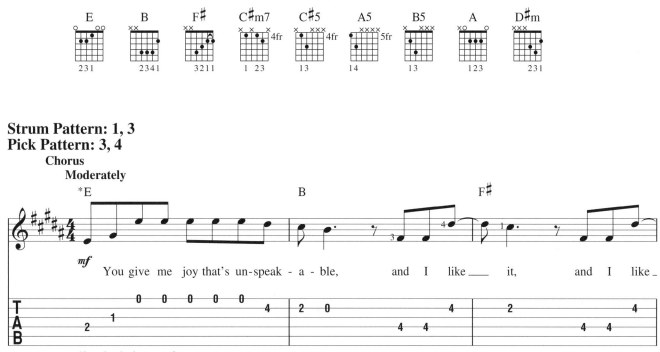

Strum Pattern: 1, 3
Pick Pattern: 3, 4

Chorus
Moderately

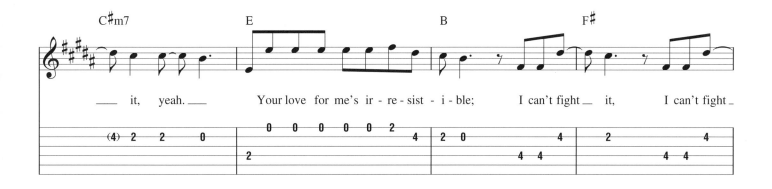

You give me joy that's un-speak - a - ble, and I like ___ it, and I like ___

*Let chords ring, next 9 meas.

___ it, yeah. ___ Your love for me's ir - re - sist - i - ble; I can't fight ___ it, I can't fight ___

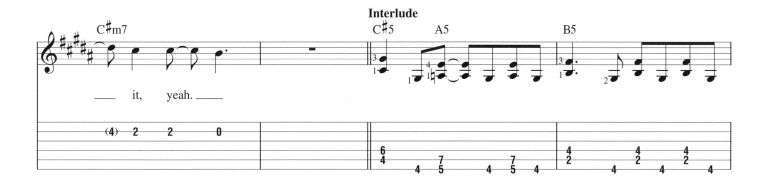

___ it, yeah. ___

Interlude

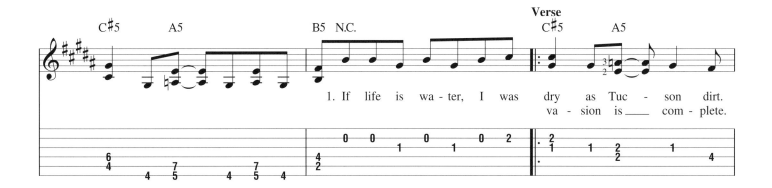

1. If life is wa-ter, I was dry as Tuc - son dirt.
va - sion is ___ com - plete.

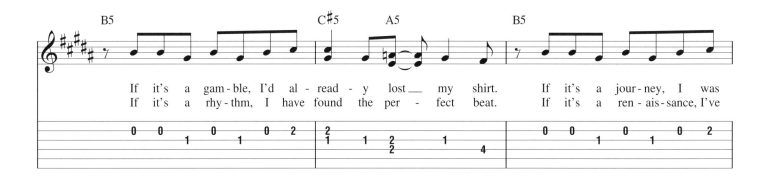

If it's a gam-ble, I'd al - read - y lost ___ my shirt. If it's a jour-ney, I was
If it's a rhy - thm, I have found the per - fect beat. If it's a ren - ais-sance, I've

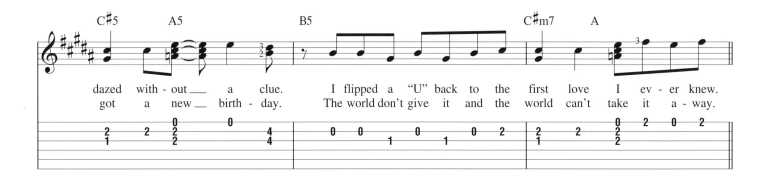

dazed with - out ___ a clue. I flipped a "U" back to the first love I ev - er knew.
got a new ___ birth - day. The world don't give it and the world can't take it a - way.

Chorus

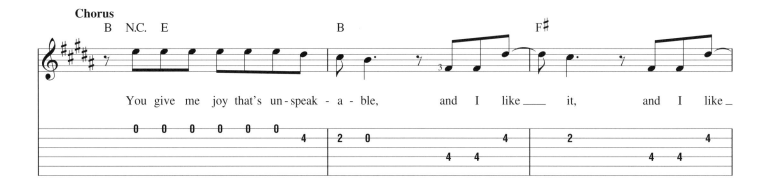

You give me joy that's un-speak - a - ble, and I like ___ it, and I like _

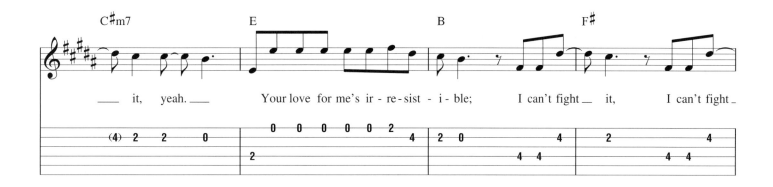

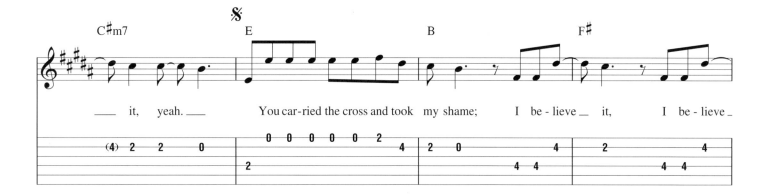

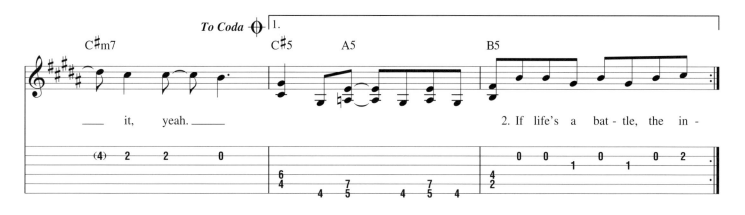

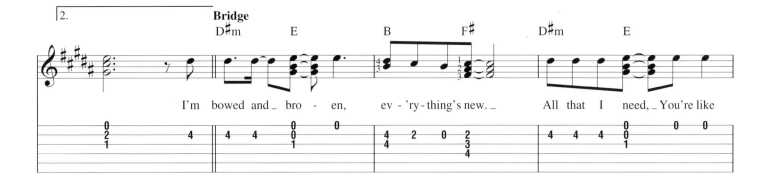

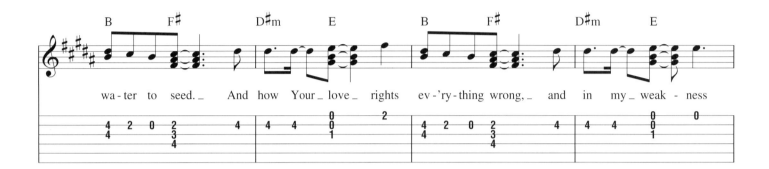

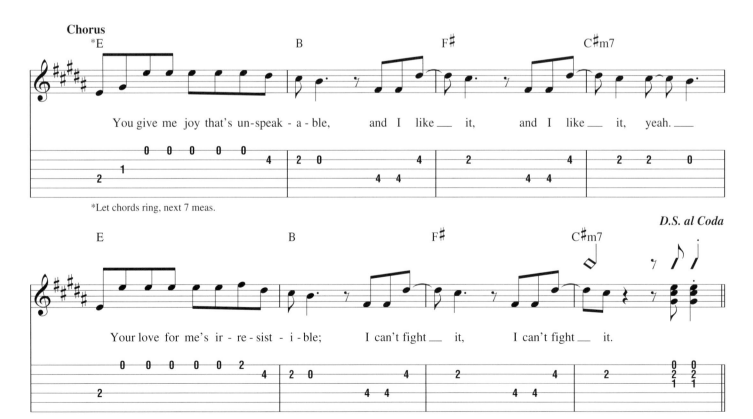

⊕ **Coda**

Outro-Chorus

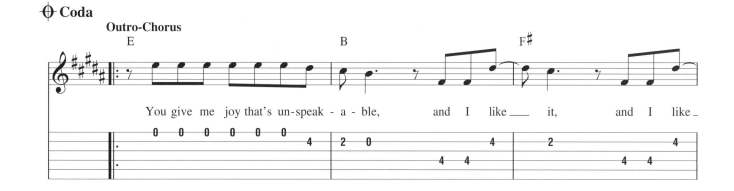

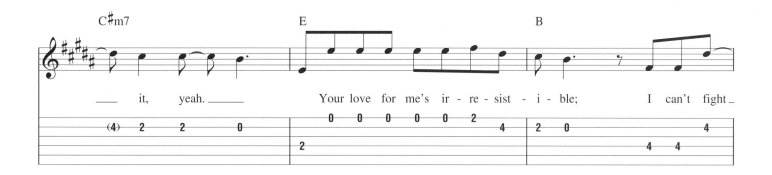

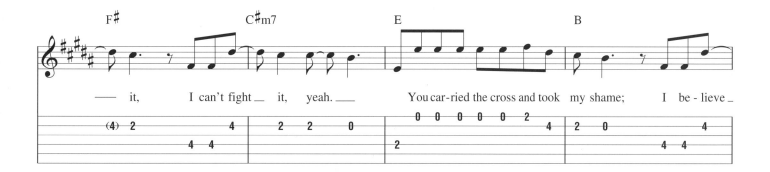

Repeat and fade

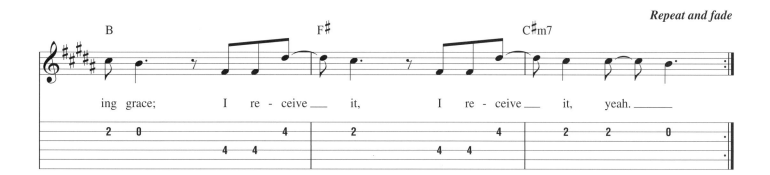

Let It Fade

Words and Music by Jeremy Camp and Adam Watts

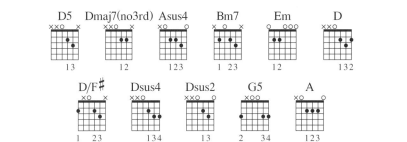

Strum Pattern: 1, 3
Pick Pattern: 3, 4

Intro
Moderately, in 2

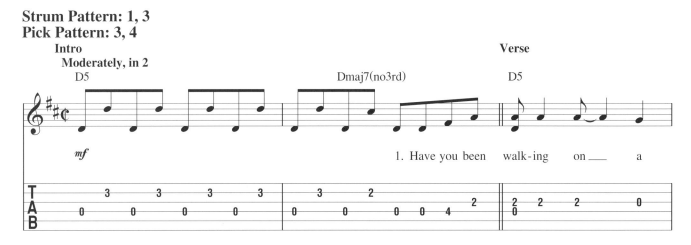

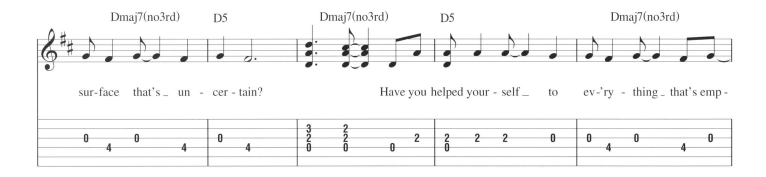

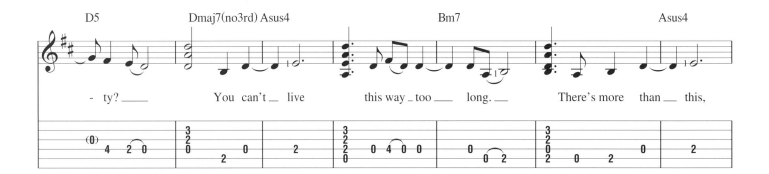

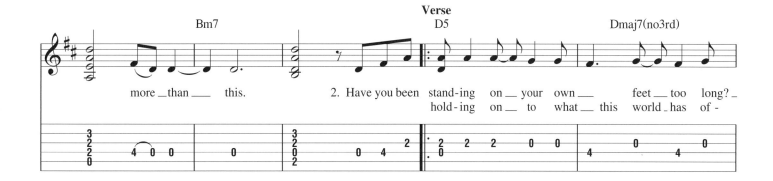

more _ than _ this. 2. Have you been stand-ing on _ your own _ feet _ too long? _
hold-ing on _ to what _ this world _ has of -

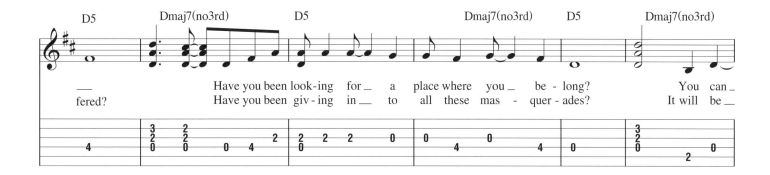

fered? Have you been look-ing for _ a place where you _ be - long? You can _
Have you been giv - ing in _ to all these mas - quer - ades? It will be _

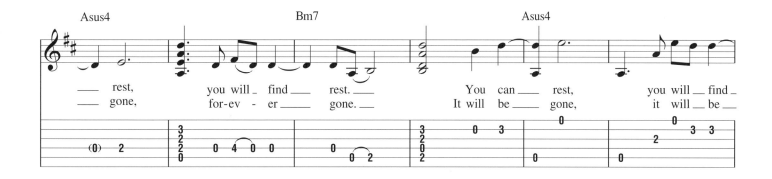

_ rest, you will _ find _ rest. _ You can _ rest, you will _ find _
_ gone, for-ev - er _ gone. _ It will be _ gone, it will _ be _

Chorus

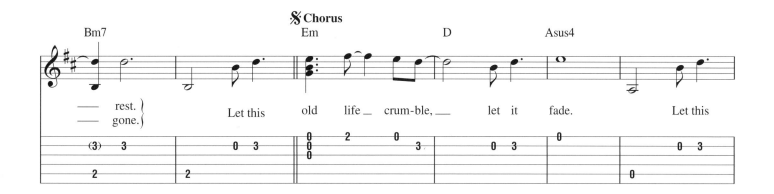

_ rest. } Let this old life _ crum-ble, _ let it fade. Let this
_ gone. }

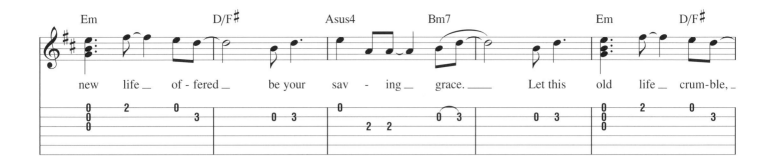

new   life __ of-fered __   be your   sav - ing __   grace. __   Let this   old   life __ crum-ble, __

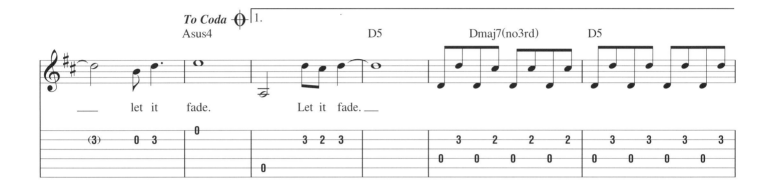

To Coda

__   let it   fade.   Let it   fade. __

3. Have you been   Let   it   fade. __

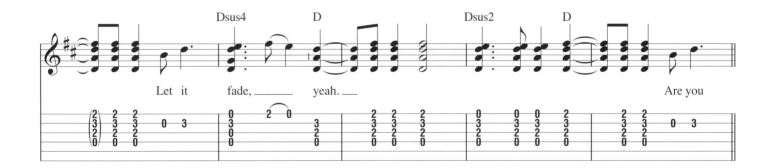

Let   it   fade, ____   yeah. __   Are you

Bridge

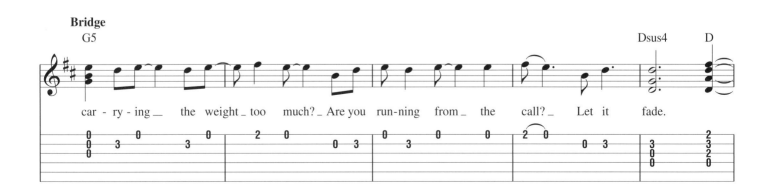

car - ry - ing __   the   weight __ too   much? __ Are you   run-ning   from __   the   call?   Let   it   fade.

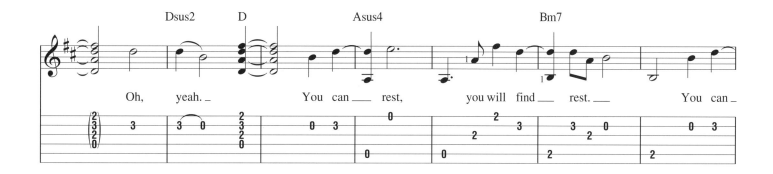

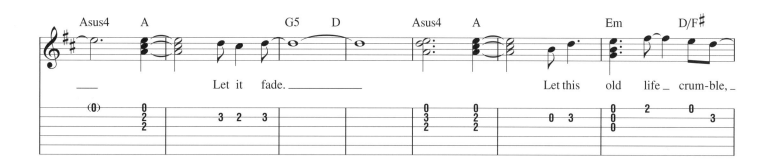

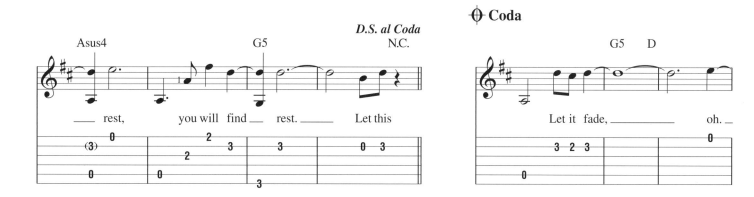

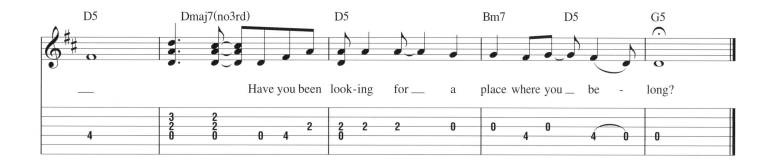

Live Out Loud

Words and Music by Steven Curtis Chapman and Geoff Moore

*Tune down 1/2 step:
(low to high) E♭-A♭-D♭-G♭-B♭-E♭

Strum Pattern: 1
Pick Pattern: 4

*Optional: To match recording, tune down 1/2 step.

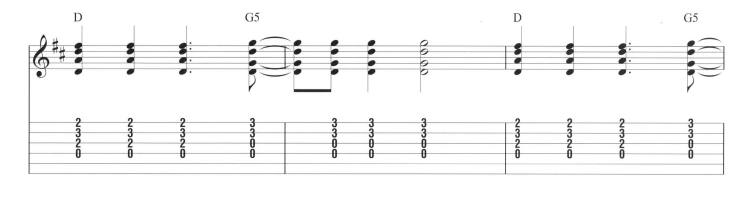

Verse

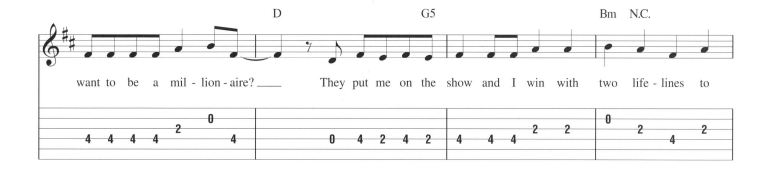

1. Im-ag-ine this: I get a phone call from Re-gis. He says, "Do you
2. *See additional lyrics*

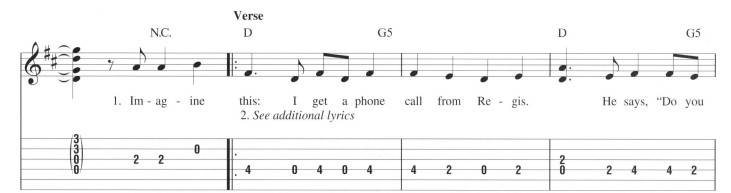

want to be a mil-lion-aire? ___ They put me on the show and I win with two life-lines to

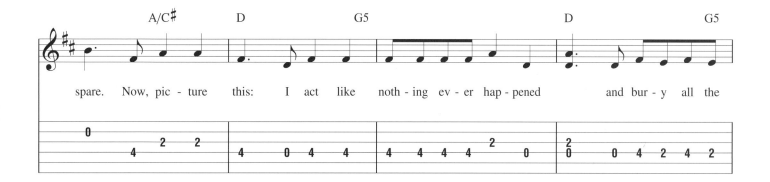

spare. Now, pic-ture this: I act like noth-ing ev-er hap-pened and bur-y all the

mon-ey in a cof-fee can. ___ Well, I've been giv-en more than Re-gis ev-er

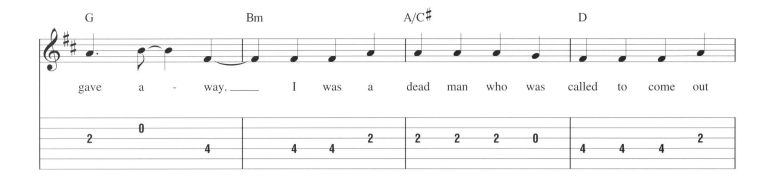

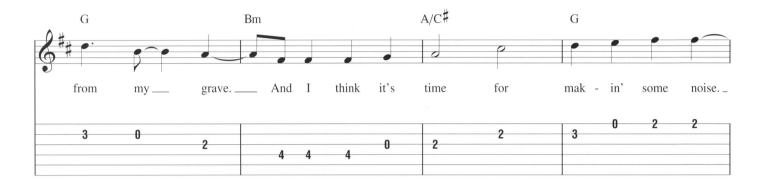

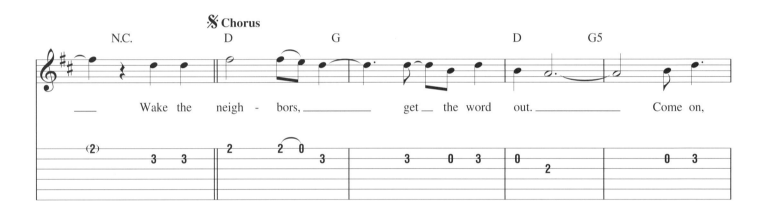

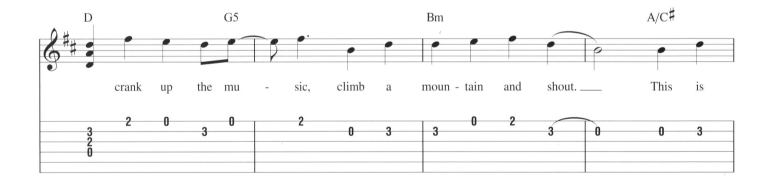

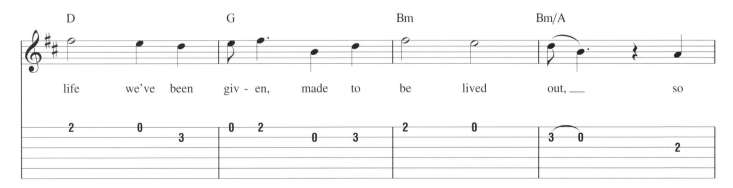

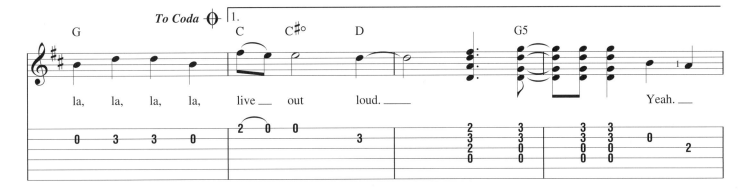

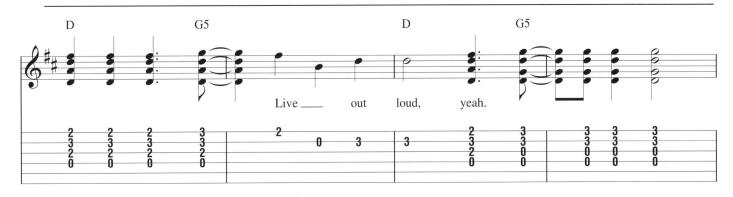

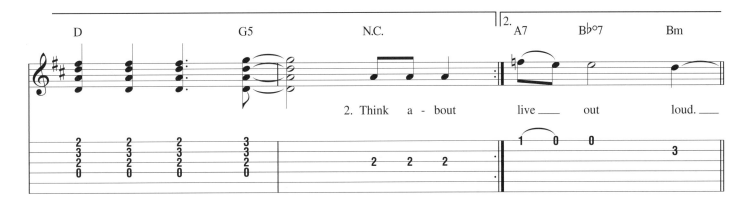

Interlude

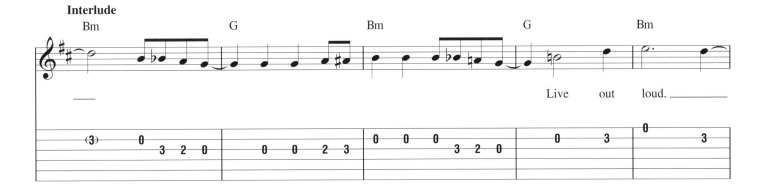

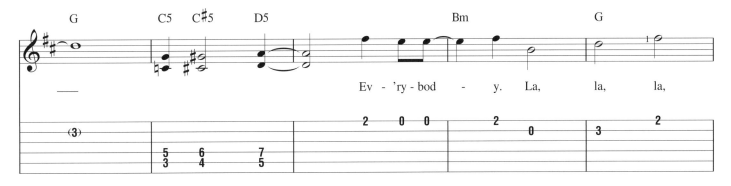

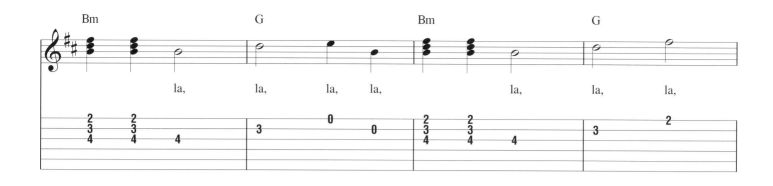

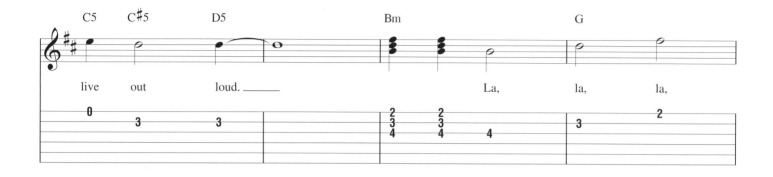

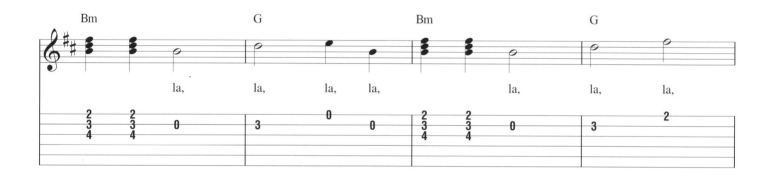

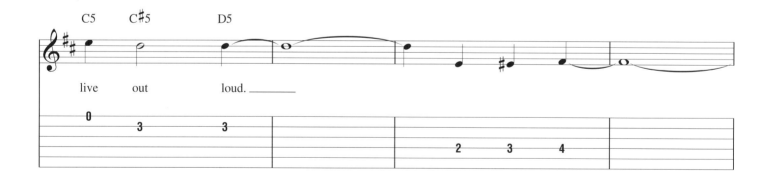

Bridge

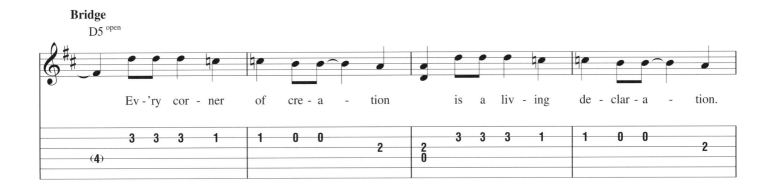

Ev-'ry cor-ner of cre-a-tion is a liv-ing de-clar-a-tion.

D.S. al Coda

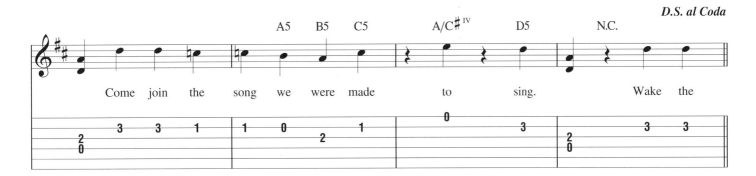

Come join the song we were made to sing. Wake the

⊕ Coda

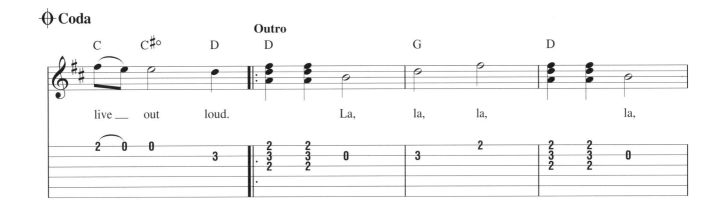

Outro

live out loud. La, la, la, la,

Repeat and fade

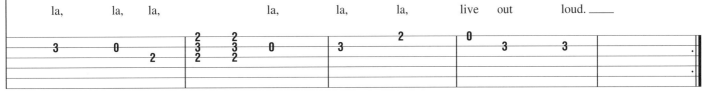

la, la, la, la, la, la, live out loud.

Additional Lyrics

2. Think about this:
   Try to keep a bird from singing
   After it's soared up in the sky,
   Give the sun a cloudless day
   And tell it not to shine.
   Now, think about this:
   If we really have been given
   The gift of life that will never end,
   And if we have been filled with living hope,
   We're gonna overflow,
   And if God's love is burning in our hearts,
   We're gonna know.
   There's just no way to keep it in.

Made to Worship

Words and Music by Chris Tomlin, Ed Cash, and Stephan Sharp

Strum Pattern: 3, 4
Pick Pattern: 4, 5

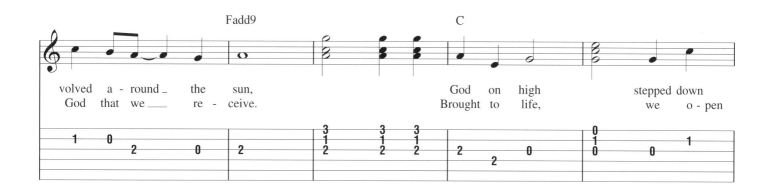

1. Be - fore the day, _ be - fore the light, _ be - fore the world _ re -
2. All we are _ and all we have _ is all a gift _ from

volved a - round _ the sun, God on high stepped down
God that we _ re - ceive. Brought to life, we o - pen

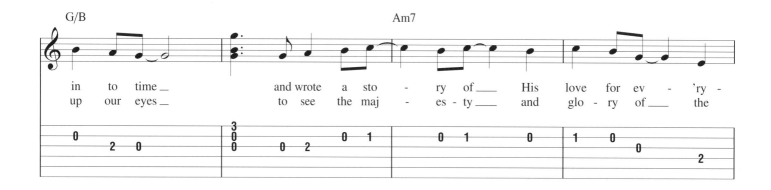

in - to time _ and wrote a sto - ry of __ His love for ev - 'ry -
up our eyes _ to see the maj - es - ty __ and glo - ry of __ the

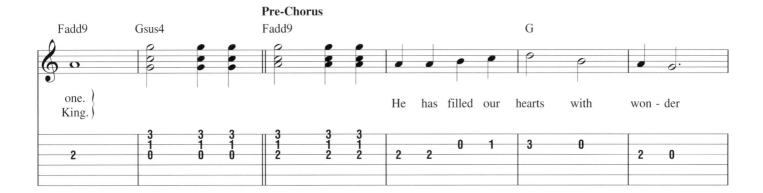

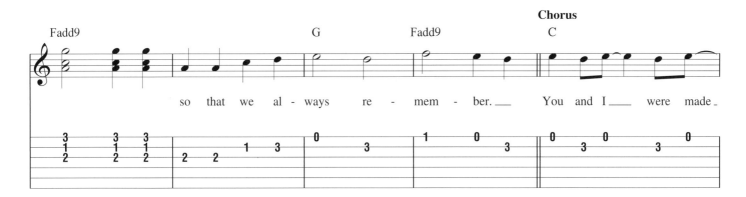

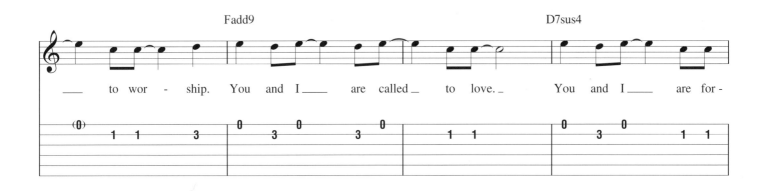

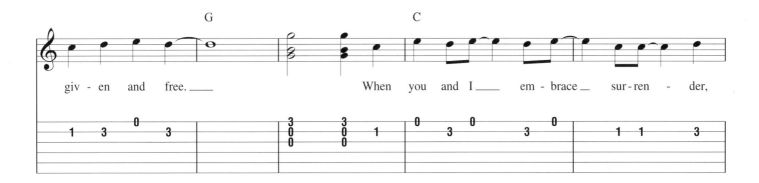

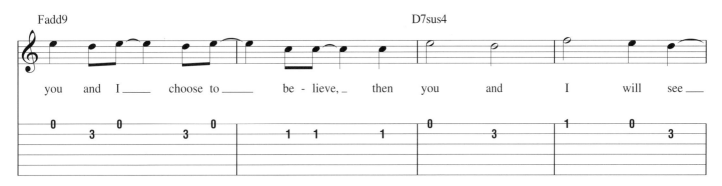

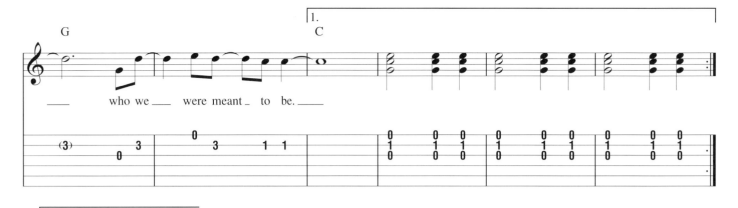

who we ___ were meant ___ to be. ___

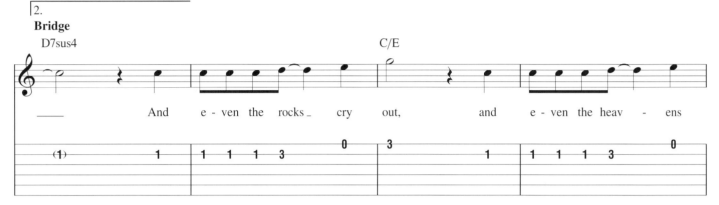

Bridge

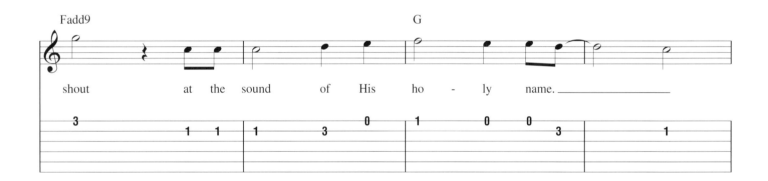

___ And e - ven the rocks ___ cry out, and e - ven the heav - ens

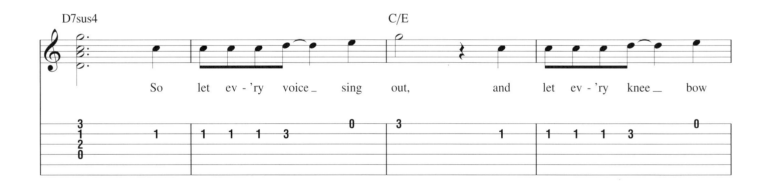

shout at the sound of His ho - ly name. ___

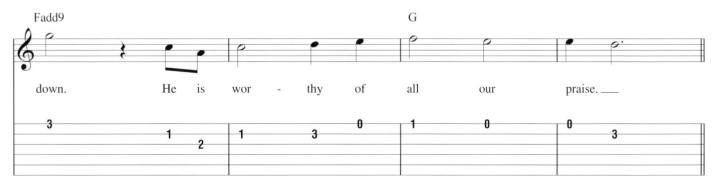

So let ev - 'ry voice ___ sing out, and let ev - 'ry knee ___ bow

down. He is wor - thy of all our praise. ___

Chorus

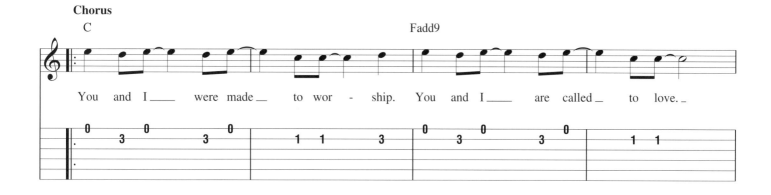

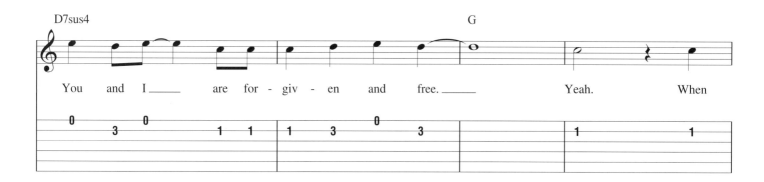

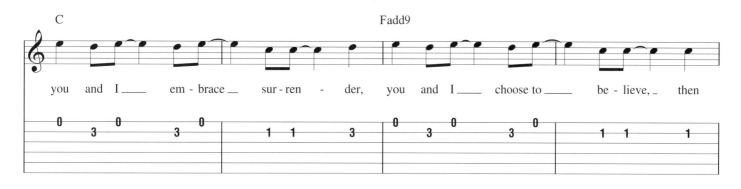

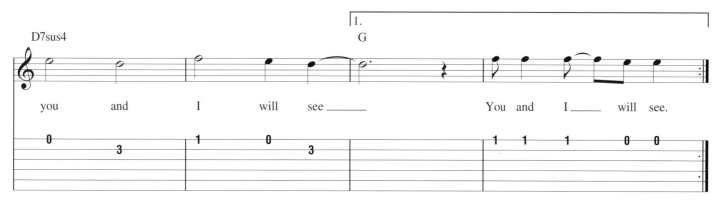

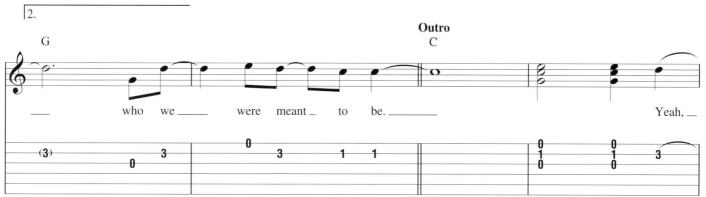

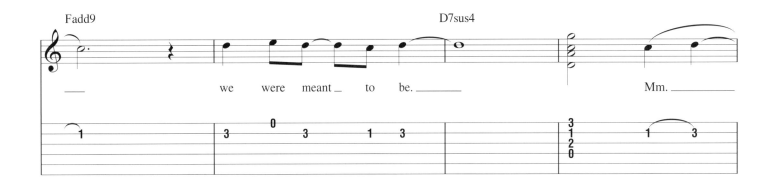

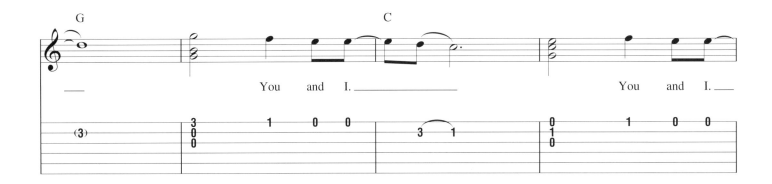

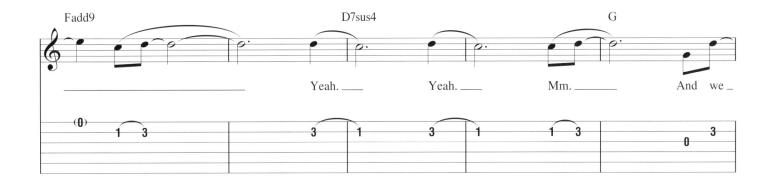

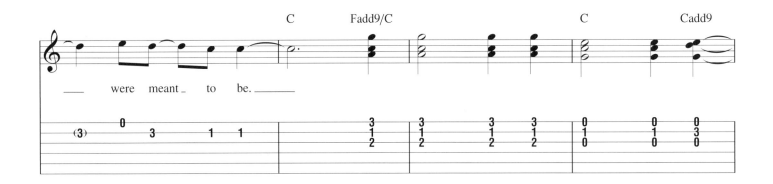

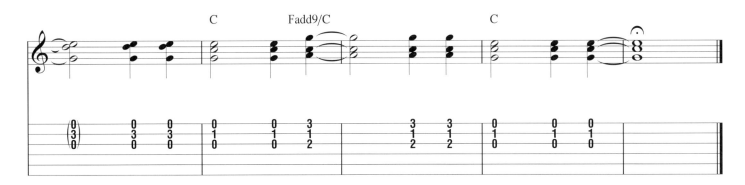

Million Pieces

Words and Music by Peter Furler and Steve Taylor

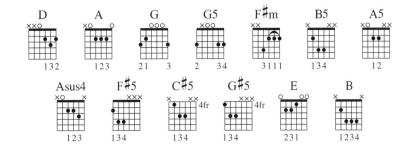

Strum Pattern: 2, 5
Pick Pattern: 1, 2

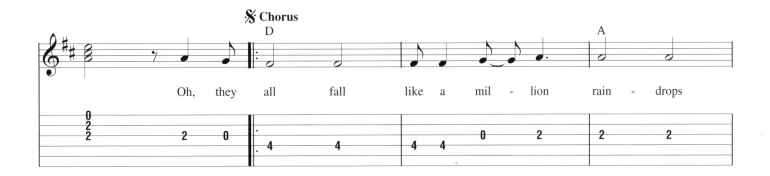

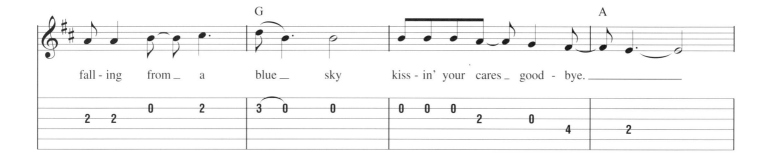

falling from _ a blue _ sky kiss - in' your cares _ good - bye. _____

Oh, __ as they all fall like a mil - lion piec - es, a

tick - er - tape _ pa - rade _ high, and now you're free _ to fly. ____

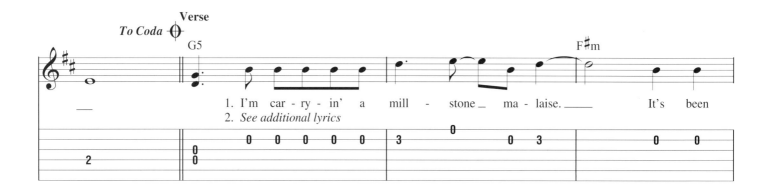

1. I'm car - ry - in' a mill - stone _ ma - laise. ____ It's been
2. *See additional lyrics*

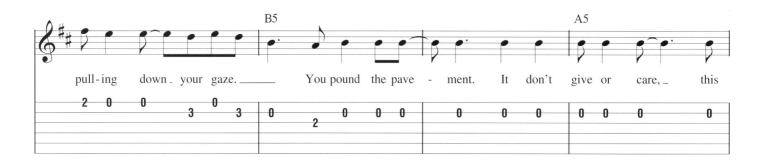

pull - ing down _ your gaze. _____ You pound the pave - ment. It don't give or care, _ this

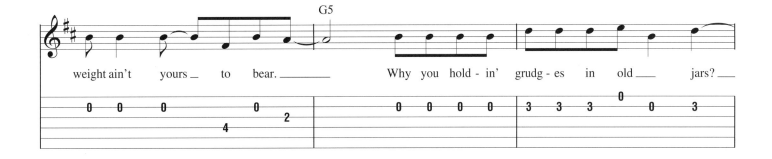

weight ain't yours __ to bear. _____ Why you hold-in' grudg-es in old __ jars? __

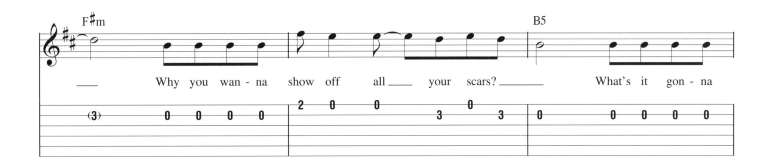

__ Why you wan-na show off all __ your scars? _____ What's it gon-na

2nd time, D.S. al Coda

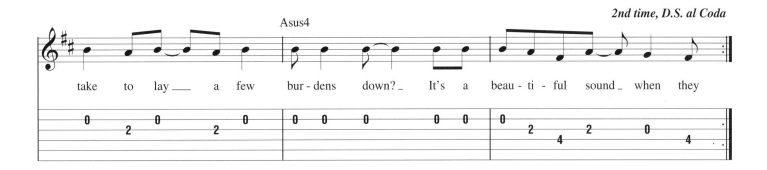

take to lay __ a few bur-dens down? _ It's a beau-ti-ful sound _ when they

Coda
Bridge

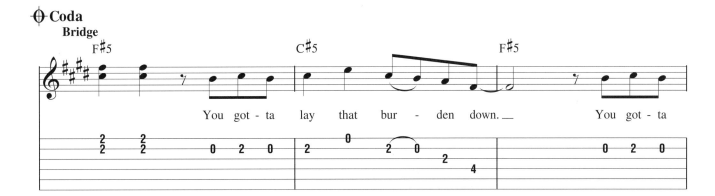

You got-ta lay that bur-den down. __ You got-ta

lay that bur-den down. __ It's time to leave your bur-dens in a pyre, _

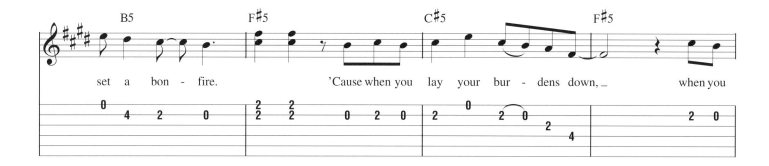

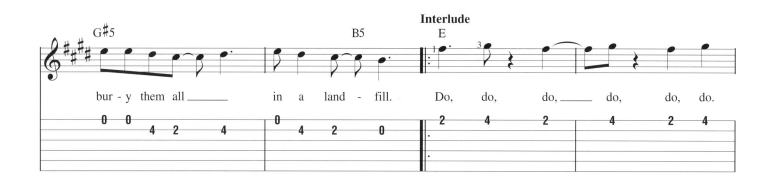

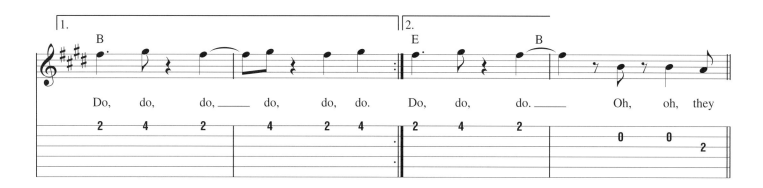

Outro-Chorus

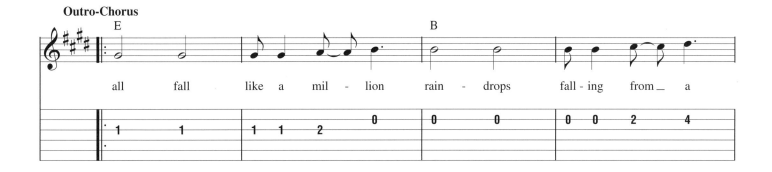

all   fall   like   a   mil - lion   rain - drops   fall - ing   from   a

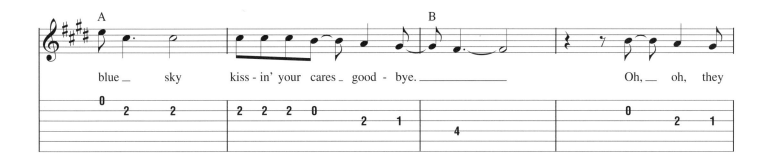

blue   sky   kiss - in' your cares good - bye.   Oh, oh, they

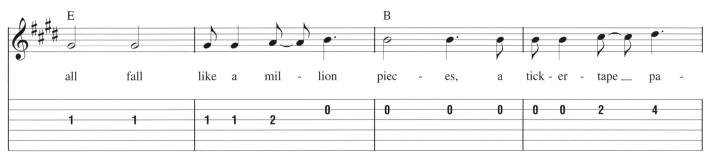

all   fall   like   a   mil - lion   piec - es,   a   tick - er - tape pa -

Repeat and fade

rade high, and now you're free to   fly.   Oh, they

Additional Lyrics

2. When that muffled sigh
   Says you're barely getting by,
   Cut your burdens loose
   And just simplify, simplify.
   This is not your floor,
   You're going higher than before.
   Drop the weight now,
   Wait for the lookout guide.
   Look outside as they...

Meant to Live

Words and Music by Jonathan Foreman and Tim Foreman

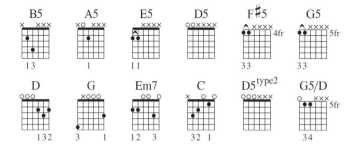

Drop D tuning:
(low to high) D–A–D–G–B–E

Strum Pattern: 2, 3

Intro

Moderately slow Rock

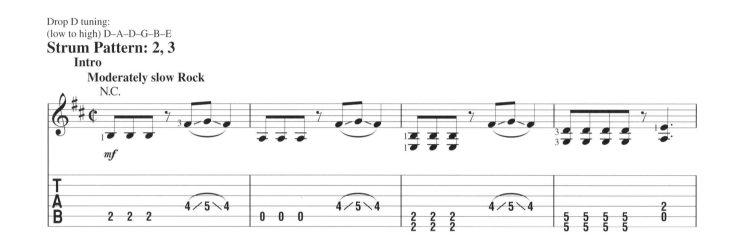

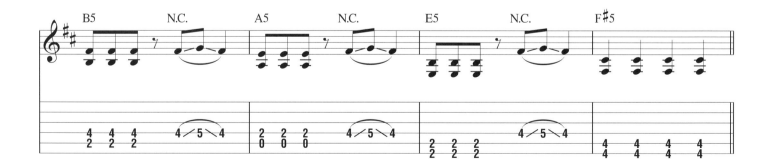

Verse

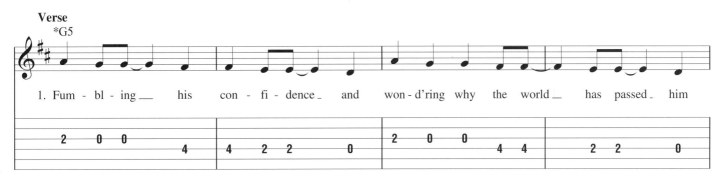

1. Fum- bl- ing ___ his con- fi- dence ___ and won- d'ring why the world ___ has passed ___ him

*Play chord once and hold through next 4 measures.

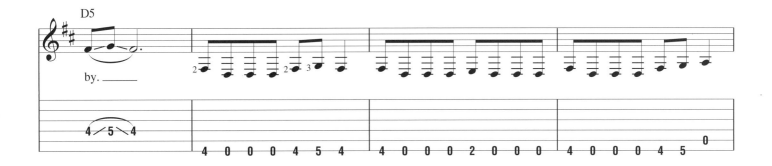

by. _____

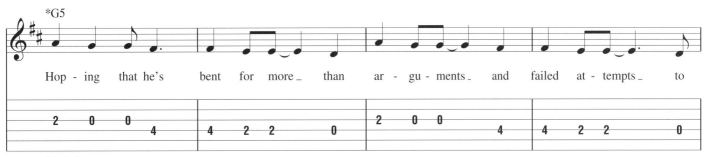

Hop- ing that he's bent for more ___ than ar- gu- ments ___ and failed at- tempts ___ to

*As before

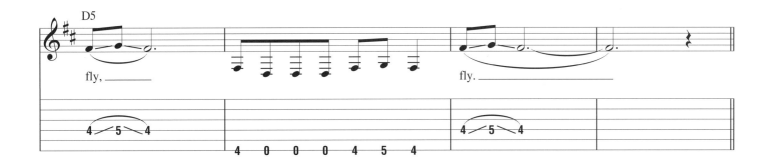

fly, _____ fly. _____

𝄋 Chorus

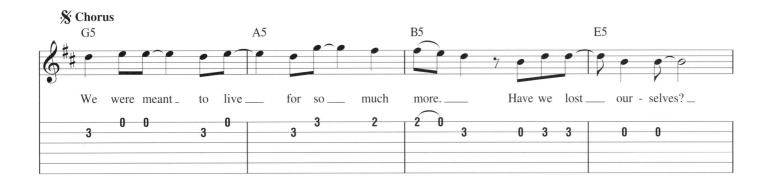

We were meant ___ to live ___ for so ___ much more. ___ Have we lost ___ our- selves? ___

Some-where we live in - side._____ Some-where we live in - side._____

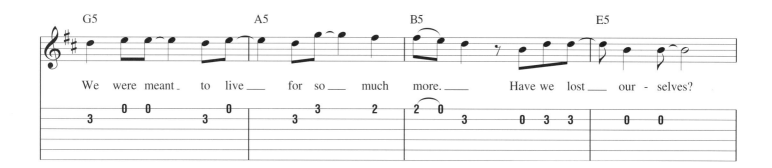

We were meant_ to live _ for so _ much more. _ Have we lost_ our - selves?

To Coda ⊕

Interlude

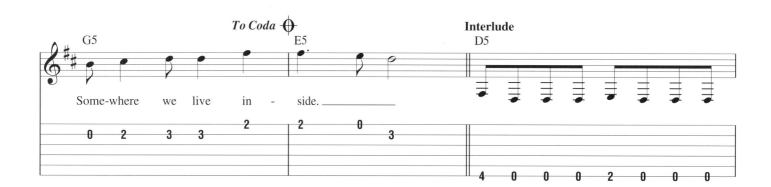

Some-where we live in - side._____

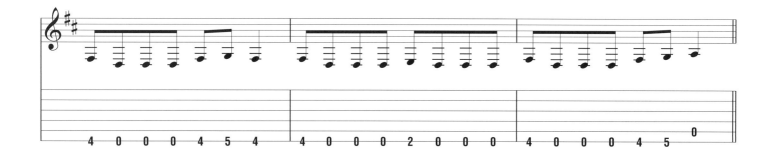

Verse

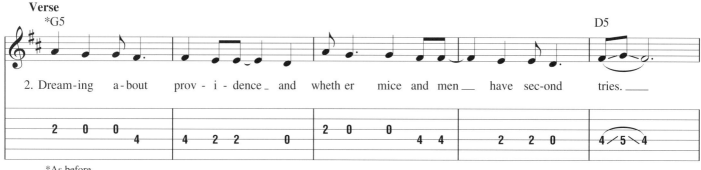

2. Dream-ing a-bout prov - i - dence _ and wheth er mice and men _ have sec-ond tries. _

*As before

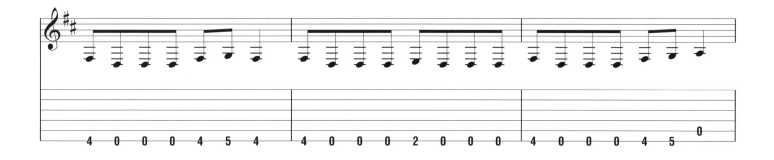

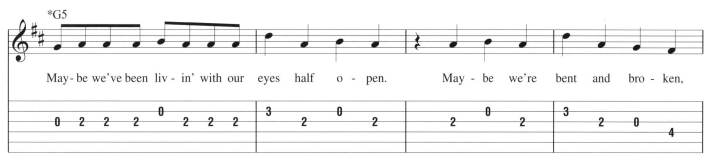

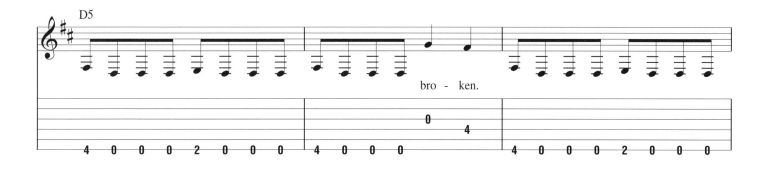

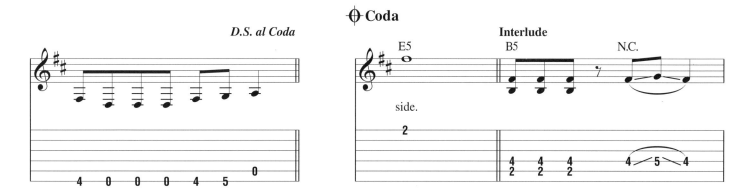

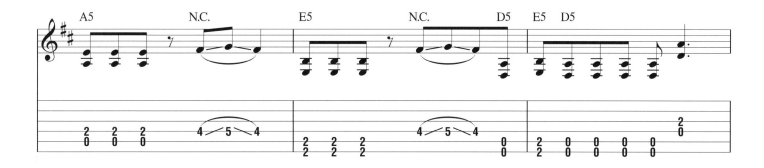

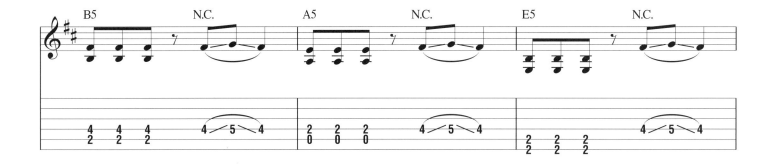

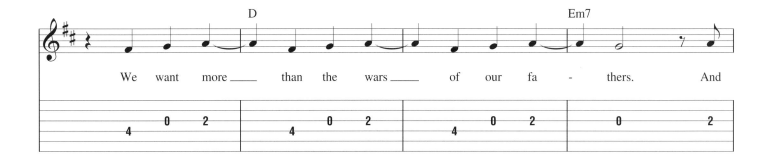

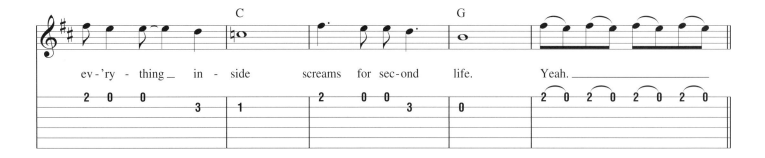

Outro-Chorus

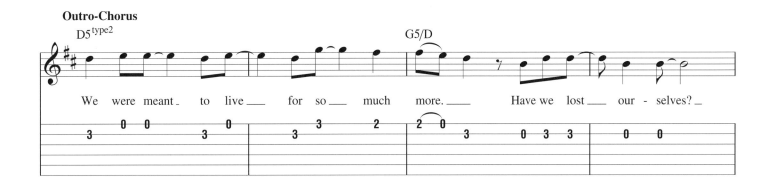

We were meant_ to live ___ for so ___ much more. ___ Have we lost ___ our - selves? _

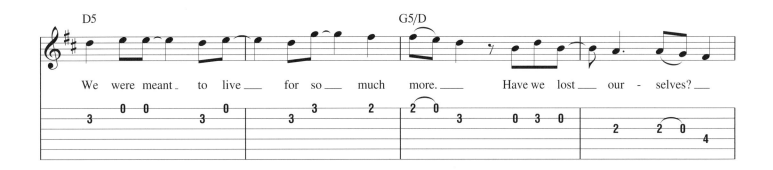

We were meant_ to live ___ for so ___ much more. ___ Have we lost ___ our - selves? _

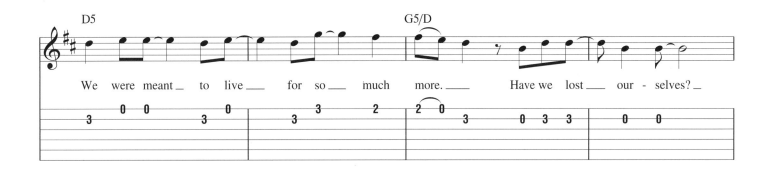

We were meant_ to live ___ for so ___ much more. ___ Have we lost ___ our - selves? _

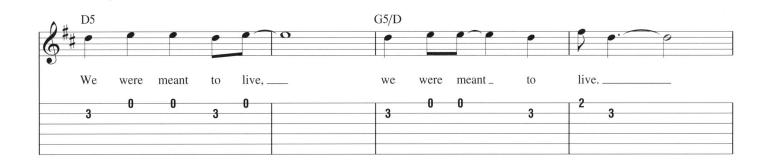

We were meant to live, ___ we were meant_ to live. _____

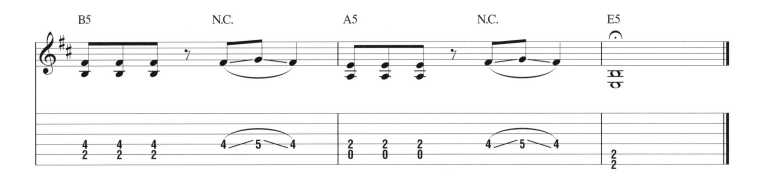

More

Words and Music by Kenny Greenberg, Jason Houser and Matthew West

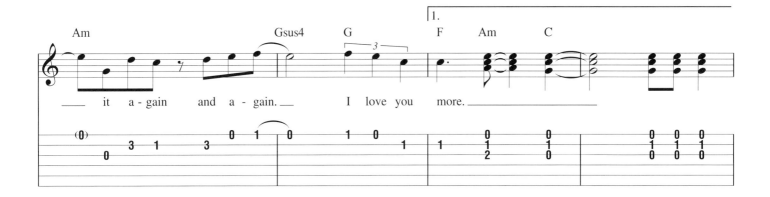

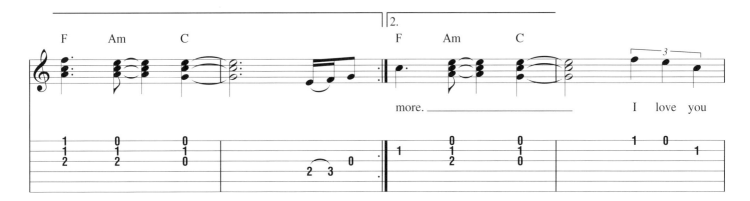

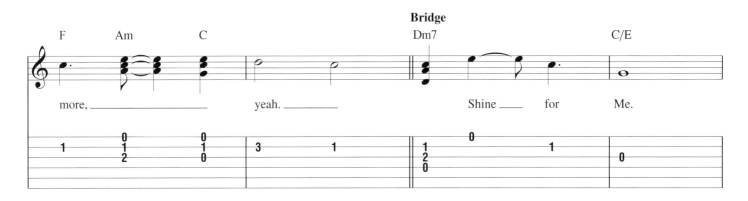

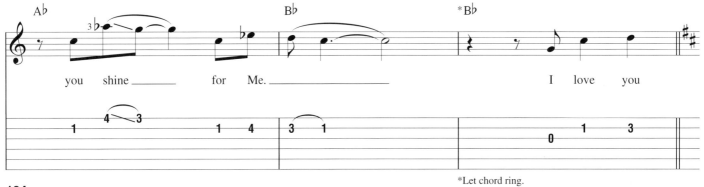

*Let chord ring.

Chorus

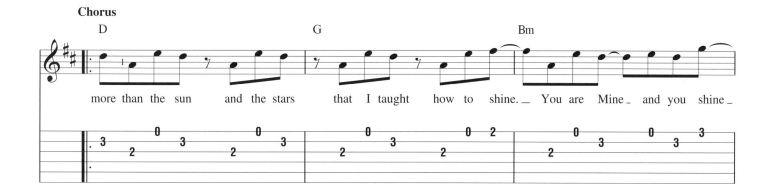

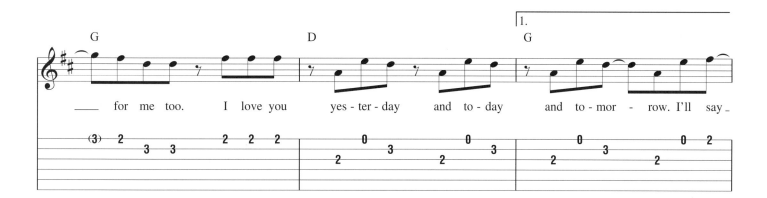

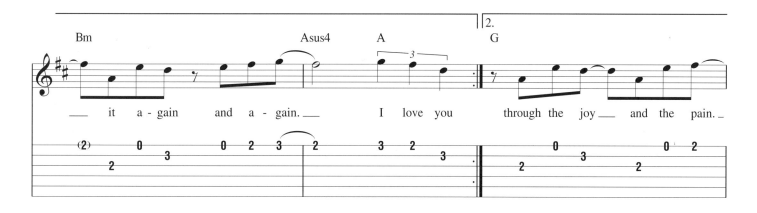

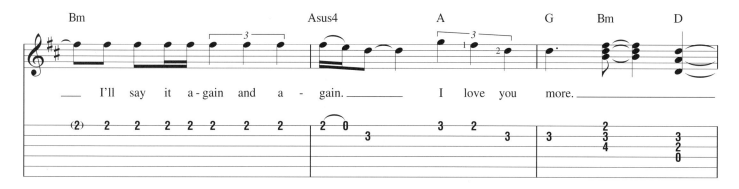

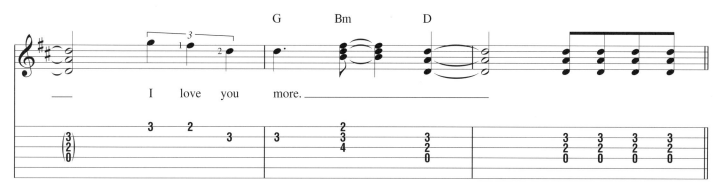

Outro

And I see ___ you. And I made ___ you. And I love ___ you

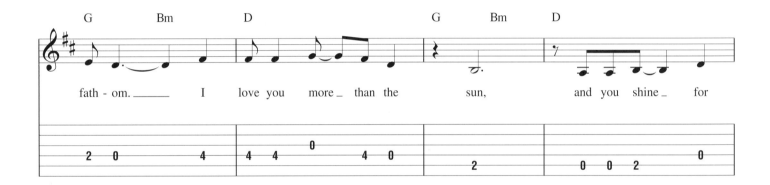

more than you ___ can im - ag - ine, _____ more than you ___ can

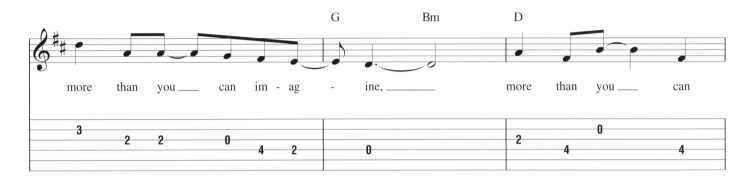

fath - om. _____ I love you more ___ than the sun, and you shine ___ for

Repeat and fade

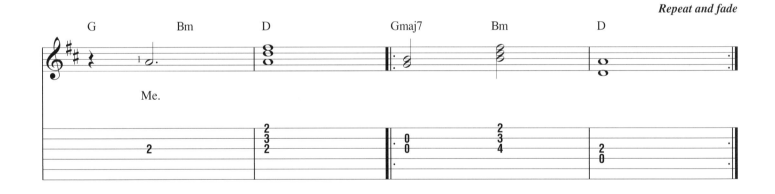

Me.

Additional Lyrics

3. Just a face in the city, just a tear on a crowded street,
   But you are one in a million, and you belong to Me.
   And I want you to know that I'm not letting go,
   Even when you come undone.

My Generation

Words and Music by Tim Neufeld, Jon Neufeld, Doug McKelvey and Shaun Huberts

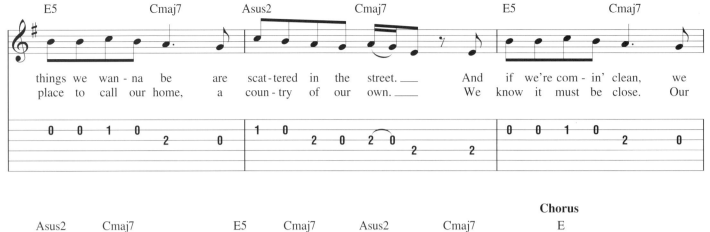

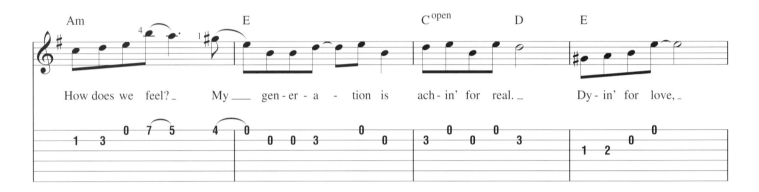

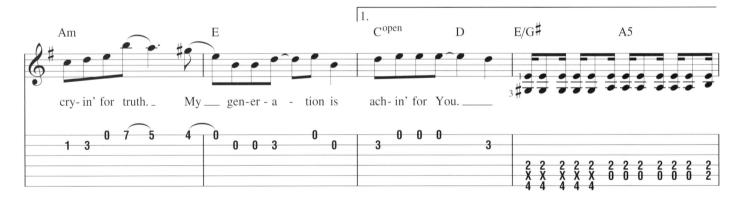

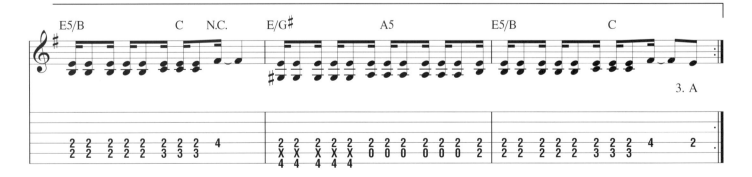

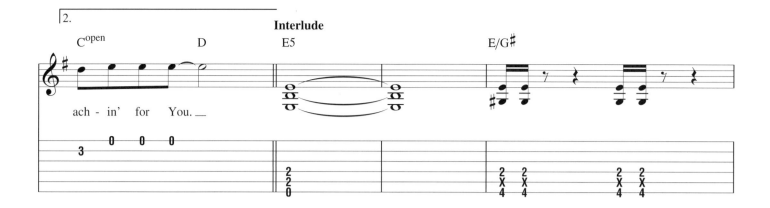

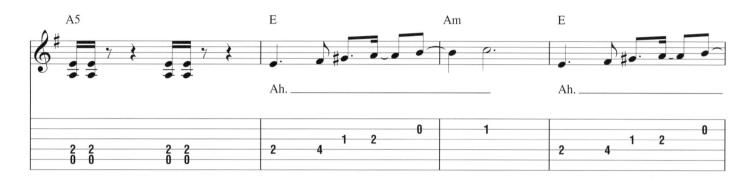

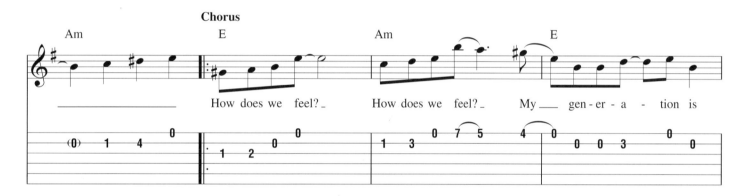

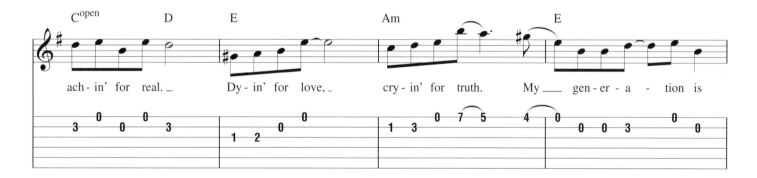

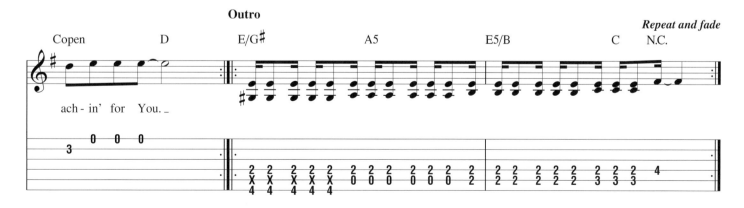

More to This Life

Words and Music by Steven Curtis Chapman and Phil Naish

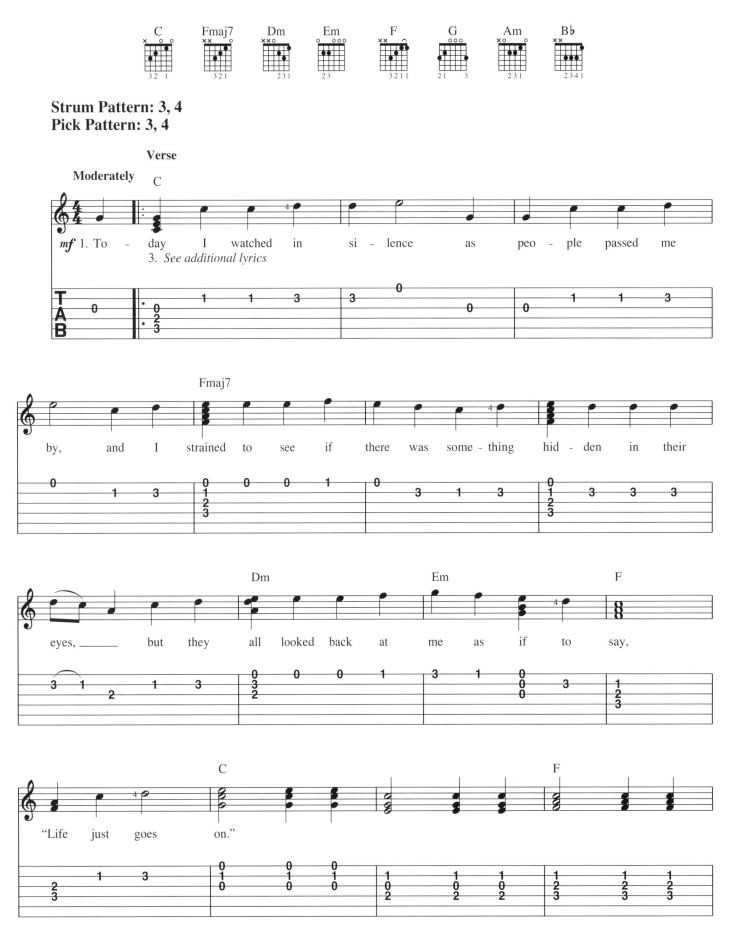

Strum Pattern: 3, 4
Pick Pattern: 3, 4

Verse

2. The old fa - mil - iar sto - ry told in dif - f'rent
4. *See additional lyrics*

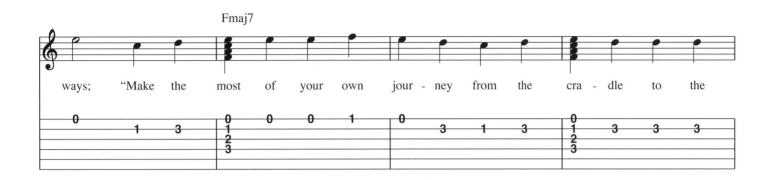

ways; "Make the most of your own jour - ney from the cra - dle to the

grave." ___ And dream your dreams to - mor - row, be - cause to - day

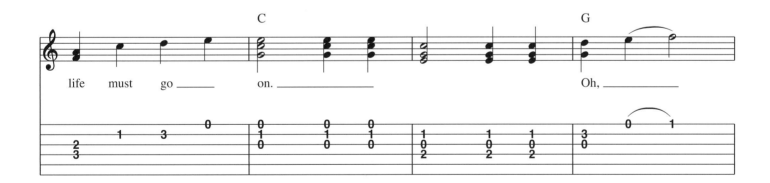

life must go ___ on. ___ Oh, ___

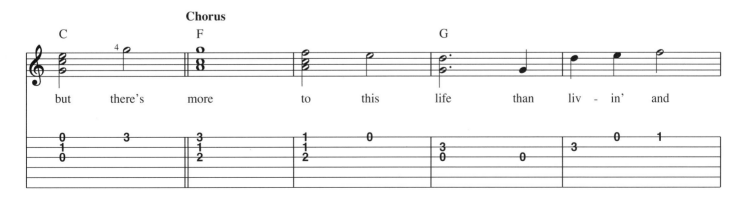

Chorus

but there's more to this life than liv - in' and

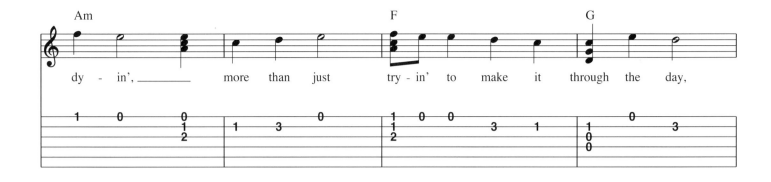

dy - in', _____ more than just try - in' to make it through the day,

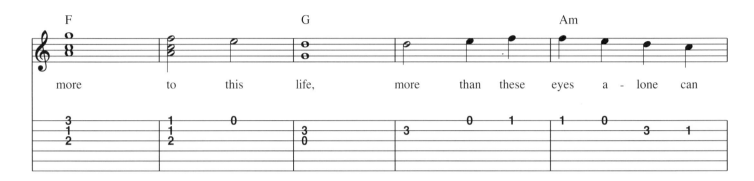

more to this life, more than these eyes a - lone can

1.

see. And there's more than this life a - lone can be.

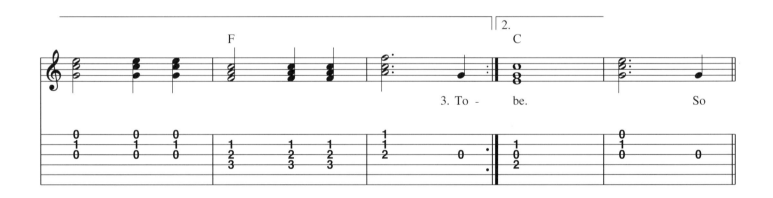

2.

3. To - be. So

Bridge

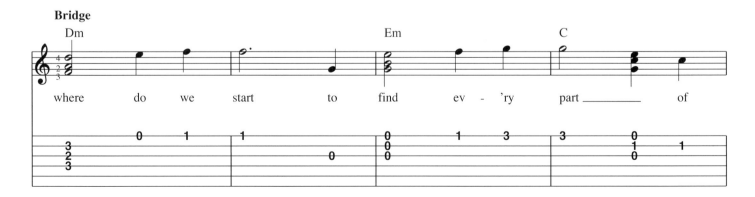

where do we start to find ev - 'ry part _____ of

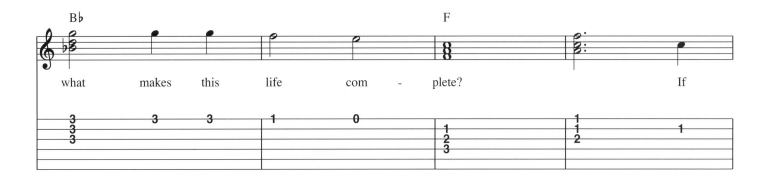

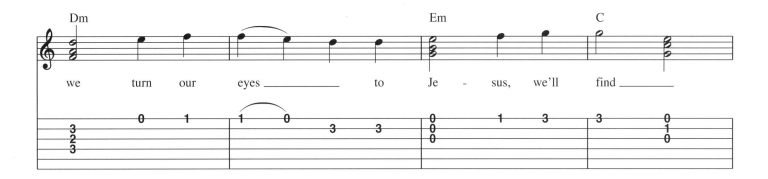

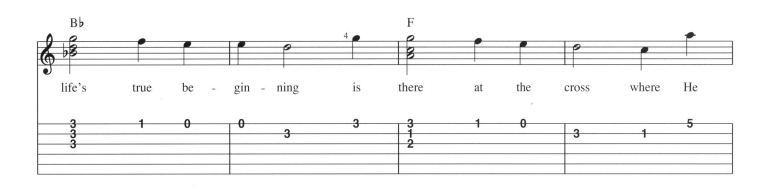

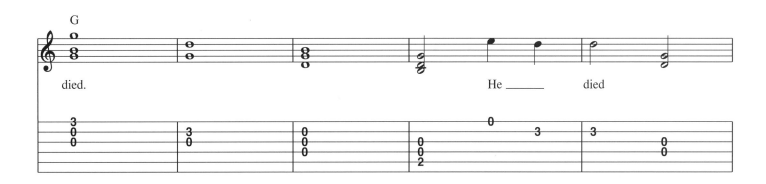

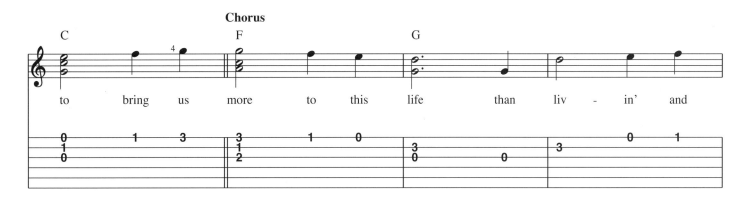

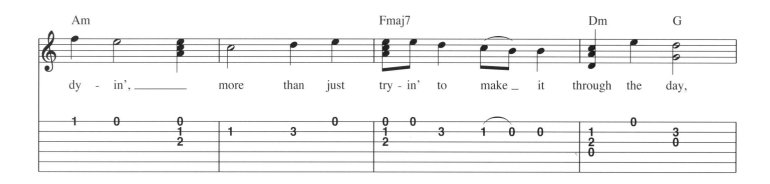

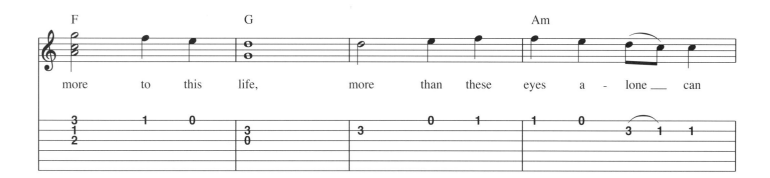

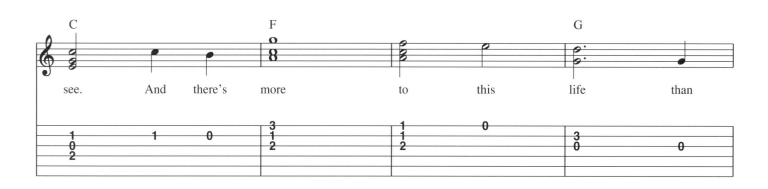

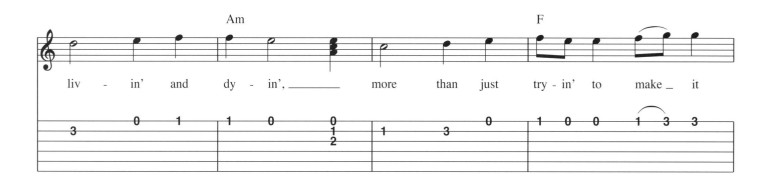

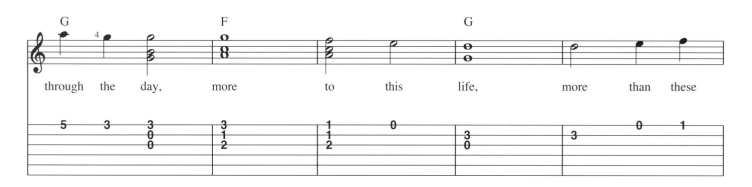

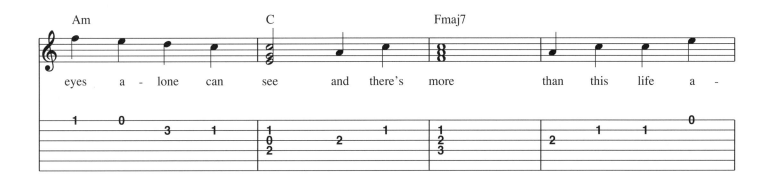

eyes a - lone can see and there's more than this life a -

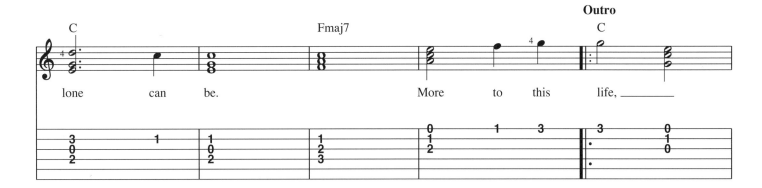

Outro

lone can be. More to this life, _____

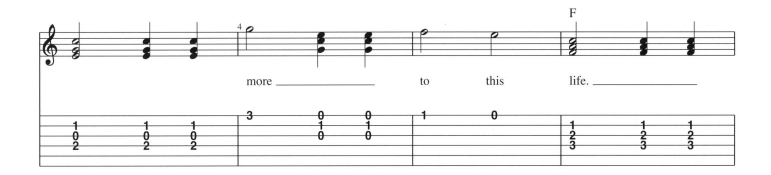

more _____ to this life. _____

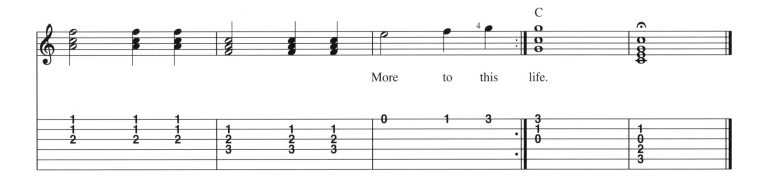

More to this life.

Additional Lyrics

3. Tonight he lies in silence, staring into space,
    And looks for ways to make tomorrow better than today.
    But in the morning light it looks the same.
    Life just goes on.

4. He takes care of his family, he takes care of his work,
    And ev'ry Sunday mornin' he takes his place at the church.
    But somehow he still feels the need to search,
    But life still goes on.

My Savior My God

Words and Music by Aaron Shust

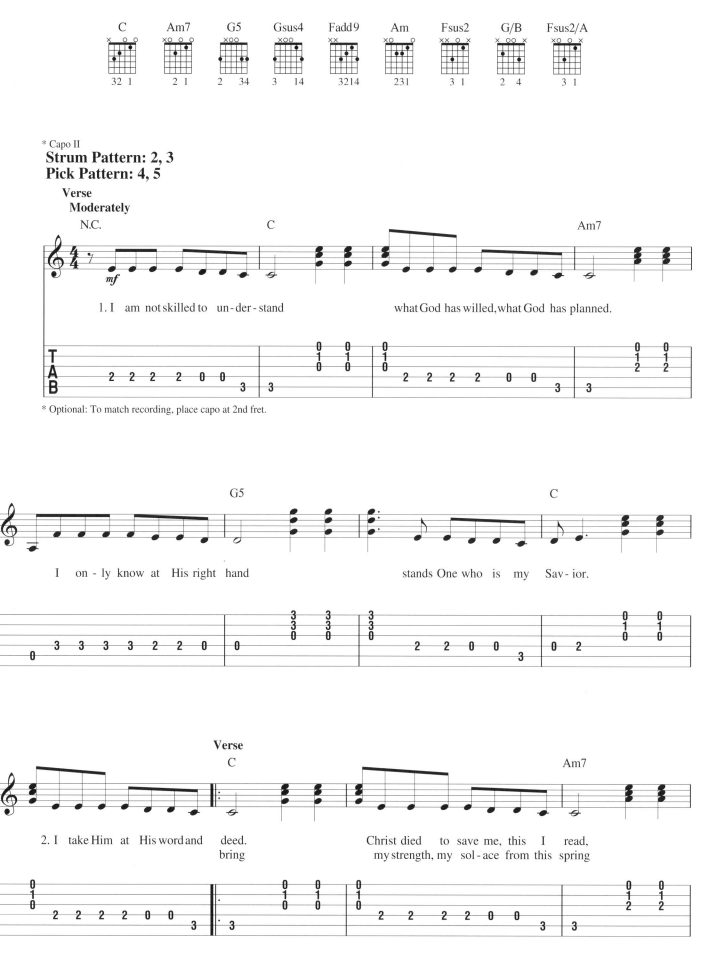

* Capo II

Strum Pattern: 2, 3
Pick Pattern: 4, 5

Verse
Moderately

1. I am not skilled to un-der-stand what God has willed, what God has planned.

* Optional: To match recording, place capo at 2nd fret.

I on-ly know at His right hand stands One who is my Sav-ior.

Verse

2. I take Him at His word and deed.
bring
Christ died to save me, this I read,
my strength, my sol-ace from this spring

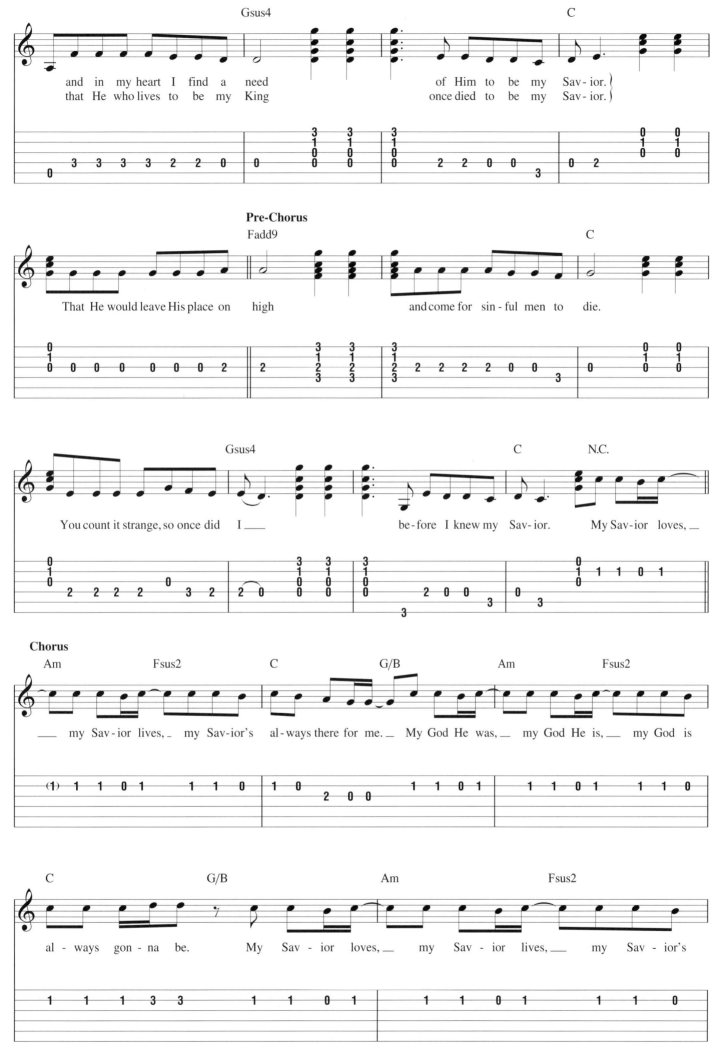

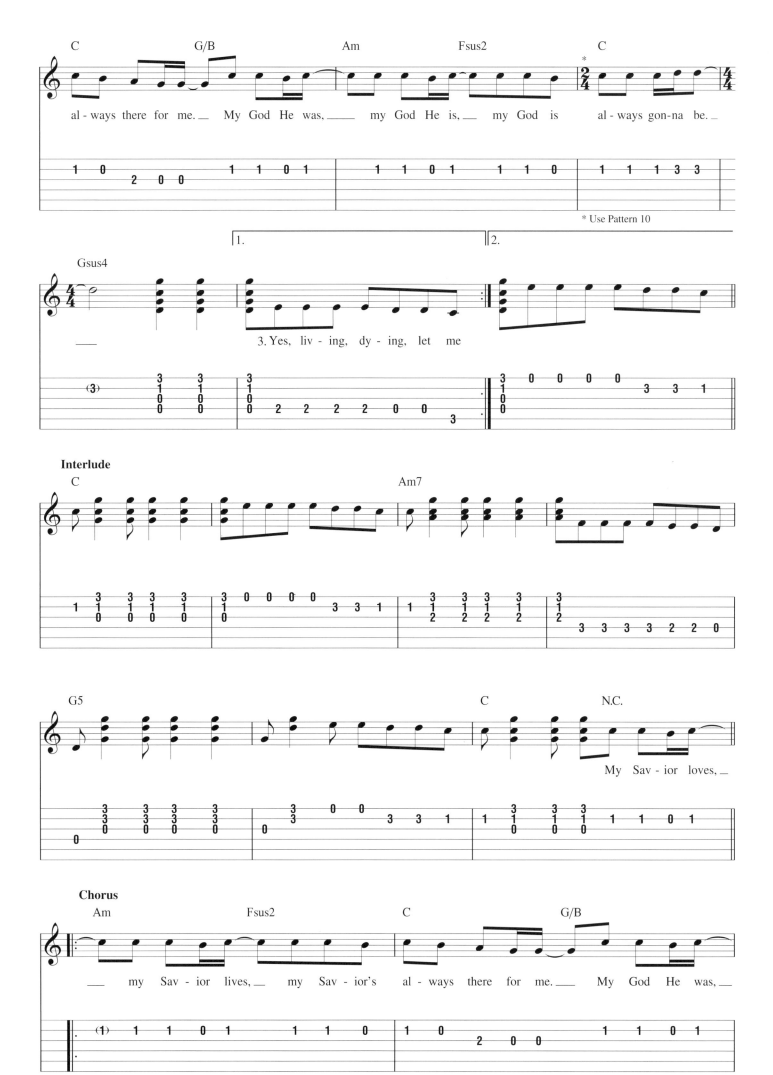

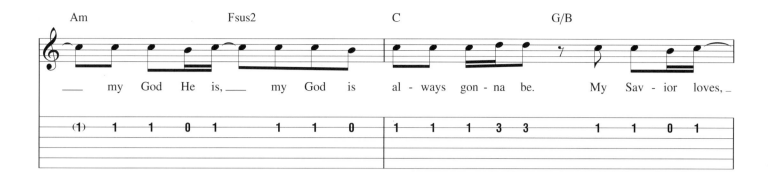

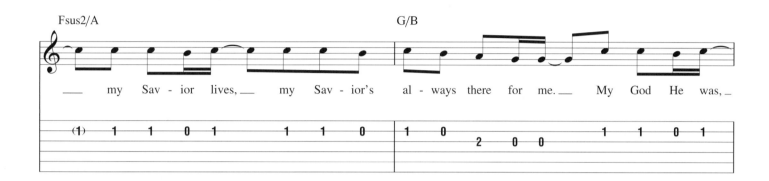

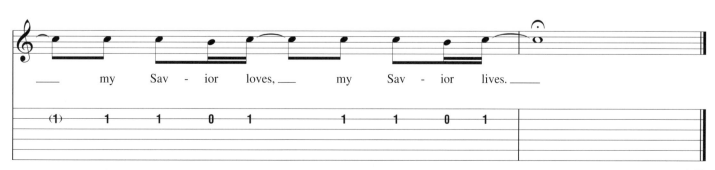

Ocean Floor

**Words and Music by Mark Stuart, Will McGinniss,
Bob Herdman, Tyler Burkum and Ben Cissell**

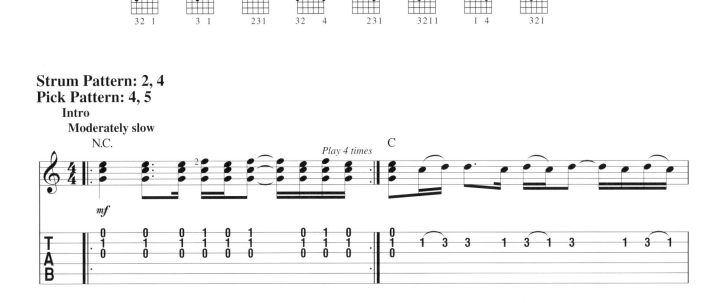

Strum Pattern: 2, 4
Pick Pattern: 4, 5

Intro
Moderately slow

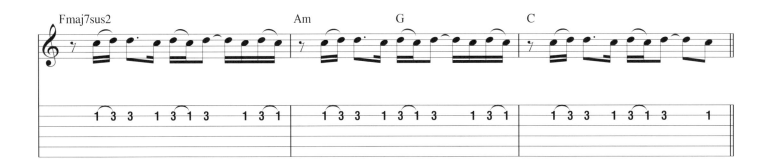

Verse

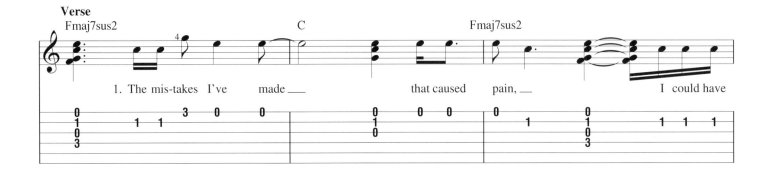

1. The mis-takes I've made ___ that caused pain, ___ I could have

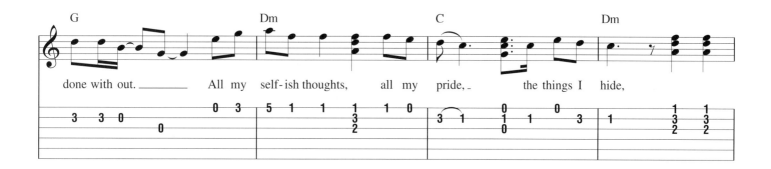

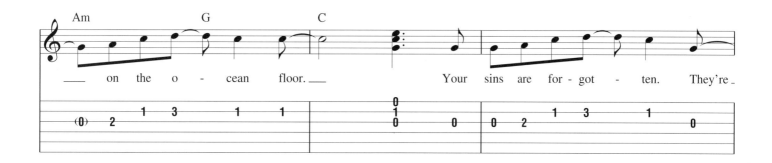

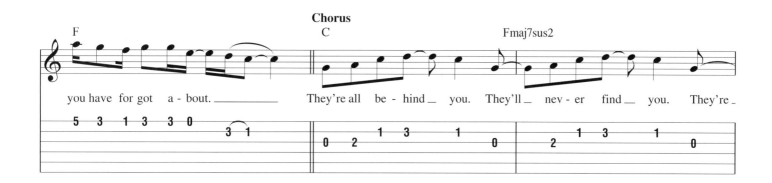

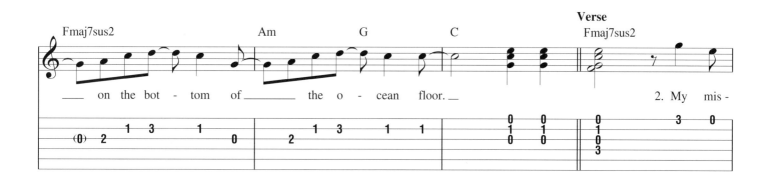

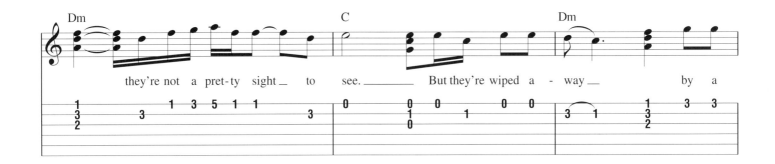

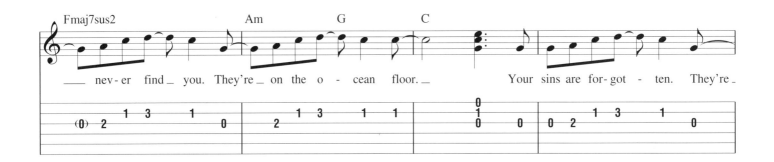

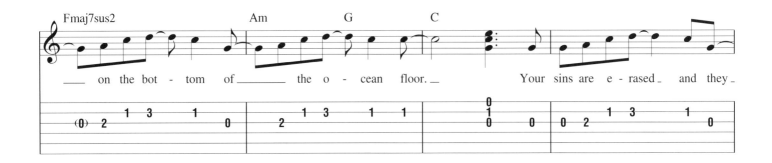

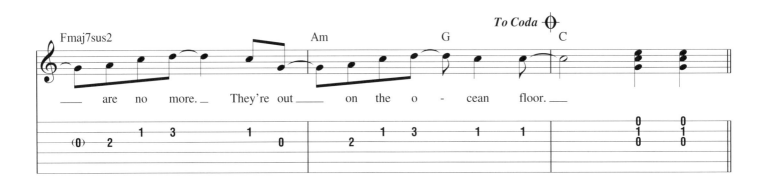

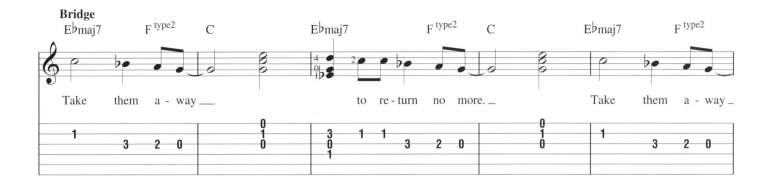

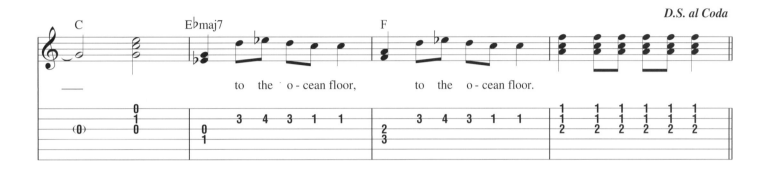

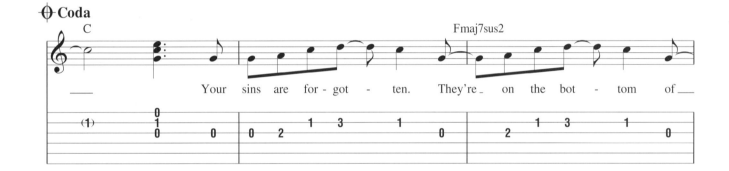

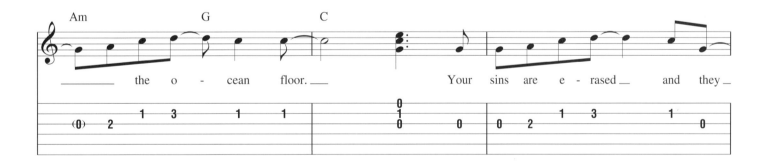

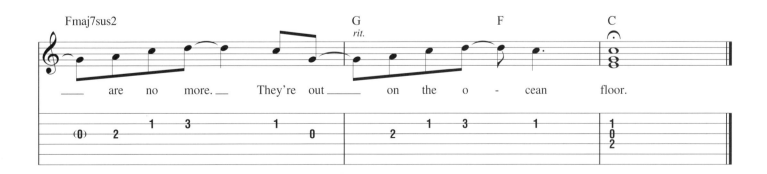

Revelation

Words by Mac Powell
Music by Third Day

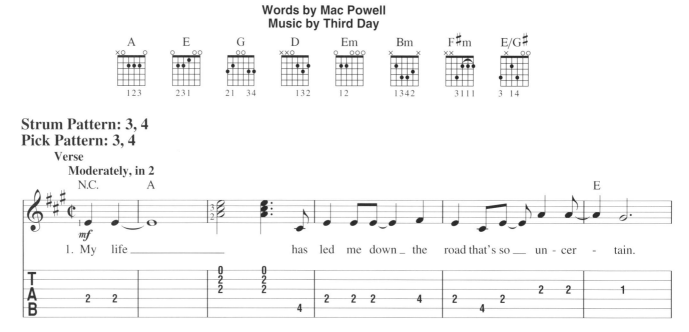

Strum Pattern: 3, 4
Pick Pattern: 3, 4

Verse
Moderately, in 2

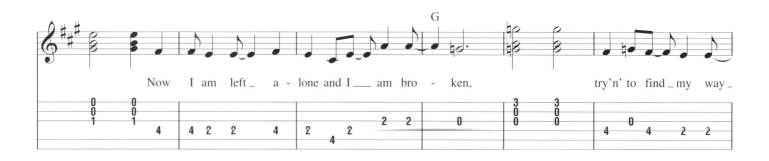

1. My life _____ has led me down _ the road that's so _ un - cer - tain.

Now I am left _ a - lone and I ___ am bro - ken, try'n' to find _ my way _

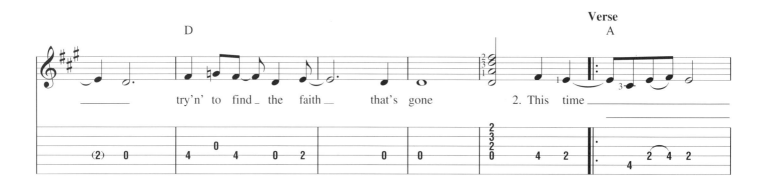

_____ try'n' to find _ the faith _ that's gone 2. This time _____

I know that You _ are hold - ing all ___ the an - swers. I'm
has led me down _ this path that's ev - er wind - ing. Through

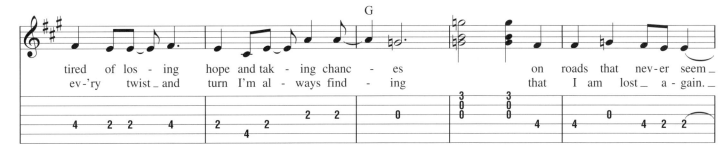

tired of los - ing hope and tak - ing chanc - es on roads that nev - er seem
ev -'ry twist _ and turn I'm al - ways find - ing that I am lost _ a - gain. _

___ to be the ones _ that bring me home. } Give me a rev-e-la - tion, _
___ Tell me when _ this road _ will ev-er end. _ }

show me what _ to do, _____ 'cause I've been try'n' to find _ my way; _ I have-n't got _ a clue. _

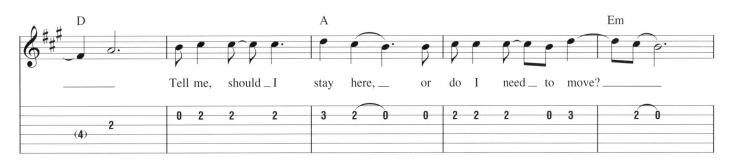

_____ Tell me, should _ I stay here, __ or do I need _ to move? _

Give me a rev-a-la - tion; I've got noth-ing with - out You, I've got noth-ing with - out

You. _____ 3. My life _ noth-ing with - out... I don't know where _

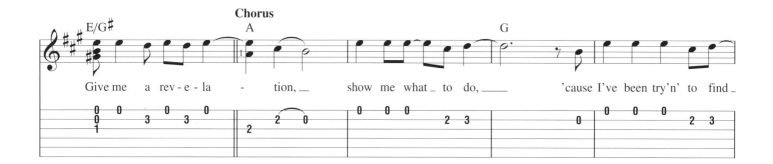

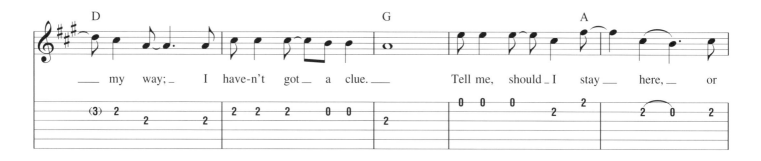

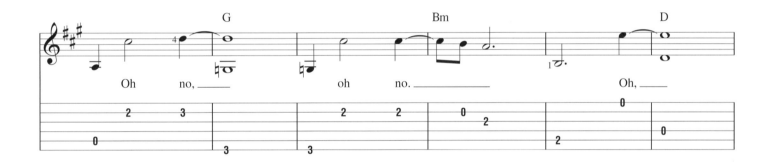

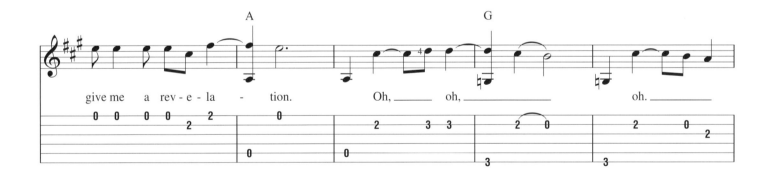

Revolutionary Love

Words and Music by David Crowder, Jack Parker and Jeremy Bush

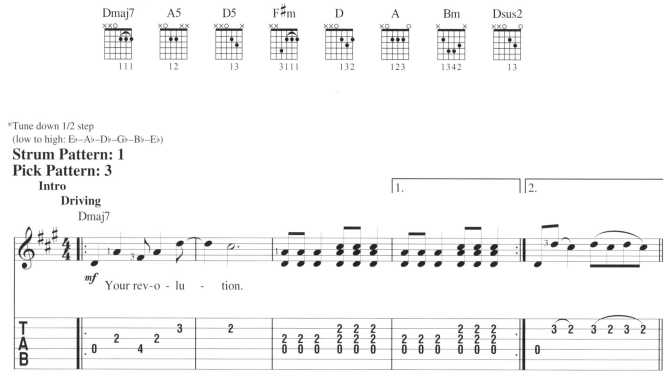

*Tune down 1/2 step
(low to high: E♭–A♭–D♭–G♭–B♭–E♭)

Strum Pattern: 1
Pick Pattern: 3

Intro
Driving

Dmaj7

Your rev-o - lu - tion.

*Optional: To match recording, tune down 1/2 step.

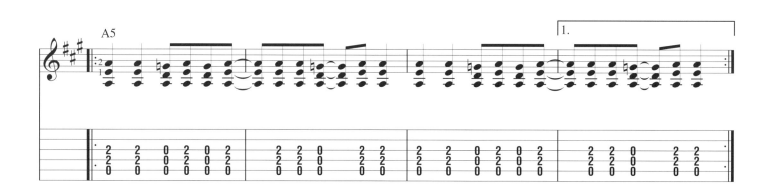

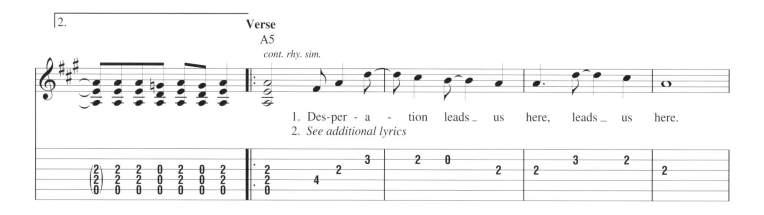

1. Des-per - a - tion leads _ us here, leads _ us here.
2. *See additional lyrics*

Il - lu - mi - na - tion meets _ us here, meets _ us here. Rev - e - la -

- tion brings _ us here, brings _ us here. Res - to - ra - tion frees _ us

Pre-Chorus

here, frees _ us here, and I don't want to leave, _ I don't want to leave _ this _ place. _

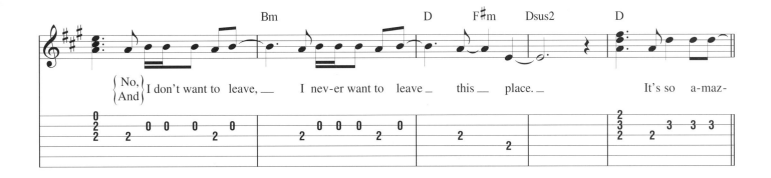

{No,} {And} I don't want to leave, _ I nev - er want to leave _ this _ place. _ It's so a - maz -

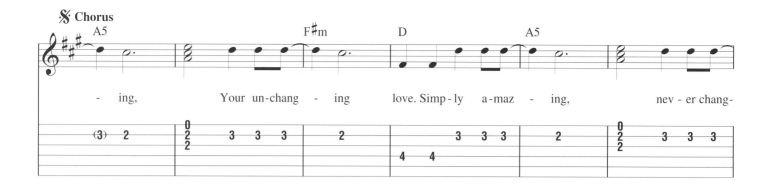

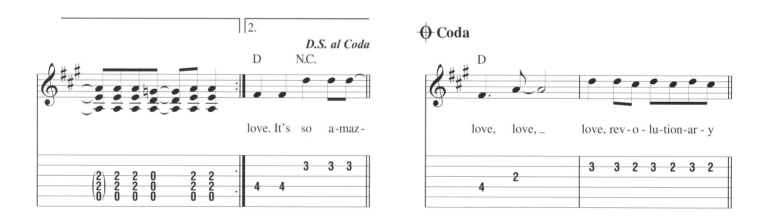

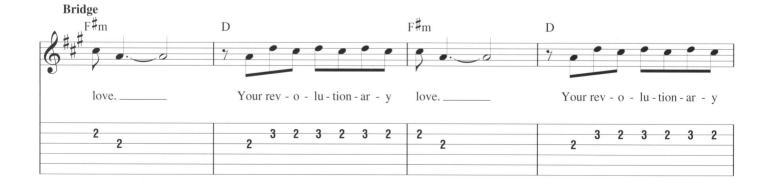

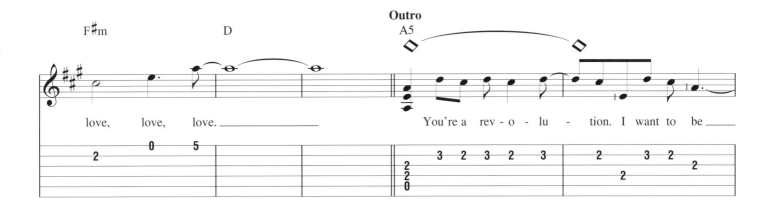

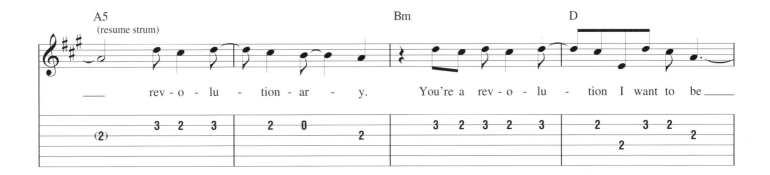

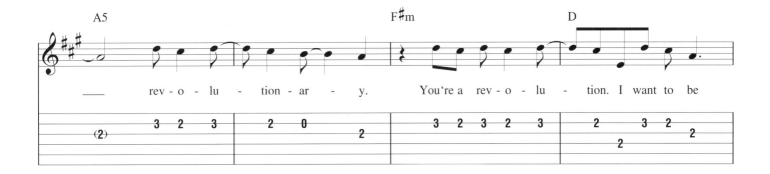

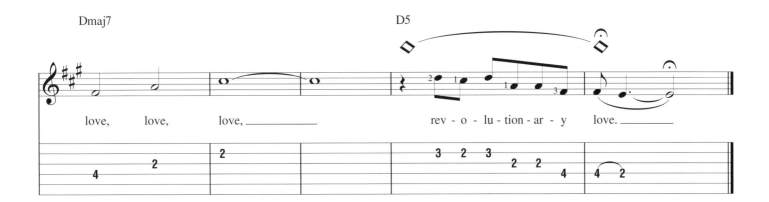

Additional Lyrics

2. Reparation leads us here, leads us here.
   Liberation meets us here, meets us here.
   Jubilation brings us here, brings us here.
   Hightened elevation frees us here, frees us here.

Say It Loud

Words and Music by Chris Rohman and Matt Hammitt

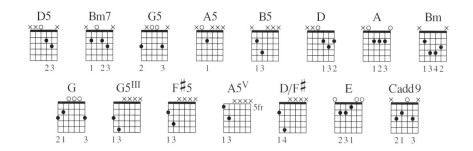

Strum Pattern: 1, 6
Pick Pattern: 2, 4

Intro
Moderately fast Rock

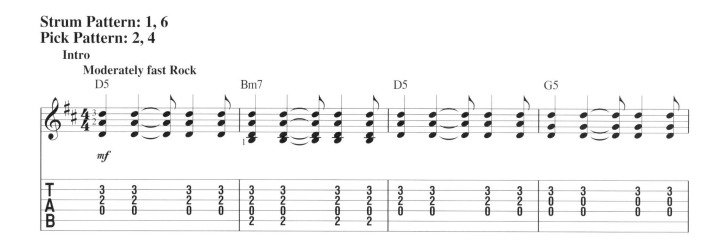

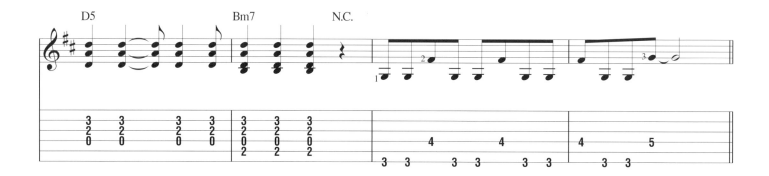

Verse

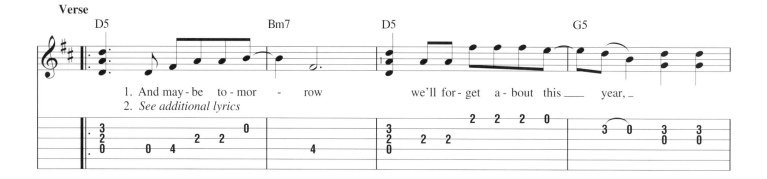

1. And may-be to-mor - row we'll for-get a-bout this ___ year, _
2. *See additional lyrics*

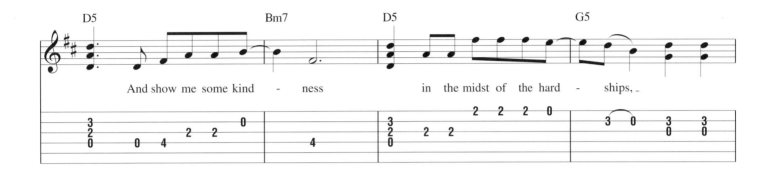

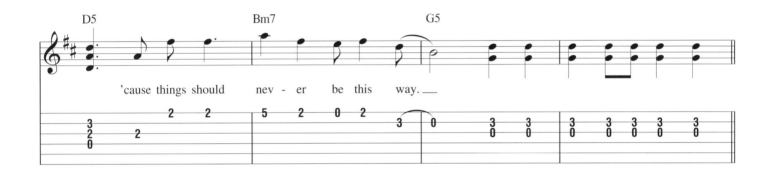

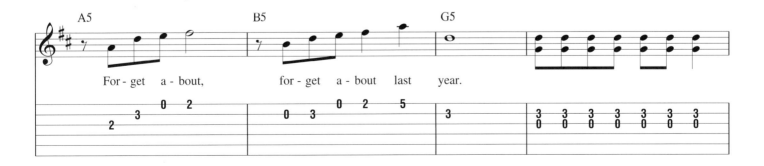

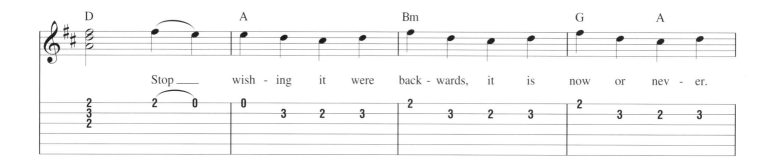

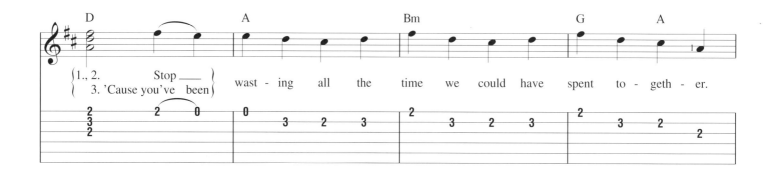

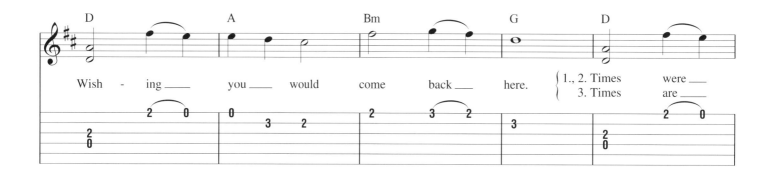

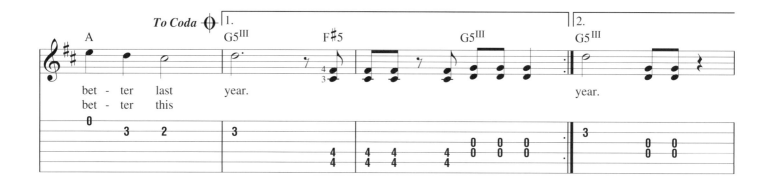

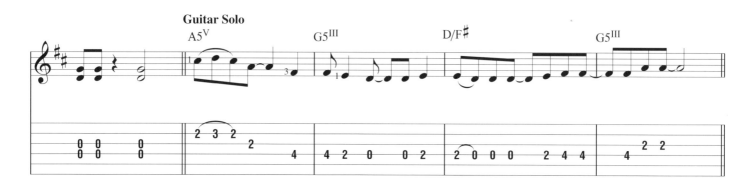

Bridge

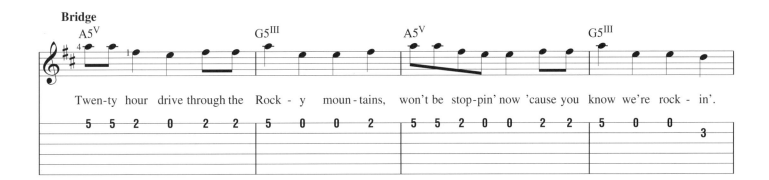

Twen-ty hour drive through the Rock - y moun - tains, won't be stop-pin' now 'cause you know we're rock - in'.

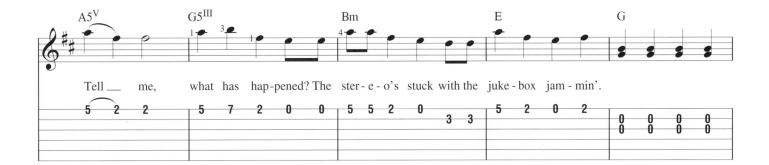

Tell __ me, what has hap-pened? The ster - e - o's stuck with the juke - box jam - min'.

Interlude

D.S. al Coda

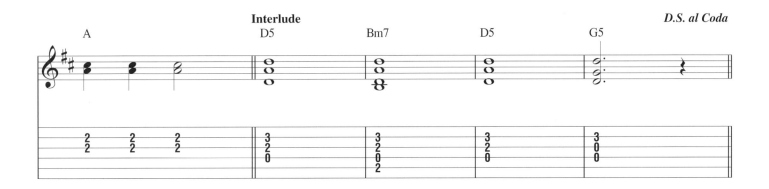

Coda

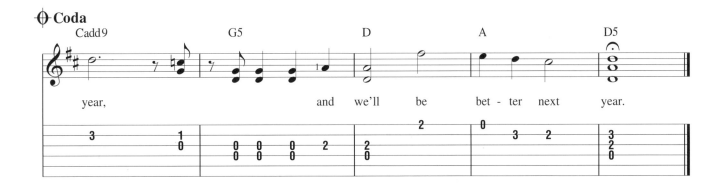

year, and we'll be bet - ter next year.

Additional Lyrics

2. And all of your reasons, they change with the seasons.
   Day by day they're not the same.
   And if you would measure all the times that we've treasured,
   Then you would see how my heart breaks.

Sea of Faces

Words and Music by Jon Micah Sumrall, Kyle Mitchell,
James Mead, Ryan Shrout and Aaron Sprinkle

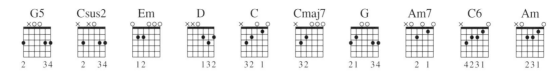

G5   Csus2   Em   D   C   Cmaj7   G   Am7   C6   Am

*Capo III

Strum Pattern: 6
Pick Pattern: 3, 4

Intro
Moderately

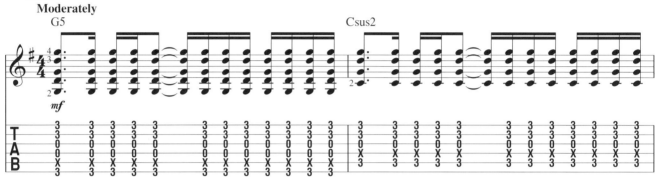

*Optional: To match recording, place capo at 3rd fret.

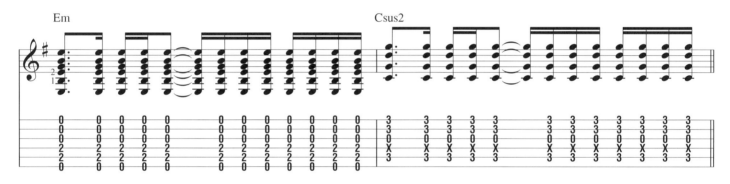

Verse

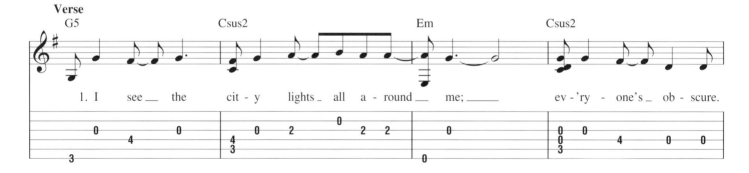

1. I see the cit-y lights all a-round me; ev-'ry-one's ob-scure.

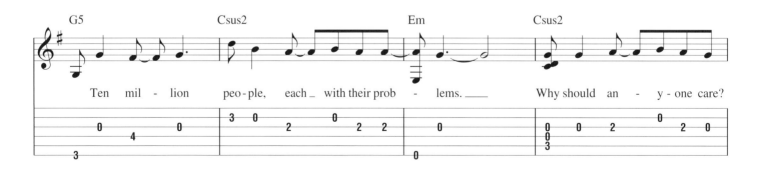

Ten mil-lion peo-ple, each with their prob-lems. Why should an-y-one care?

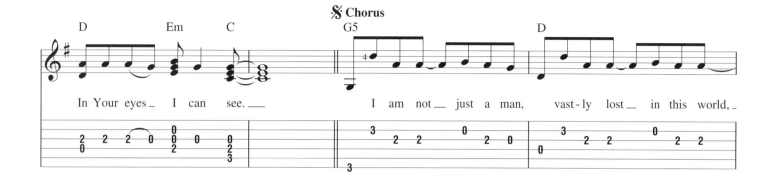

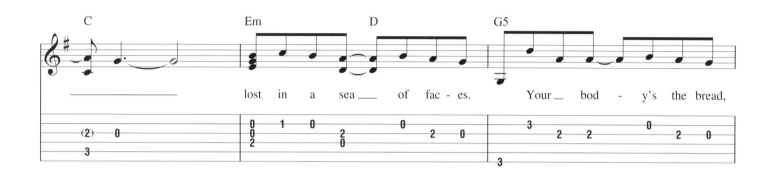

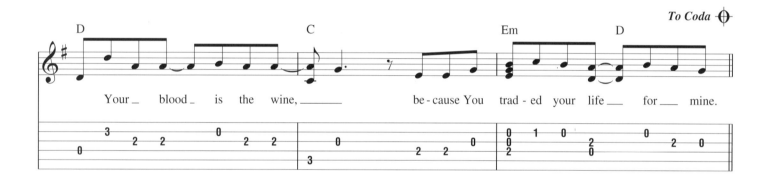

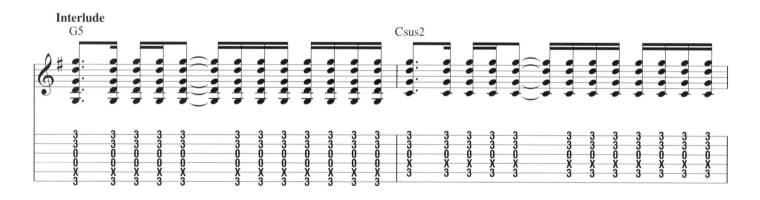

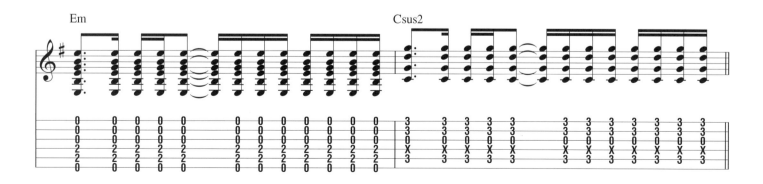

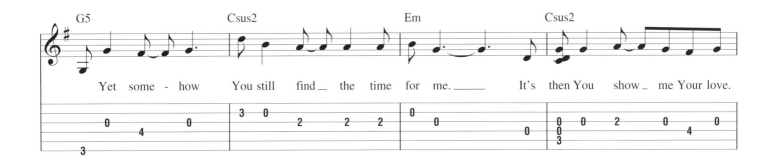

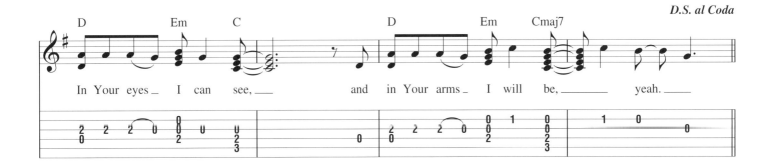

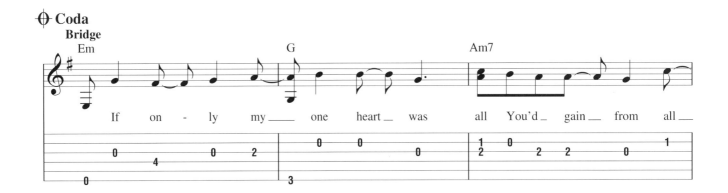

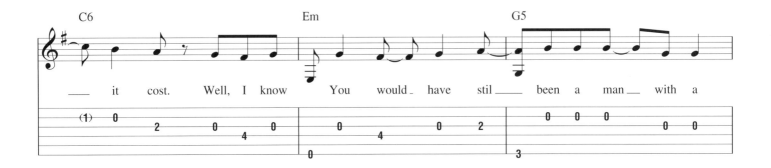

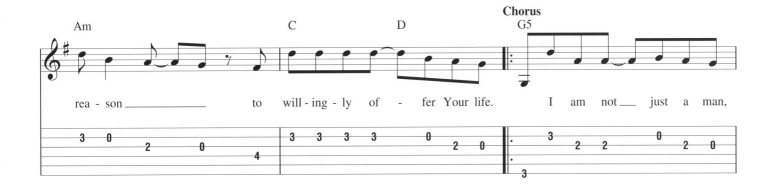

rea - son _____ to will - ing - ly of - fer Your life. I am not ___ just a man,

*Play 2nd time.   **2nd time, substitute C.

vast - ly lost ___ in this world, _____ lost in a sea ___ of fac - es.

Your ___ bod - y's the bread, Your ___ blood ___ is the wine, _____ be - cause You

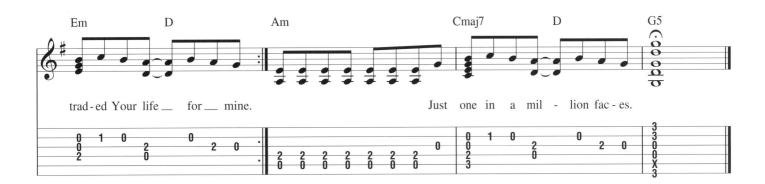

trad - ed Your life ___ for ___ mine. Just one in a mil - lion fac - es.

So Long Self

Words and Music by Bart Millard, Barry Graul, Jim Bryson, Nathan Cochran, Mike Scheuchzer and Robby Shaffer

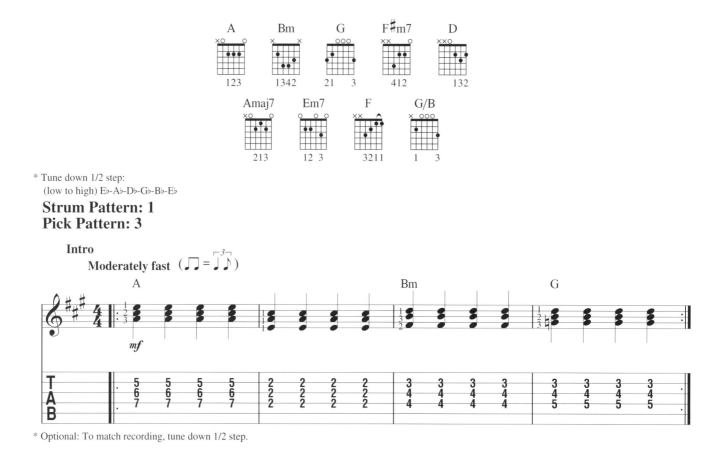

* Tune down 1/2 step:
(low to high) E♭-A♭-D♭-G♭-B♭-E♭

Strum Pattern: 1
Pick Pattern: 3

Intro
Moderately fast

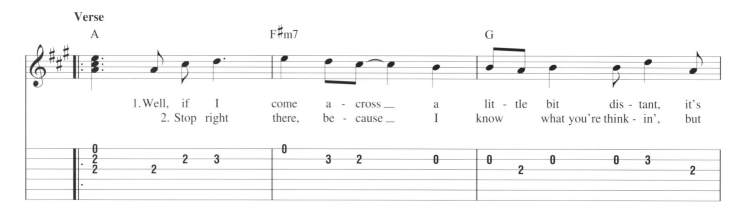

* Optional: To match recording, tune down 1/2 step.

Verse

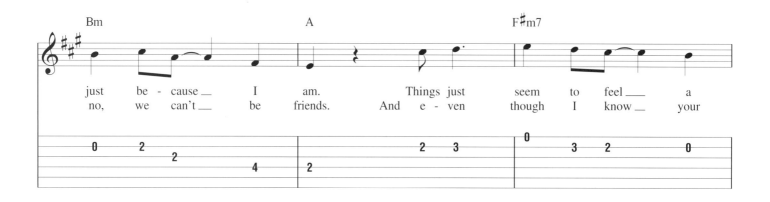

1. Well, if I come a - cross __ a lit - tle bit dis - tant, it's
2. Stop right there, be - cause __ I know what you're think - in', but

just be - cause __ I am. Things just seem to feel __ a
no, we can't __ be friends. And e - ven though I know __ your

lit - tle bit dif - f'rent, you un - der - stand. Be - lieve it or not, ___ but life ___ is
heart ___ is break - ing, this has to end. And come ___ to think ___ of it, ___ the

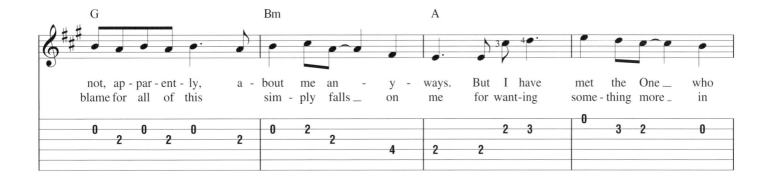

not, ap - par - ent - ly, a - bout me an - y - ways. But I have met the One ___ who
blame for all of this sim - ply falls ___ on me for want - ing some - thing more ___ in

𝄋 Chorus

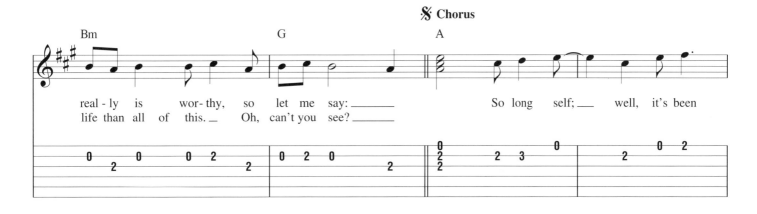

real - ly is wor - thy, so let me say: _____ So long self; ___ well, it's been
life than all of this. ___ Oh, can't you see? _____

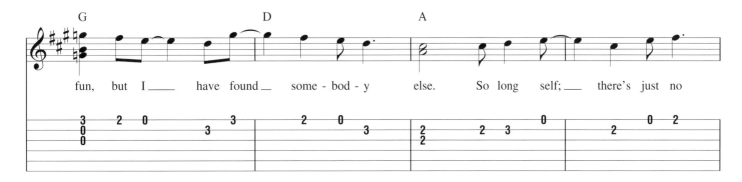

fun, but I ___ have found ___ some - bod - y else. So long self; ___ there's just no

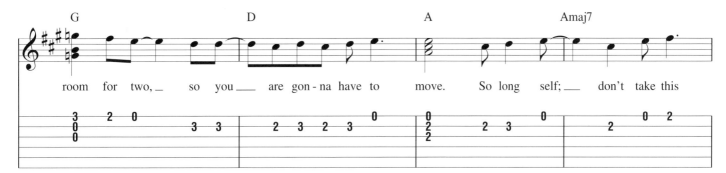

room for two, ___ so you ___ are gon - na have to move. So long self; ___ don't take this

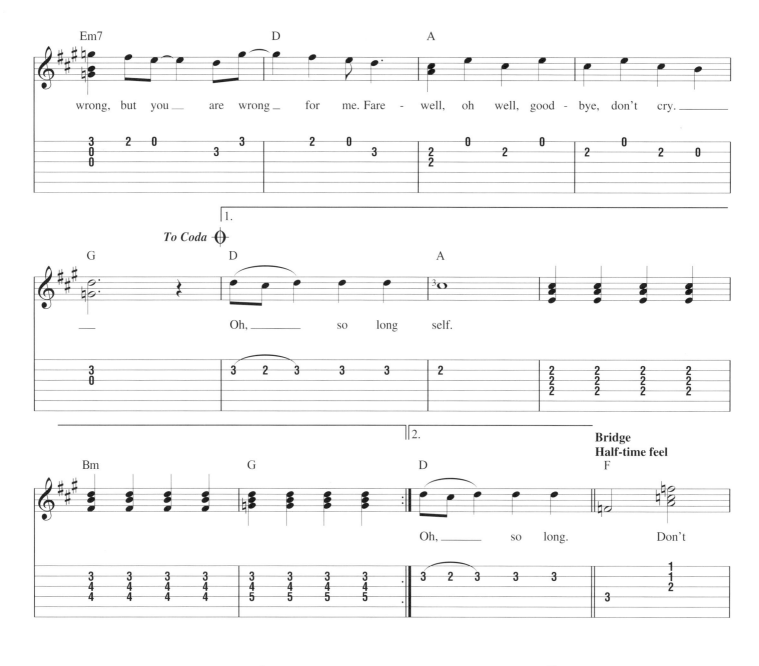

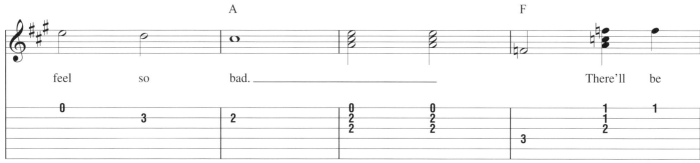

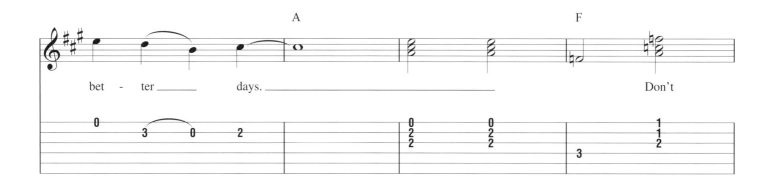

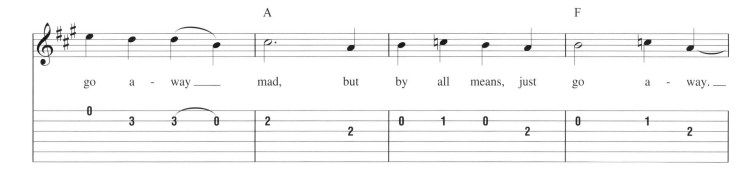

go a - way ___ mad, but by all means, just go a - way. ___

Interlude
End half-time feel

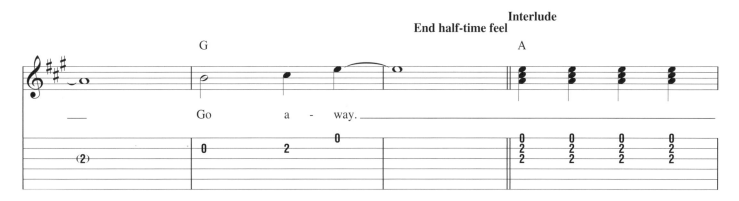

___ Go a - way. ___

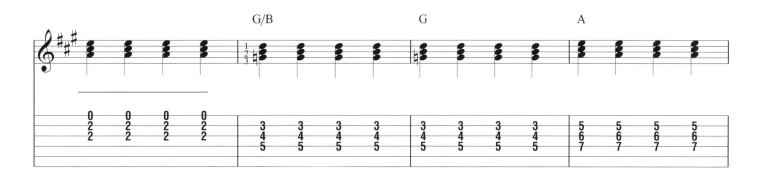

D.S. al Coda

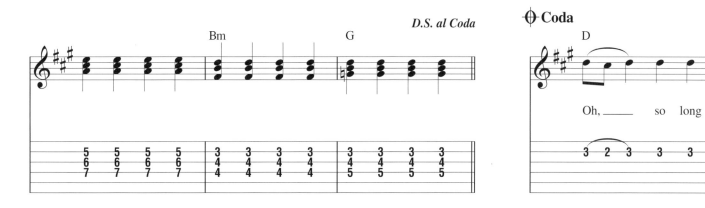

⊕ Coda

Oh, ___ so long

Outro

Repeat and fade

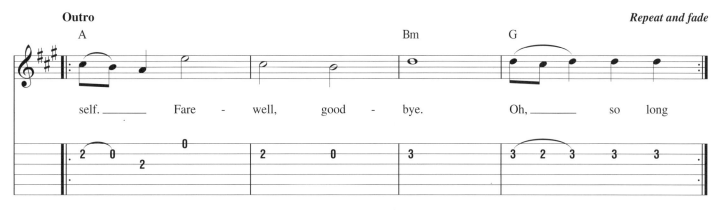

self. ___ Fare - well, good - bye. Oh, ___ so long

Song of Hope

Words and Music by Robbie Seay, Taylor Johnson, Ryan Owens, Chase Jenkins, Dan Hamilton and Tedd Tjornhom

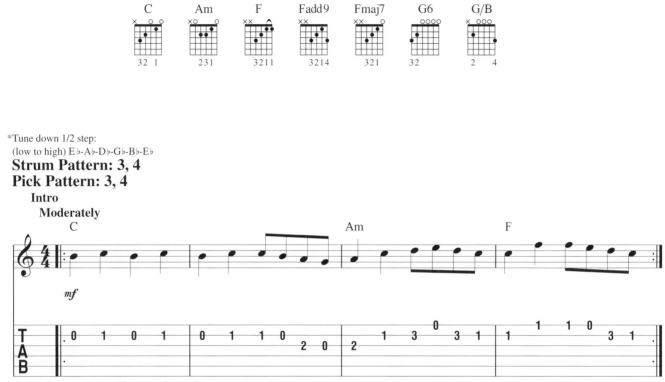

*Tune down 1/2 step:
(low to high) E♭-A♭-D♭-G♭-B♭-E♭

Strum Pattern: 3, 4
Pick Pattern: 3, 4

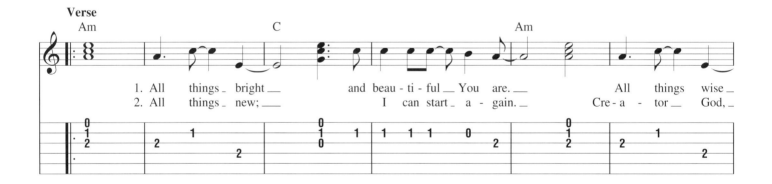

*Optional: To match recording, tune down 1/2 step.

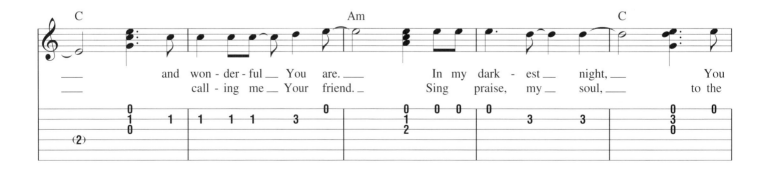

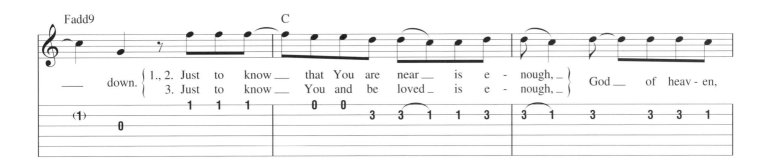

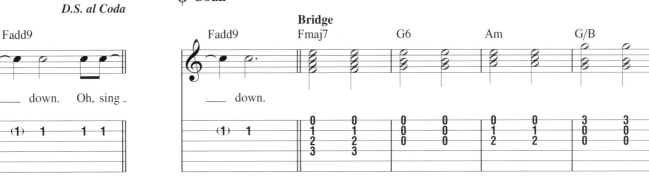

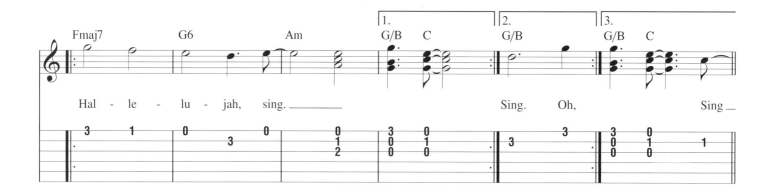

Hal - le - lu - jah, sing. _____ Sing. Oh, Sing __

Chorus

_____ a song of hope, sing a - long. _ God _ of heav - en, come down, heav - en come _ down. Just to know _

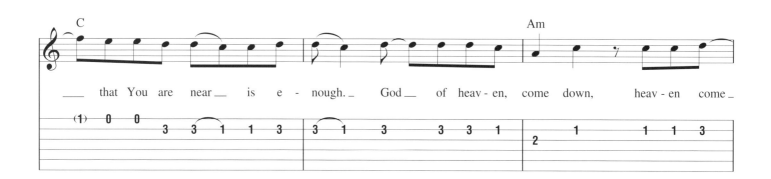

_____ that You are near _ is e - nough. _ God _ of heav - en, come down, heav - en come _

_____ down. Oh sing _____ a song of hope, sing a - long. _ God _ of heav - en,

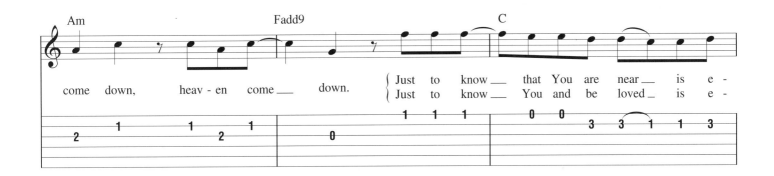

come down, heav - en come ___ down. Just to know ___ that You are near ___ is e -
Just to know ___ You and be loved ___ is e -

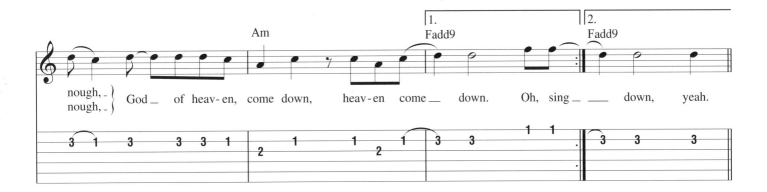

nough, - God ___ of heav - en, come down, heav - en come ___ down. Oh, sing ___ ___ down, yeah.
nough, -

Outro

Heav - en come ___

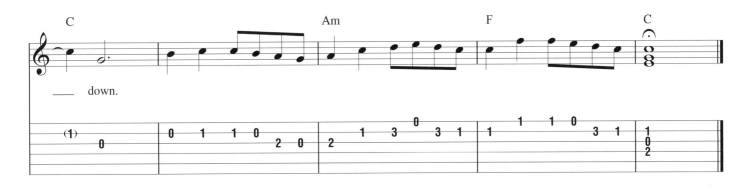

___ down.

Sunday!

Words and Music by John Ellis

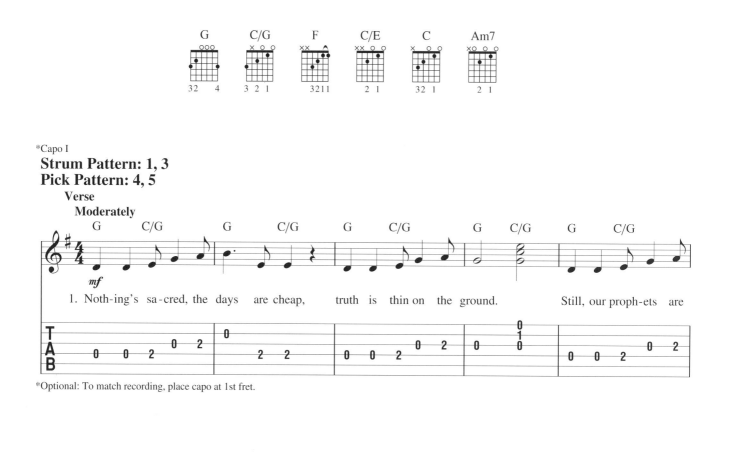

*Capo I

Strum Pattern: 1, 3
Pick Pattern: 4, 5

Verse
Moderately

1. Noth-ing's sa-cred, the days are cheap, truth is thin on the ground. Still, our proph-ets are

*Optional: To match recording, place capo at 1st fret.

cru - ci-fied. No - bod-y be-lieves we're stum-bling. It's Fri - day, but Sun-day is com- ing.

Verse

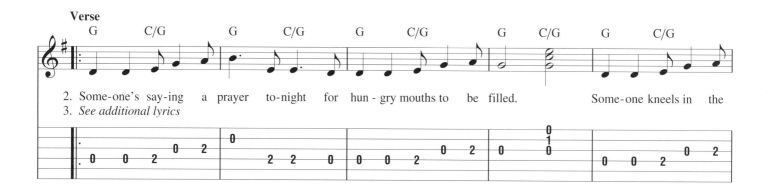

2. Some-one's say-ing a prayer to-night for hun-gry mouths to be filled. Some-one kneels in the
3. *See additional lyrics*

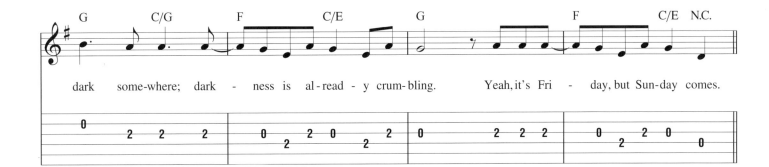

dark some-where; dark - ness is al-read - y crum-bling. Yeah, it's Fri - day, but Sun-day comes.

Chorus

Sun - day, hal-le-lu - jah! It's not ___ so far, ___ it's not ___ so far ___ a - way.

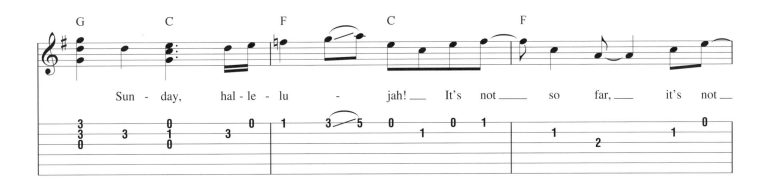

Sun - day, hal-le-lu - jah! It's not ___ so far, ___ it's not ___

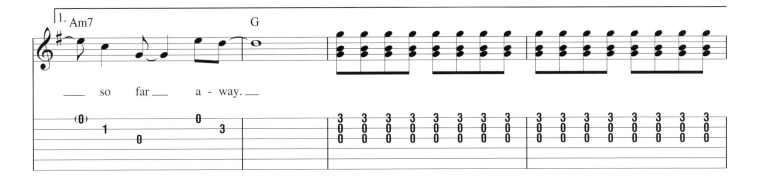

___ so far ___ a - way. ___

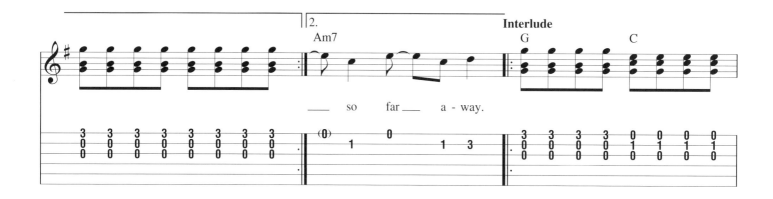

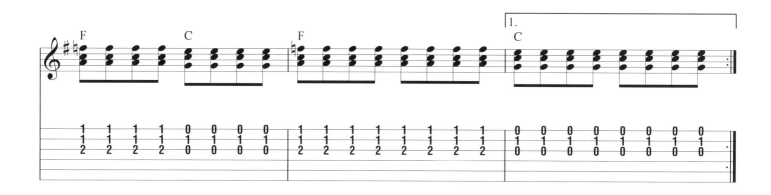

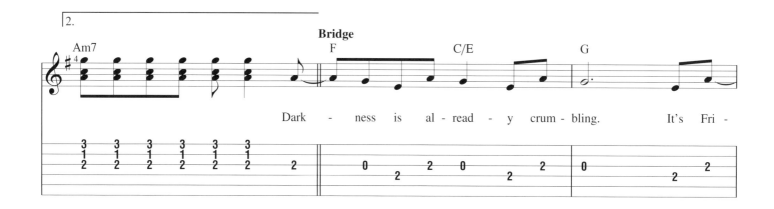

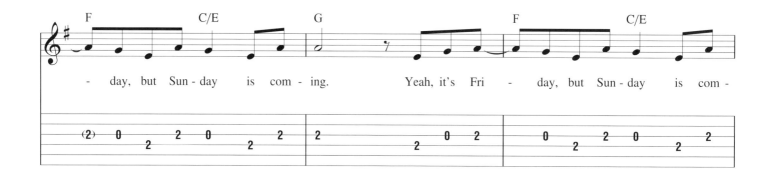

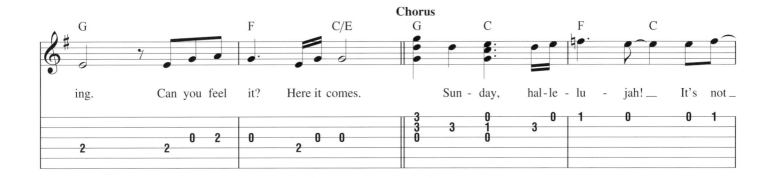

ing. Can you feel it? Here it comes. Sun-day, hal-le-lu - jah! __ It's not__

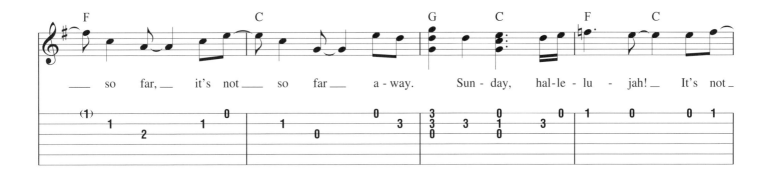

__ so far, __ it's not __ so far __ a - way. Sun-day, hal-le-lu - jah! __ It's not__

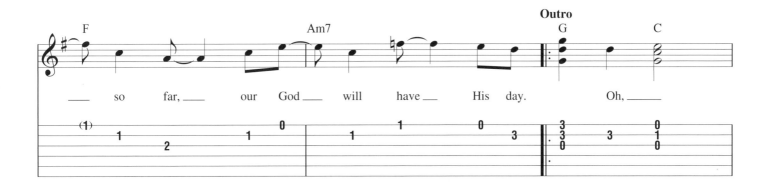

__ so far, __ our God __ will have __ His day. Oh, __

oh, __ oh, oh, __ oh, oh, __ oh, oh, __ oh, oh, __ oh. __

Additional Lyrics

3. Broken promises, weary hearts,
   But one promise remains.
   Crucified, he will come again.
   It's Friday, but Sunday is coming.
   Yeah, it's Friday, but Sunday is coming.

There Will Be a Day

Words and Music by Jeremy Camp

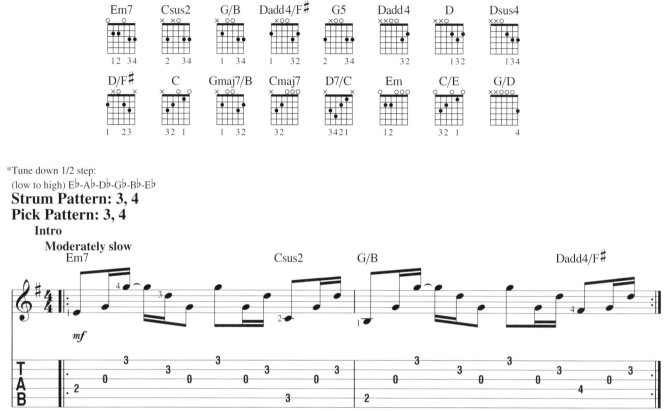

*Tune down 1/2 step:
(low to high) E♭-A♭-D♭-G♭-B♭-E♭

Strum Pattern: 3, 4
Pick Pattern: 3, 4

Intro

Moderately slow

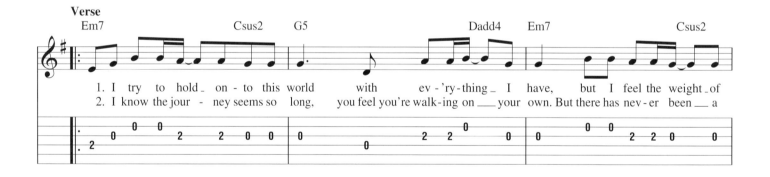

*Optional: To match recording, tune down 1/2 step.

Verse

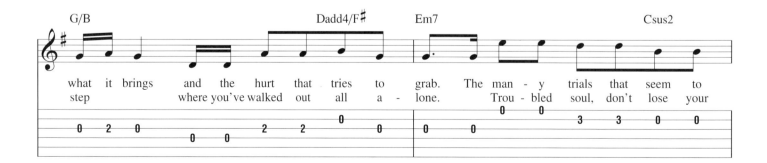

1. I try to hold_ on-to this world with ev-'ry-thing_ I have, but I feel the weight_of
2. I know the jour-ney seems so long, you feel you're walk-ing on ___ your own. But there has nev-er been ___ a

what it brings and the hurt that tries to grab. The man-y trials that seem to
step where you've walked out all a-lone. Trou-bled soul, don't lose your

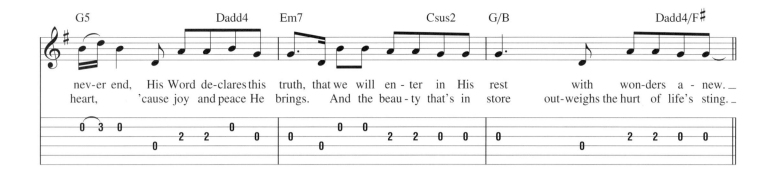

never end,   His Word de-clares this   truth, that we will en - ter in His   rest   with   won-ders a - new. __
heart,   'cause joy and peace He   brings.   And the beau - ty that's in   store   out-weighs the hurt of life's sting. __

Pre-Chorus

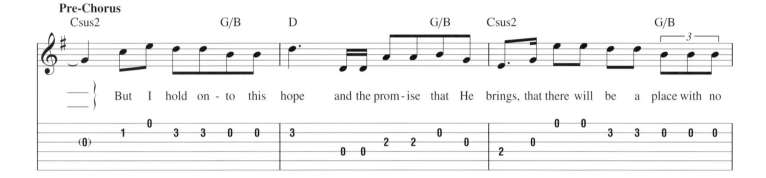

But   I   hold on - to   this   hope   and the prom - ise   that   He   brings, that there will be   a   place with no

𝄉 **Chorus**

more suf-fer-ing. There will be   a   day   with no   more _ tears, _   no   more _ pain __   and no   more _ fears. __

*3rd time, let chords ring, next 7 meas.

To Coda ⊕

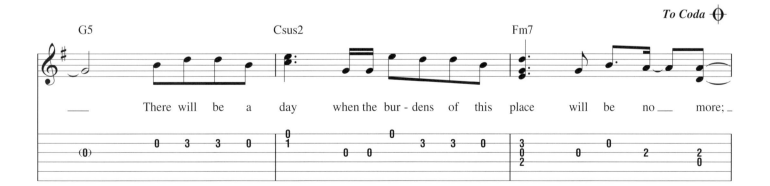

__   There will be   a   day   when the bur - dens of   this   place   will be   no __   more; __

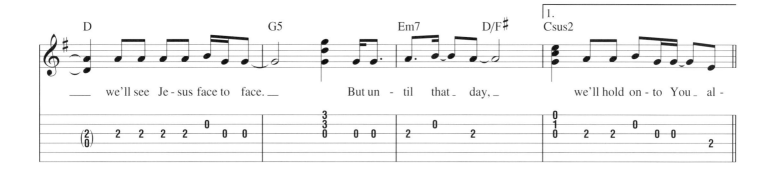

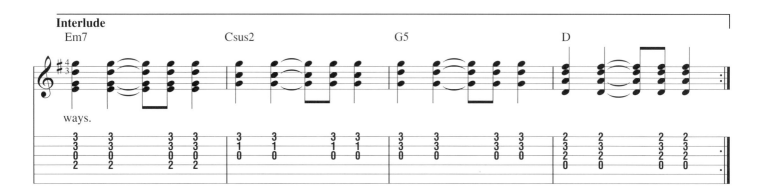

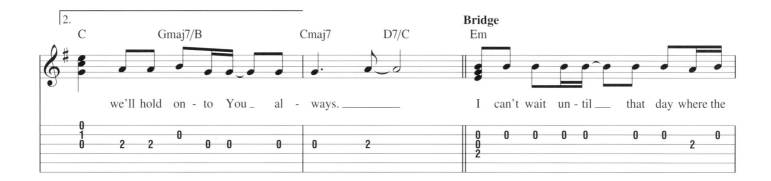

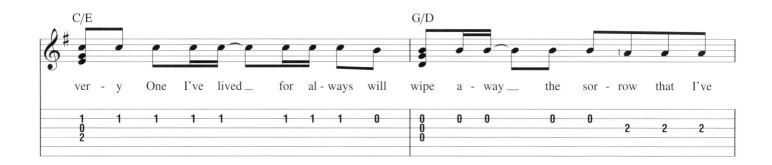

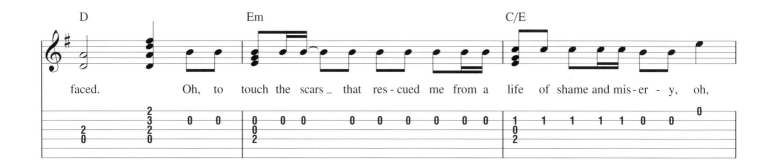

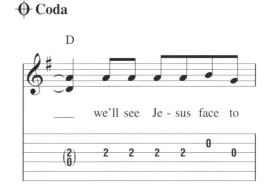

D.S. al Coda

Tunnel

Words by Mac Powell
Music by Mac Powell, David Carr, Tai Anderson, Brad Avery and Mark Lee

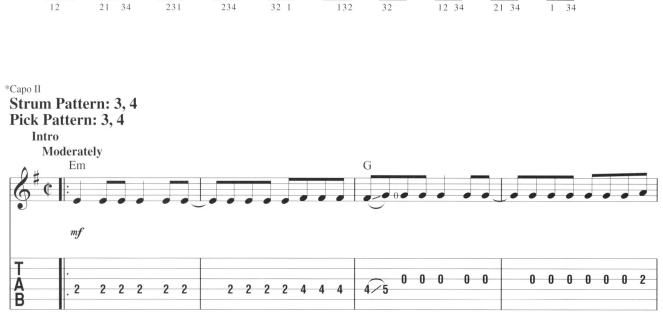

*Capo II

Strum Pattern: 3, 4
Pick Pattern: 3, 4

Intro
Moderately

*Optional: To match recording, place capo at 2nd fret.

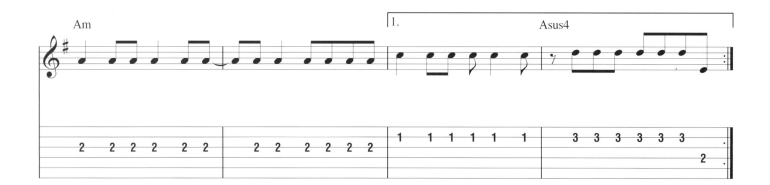

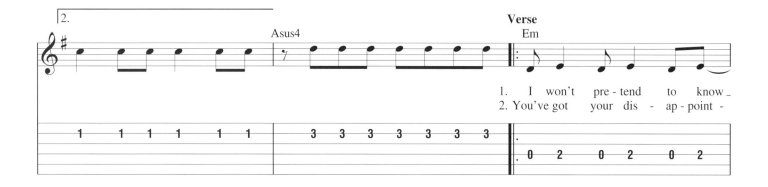

1. I won't pre-tend to know
2. You've got your dis-ap-point-

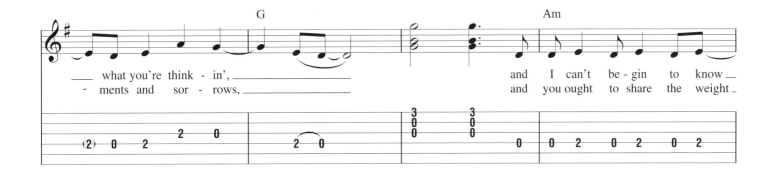

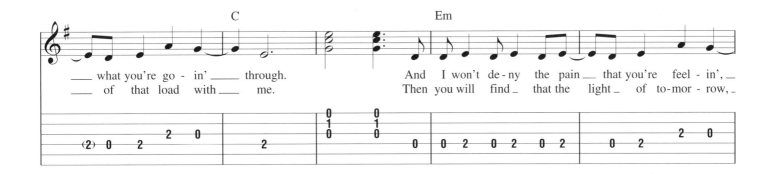

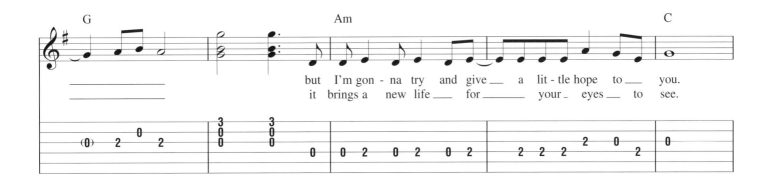

187

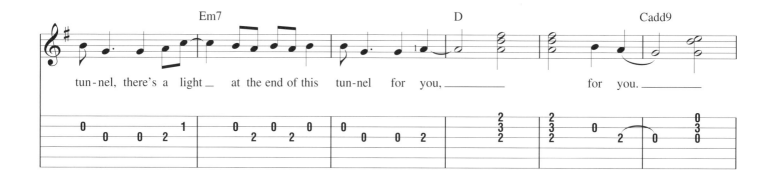

tun-nel, there's a light __ at the end of this tun-nel for you, _____ for you. _____

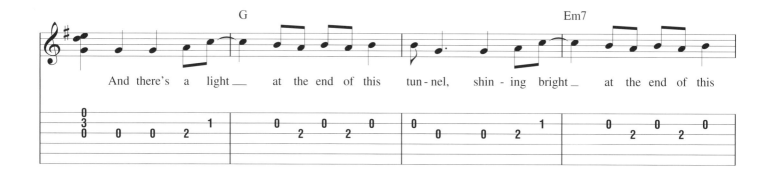

And there's a light ___ at the end of this tun-nel, shin-ing bright __ at the end of this

tun-nel for you, _____ for __ you. __ So keep hold - ing on. _____

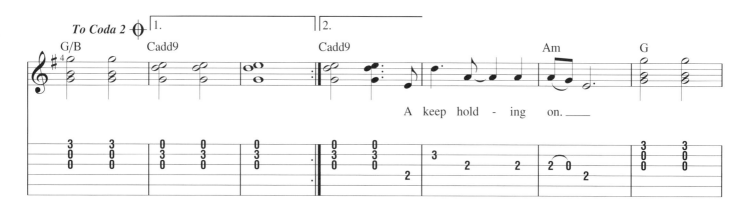

A keep hold - ing on. _____

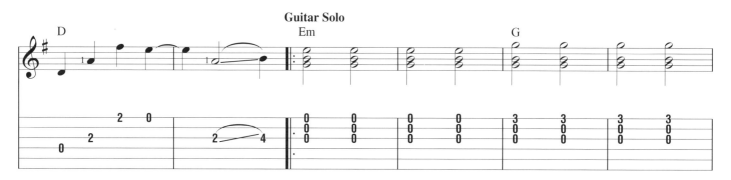

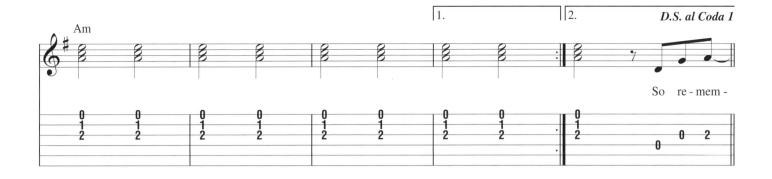

D.S. al Coda 1

So re-mem-

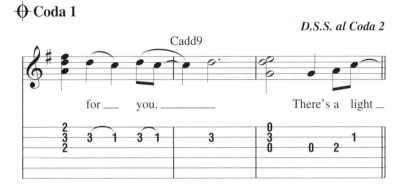

Coda 1

D.S.S. al Coda 2

Cadd9

for ___ you. ___ There's a light ___

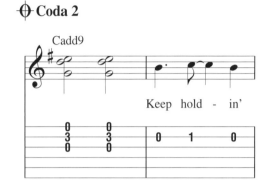

Coda 2

Cadd9

Keep hold - in'

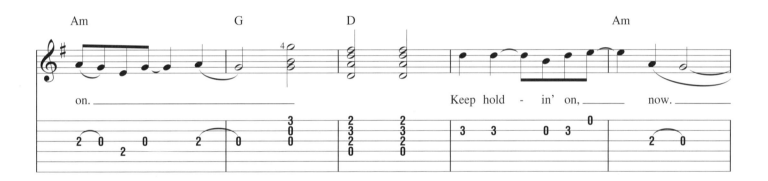

Am   G   D   Am

on. ___   Keep hold - in' on, ___ now.

G/B   Cadd9   **Outro**   Em

___   You've got your dis - ap-point - ments and sor - rows, ___

G   *Am   G/B   C

___   but I'm gon - na try to give ___ a lit - tle hope to you. ___

*Let chord ring.

Undo

Words and Music by Scott Davis, Wes Willis and Kevin Huguley

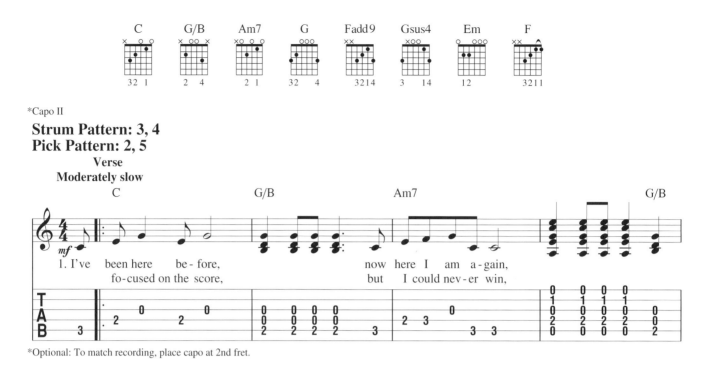

*Capo II

Strum Pattern: 3, 4
Pick Pattern: 2, 5

Verse
Moderately slow

1. I've been here be-fore, now here I am a-gain,
fo-cused on the score, but I could nev-er win,

*Optional: To match recording, place capo at 2nd fret.

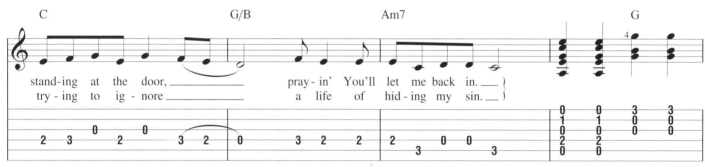

stand-ing at the door, _____ pray-in' You'll let me back in. __
try-ing to ig-nore _____ a life of hid-ing my sin. __

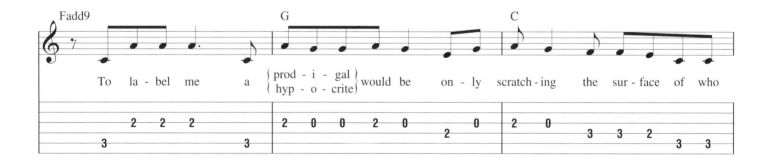

To la-bel me a { prod-i-gal } would be on-ly scratch-ing the sur-face of who
{ hyp-o-crite }

Chorus

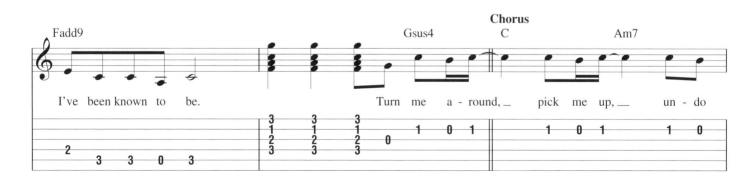

I've been known to be. Turn me a-round, _ pick me up, _ un-do

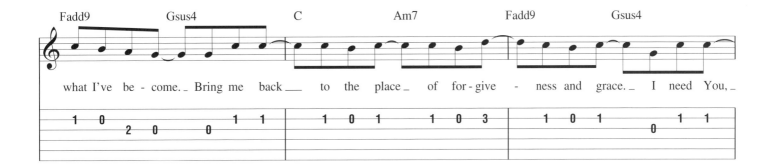

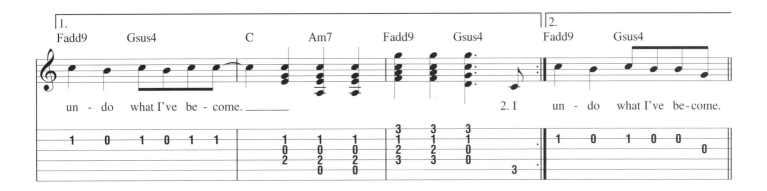

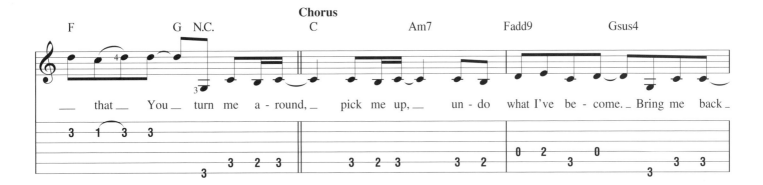

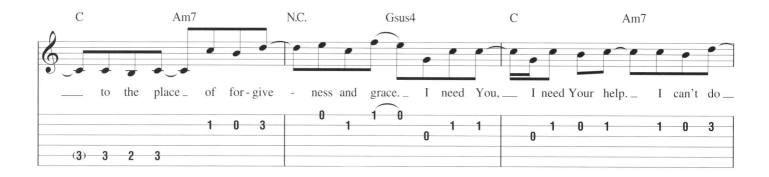

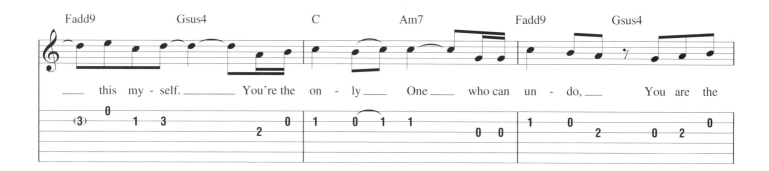

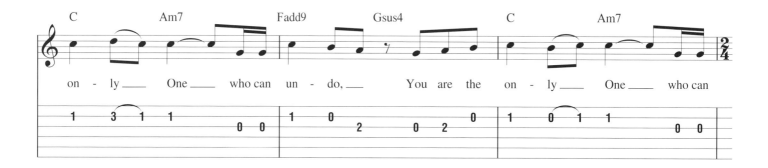

*Use Pattern 10 **Let chord ring.

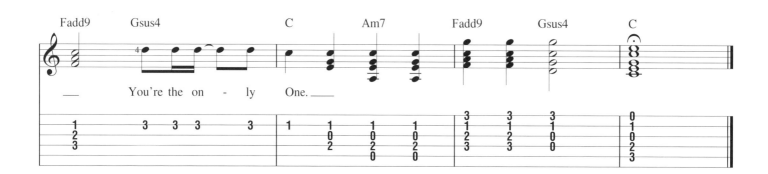

What If His People Prayed

Words and Music by Mark Hall and Steven Curtis Chapman

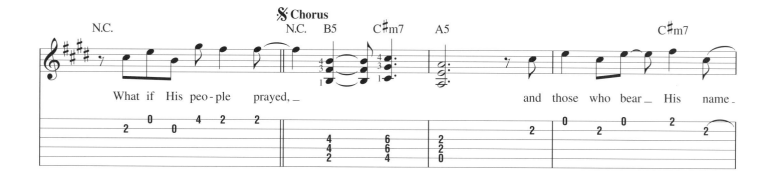

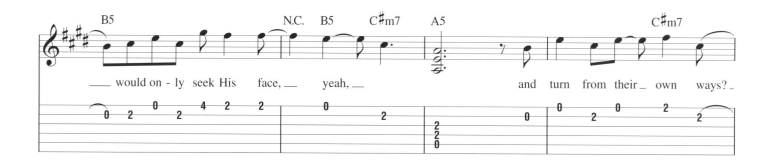

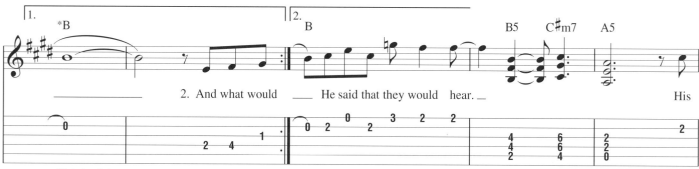

*Let chord ring.

To Coda

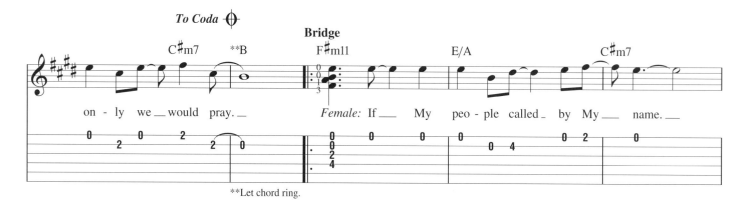

**Let chord ring.

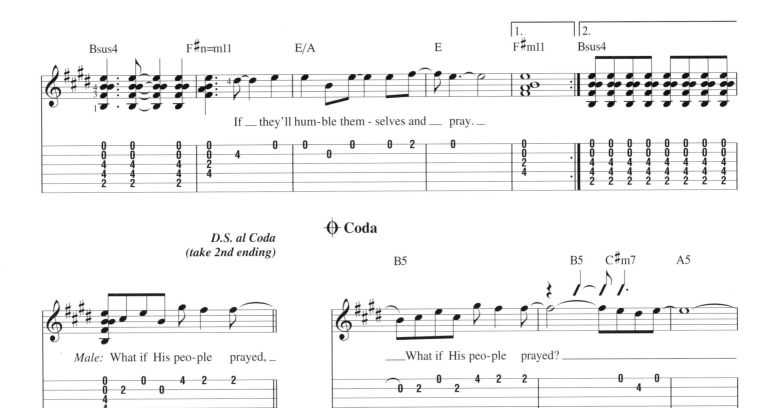

If __ they'll hum-ble them-selves and __ pray. __

⊕ **Coda**

D.S. al Coda
(take 2nd ending)

Male: What if His peo-ple prayed, __

__ What if His peo-ple prayed? __

(If __ they'll hum - ble them - selves and __ pray.

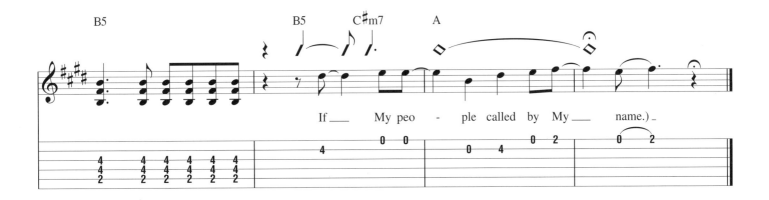

If __ My peo - ple called by My __ name.) __

Additional Lyrics

2. And what would happen if we prayed
For those raised up to lead the way?
Then maybe kids in school could pray
And unborn children see light of day.
What if the life that we pursue
Came from a hunger for the truth?
What if the fam'ly turned to Jesus,
Stopped asking Oprah what to do?

Whatever You're Doing
(Something Heavenly)

Words and Music by Matt Hammitt, Chris Rohman,
Mark Graalman, Dan Gartley and Peter Provost

Strum Pattern: 1, 3
Pick Pattern: 3, 4

Verse
Moderately slow

1. It's time for heal - ing, time to move on. ___ It's time to fix ___ what's been bro - ken too long. _

Time to make right ___ what has been ___ wrong. It's time to find ___ my way to where I be - long. _

There's a wave ___ that's crash-ing o - ver me, and all I can do ___ is sur - ren-

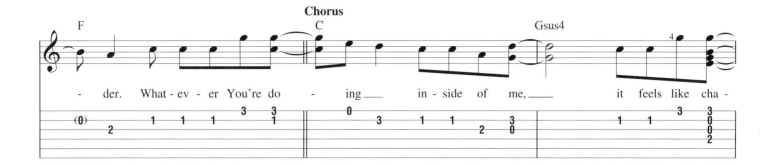

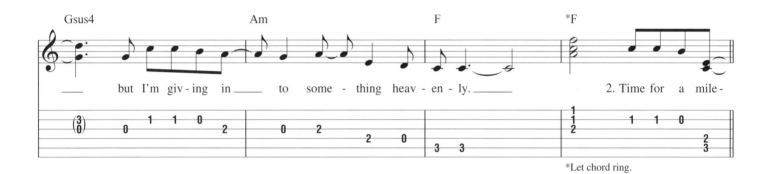

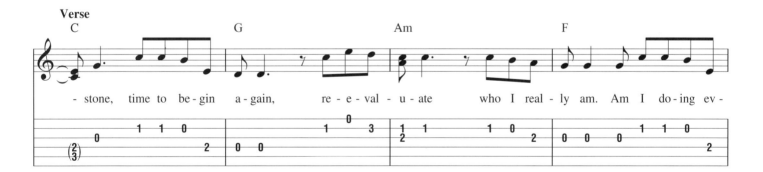

*Let chord ring.

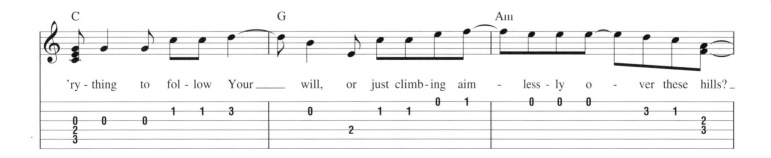

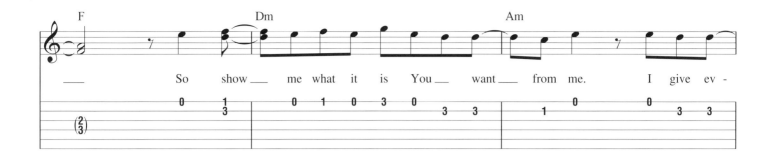

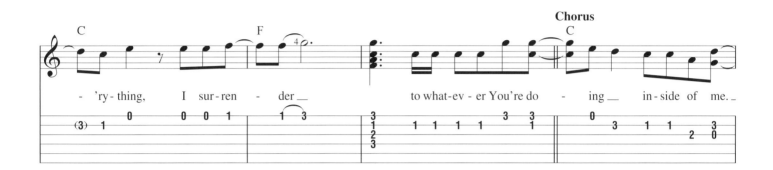

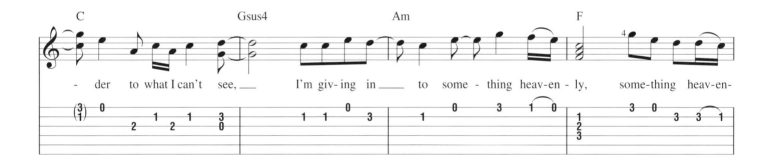

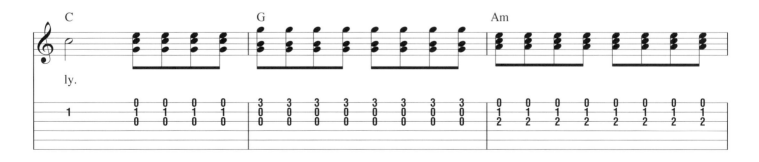

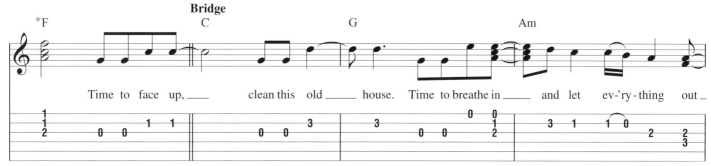

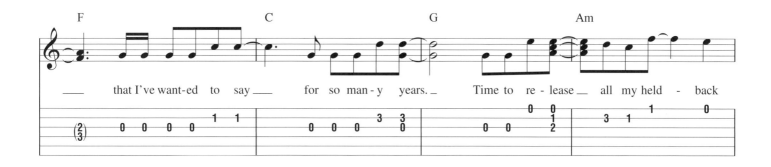

*Let chords ring, next 9 meas.

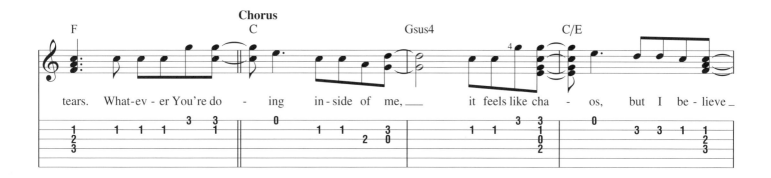

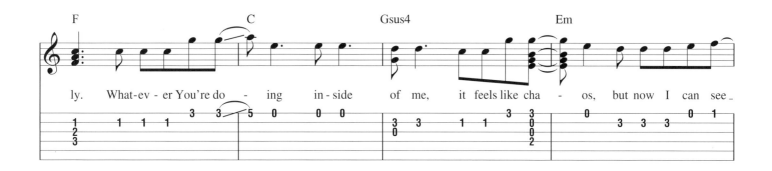

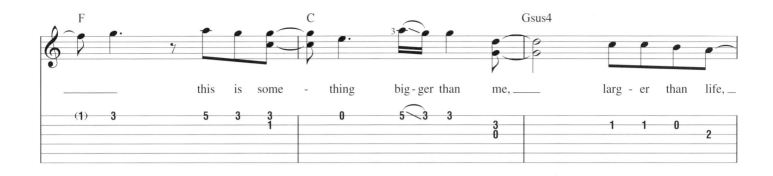

this is some - thing big-ger than me, _____ larg - er than life, _____

Outro

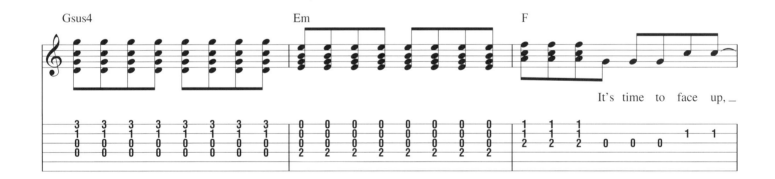

_____ some - thing heav-en - ly, some-thing heav-en - ly.

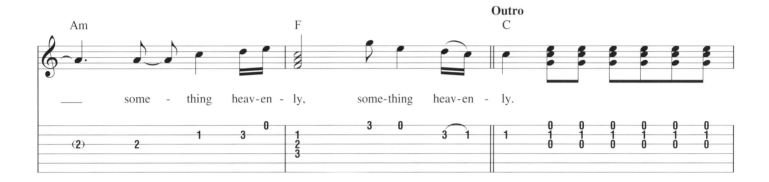

It's time to face up, _____

_____ clean this old _____ house. Time to breathe in _____ and let ev-'ry-thing out. _____

*Let chords ring till end.

The Word Is Alive

Words and Music by Mark Hall and Steven Curtis Chapman

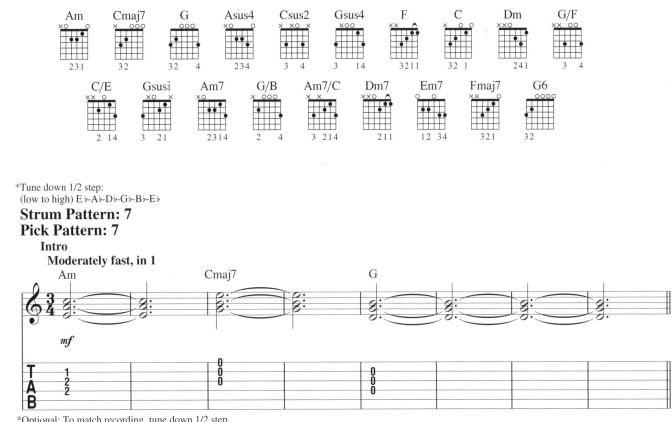

*Tune down 1/2 step:
(low to high) E♭-A♭-D♭-G♭-B♭-E♭

Strum Pattern: 7
Pick Pattern: 7

Intro
Moderately fast, in 1

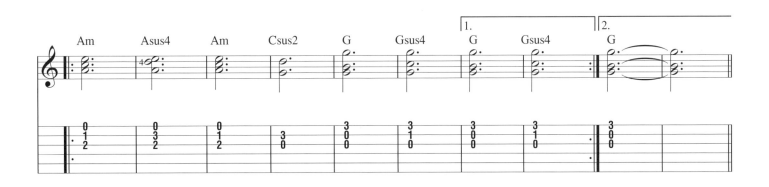

*Optional: To match recording, tune down 1/2 step.

Verse

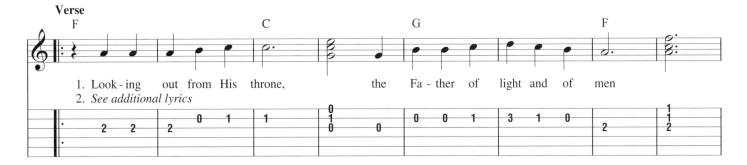

1. Look-ing out from His throne, the Fa-ther of light and of men
2. *See additional lyrics*

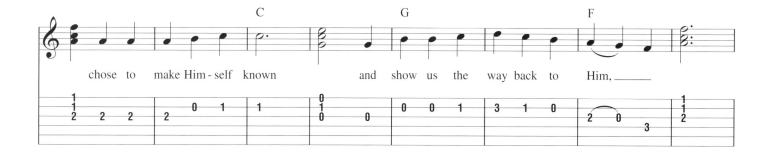

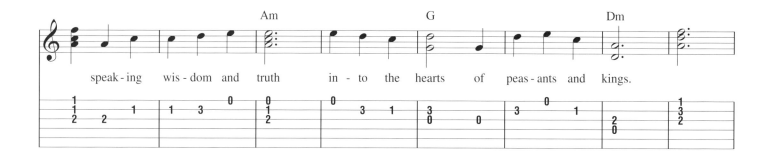

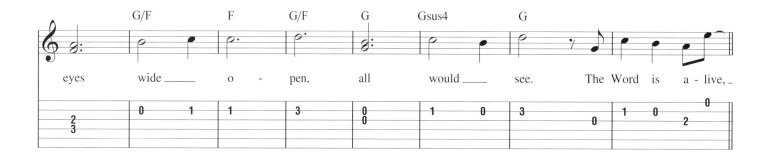

𝄋 Chorus

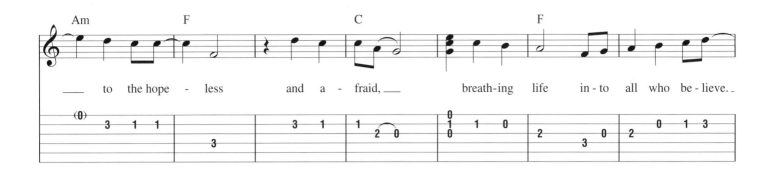

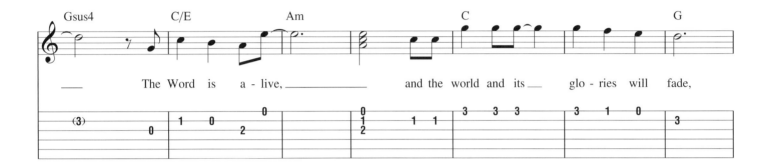

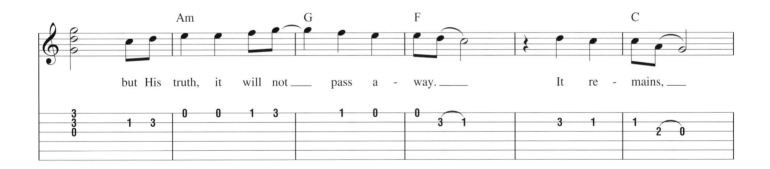

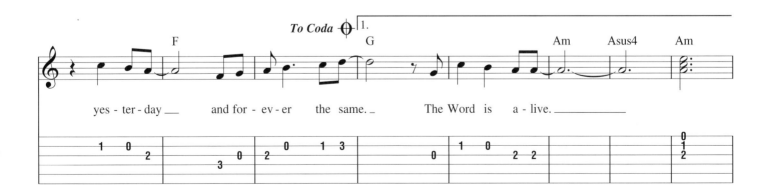

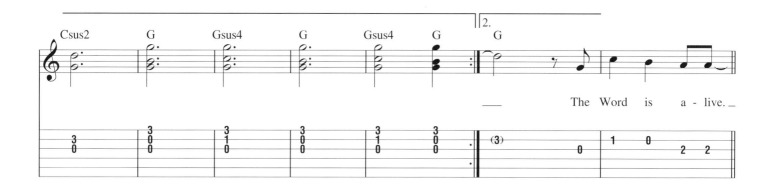

The Word is a-live.

Bridge

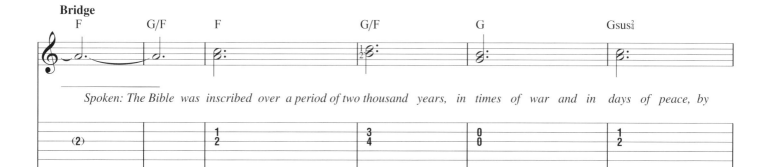

Spoken: The Bible was inscribed over a period of two thousand years, in times of war and in days of peace, by

kings, physicians, tax collectors, farmers, fishermen, singers and shepherds. The marvel is that a library so perfectly

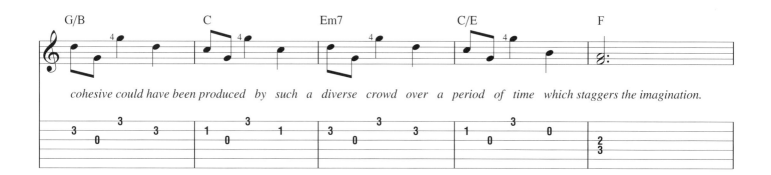

cohesive could have been produced by such a diverse crowd over a period of time which staggers the imagination.

Jesus is its grand subject, our good its design, and the glory of God is its end.

The Word is a - live. _

Coda

Outro

_ The Word is a - live. _____

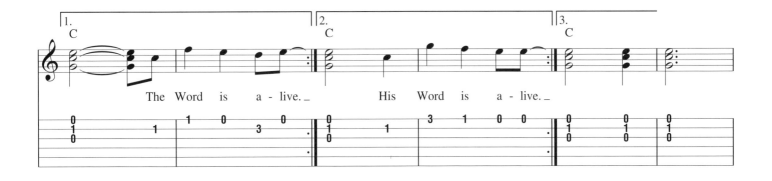

1.
The Word is a - live. _

2.
His Word is a - live. _

3.

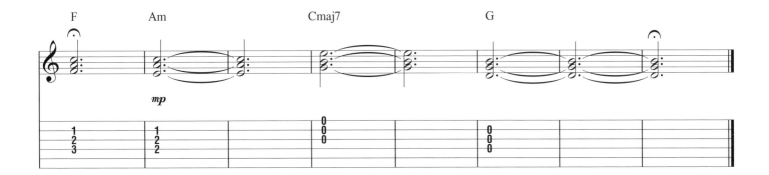

mp

Additional Lyrics

2. Simple strokes on a page, eternity's secrets revealed,
   Carried on from age to age. It speaks the truth to us even still.
   And as the rain falls from heaven, feeds the earth before it returns,
   Lord, let Your Word fall on us and bring forth the fruit you deserve.
   With eyes wide open, let us see.

Wholly Yours

Words and Music by David Crowder

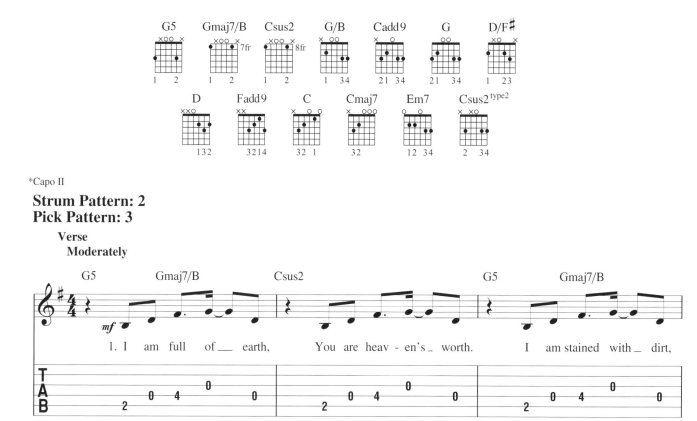

*Capo II

Strum Pattern: 2
Pick Pattern: 3

Verse
Moderately

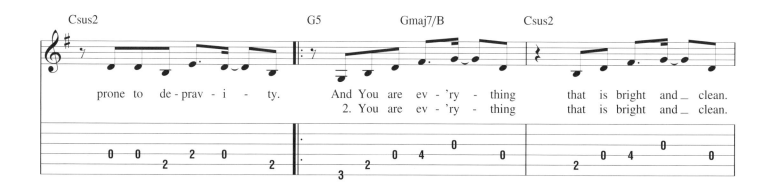

1. I am full of __ earth, You are heav-en's __ worth. I am stained with __ dirt,

*Optional: To match recording, place capo at 2nd fret.

prone to de-prav-i-ty. And You are ev-'ry-thing that is bright and __ clean.
2. You are ev-'ry-thing that is bright and __ clean.

The an-to-nym of __ me, You are di-vin-i-ty. What a cer-tain side __ of
And You're cov-er-ing me with Your maj-es-ty. And the tru-est sign __ of

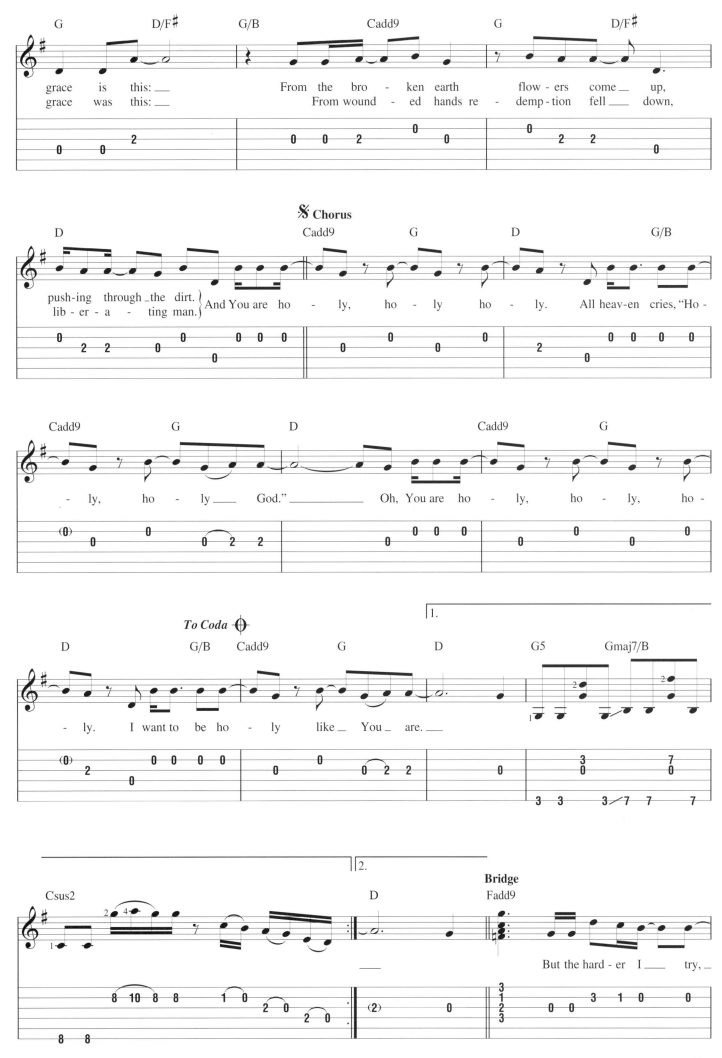

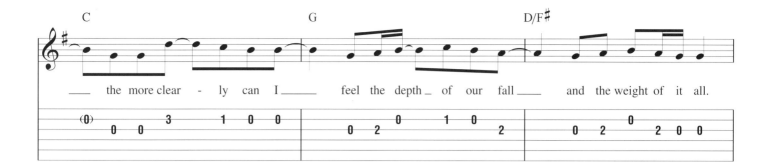

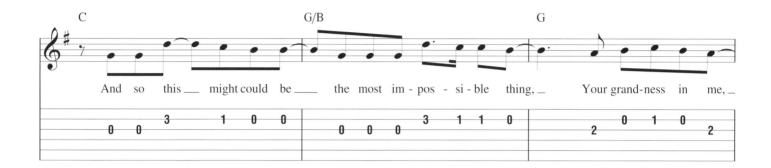

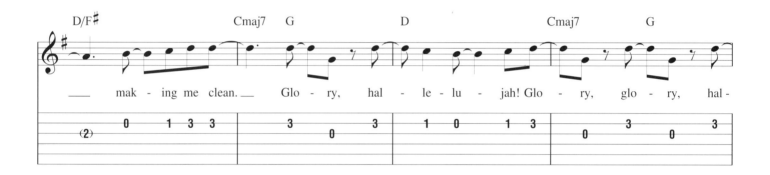

D.S. al Coda

⊕ **Coda**

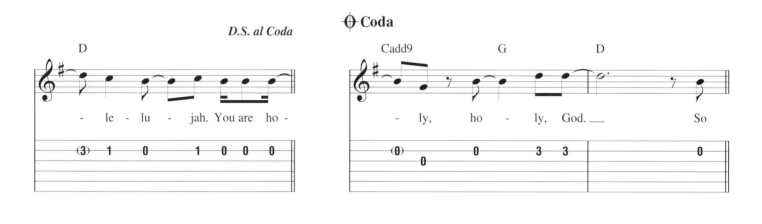

Pre-Chorus

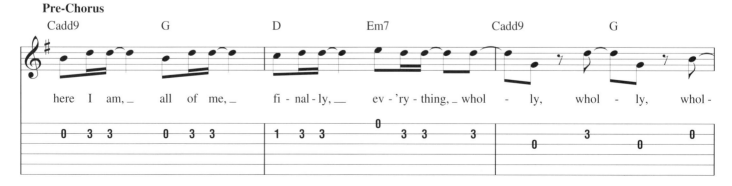

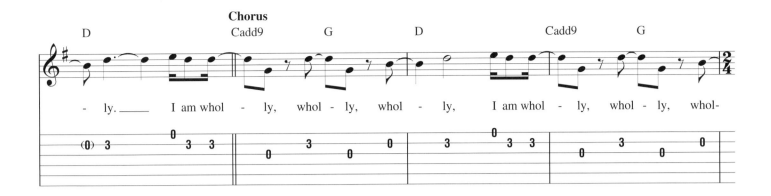

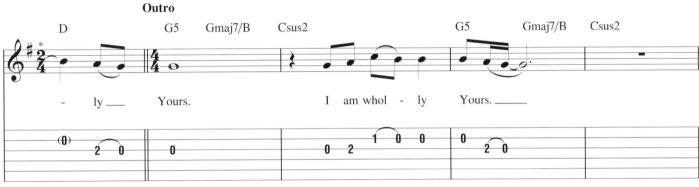

*Use Pattern 10

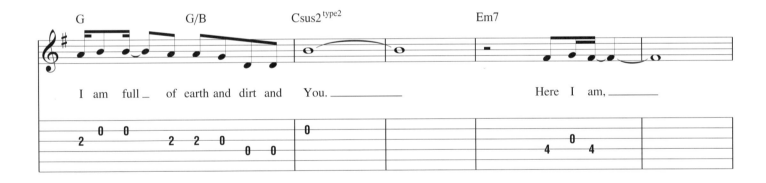

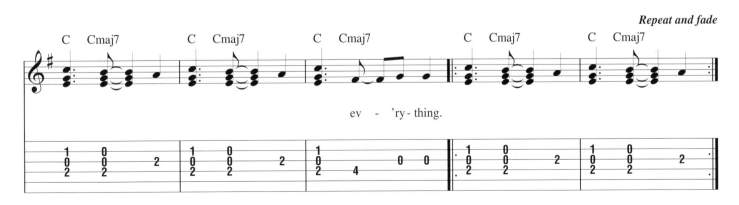

You Already Take Me There

Words and Music by Jonathan Foreman and Tim Foreman

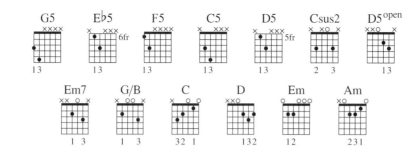

Intro
Moderate Rock

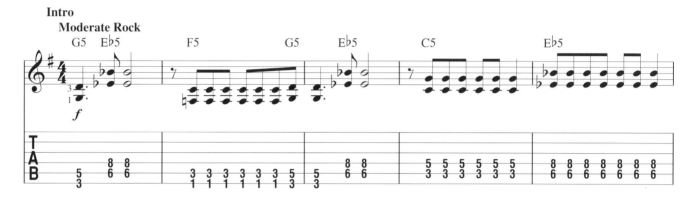

Strum Pattern: 5
Verse

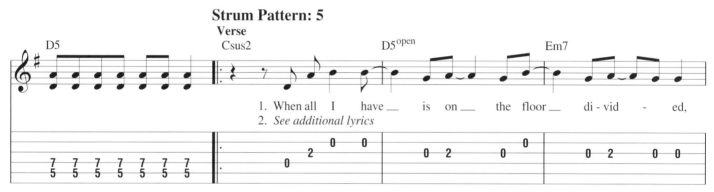

1. When all I have __ is on __ the floor __ di - vid - ed,
2. *See additional lyrics*

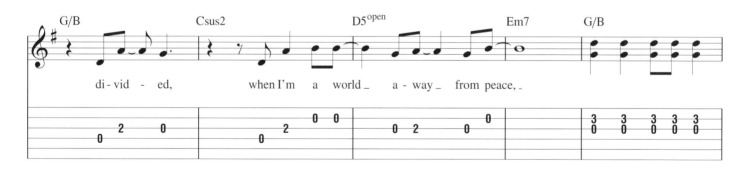

di - vid - ed, when I'm a world __ a - way __ from peace,

be - hind Your eyes __ is where __ I know I'll find __ it, I'll find __ it.

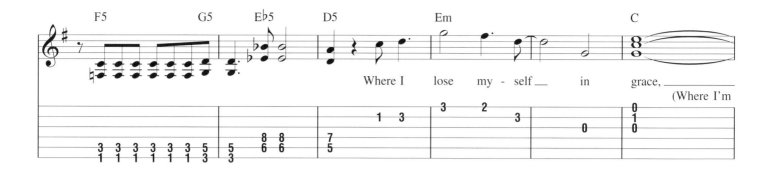

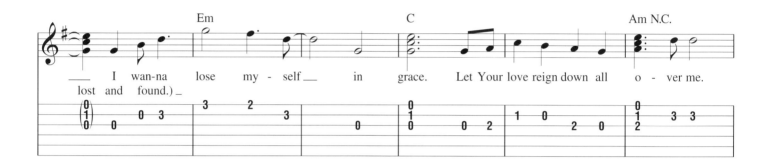

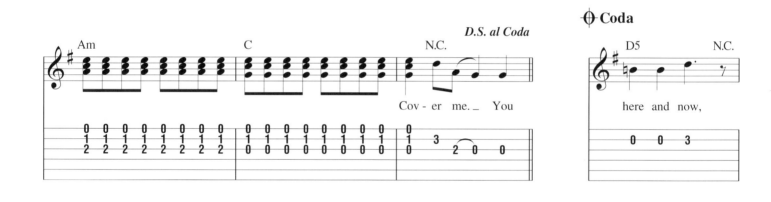

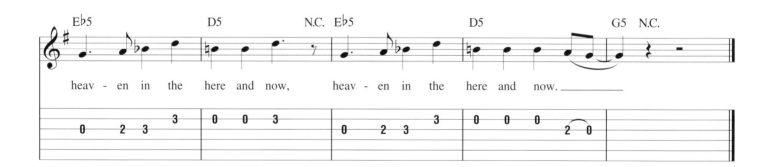

Additional Lyrics

2. (When) I'm a broken-hearted man complacent and tired,
   When I've been knocked out of the race,
   I've been a fool for long enough to fight it, to fight it.
   It's in Your arms I find my place.

EASY GUITAR WITH NOTES & TAB

This series features simplified arrangements with notes, tab, chord charts, and strum and pick patterns.

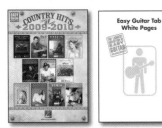

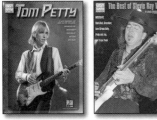

MIXED FOLIOS

00702287	Acoustic	$14.99
00702002	Acoustic Rock Hits for Easy Guitar	$12.95
00702166	All-Time Best Guitar Collection	$19.99
00699665	Beatles Best	$12.95
00702232	Best Acoustic Songs for Easy Guitar	$12.99
00702233	Best Hard Rock Songs	$14.99
00698978	Big Christmas Collection	$16.95
00702115	Blues Classics	$10.95
00385020	Broadway Songs for Kids	$9.95
00702237	Christian Acoustic Favorites	$12.95
00702149	Children's Christian Songbook	$7.95
00702028	Christmas Classics	$7.95
00702185	Christmas Hits	$9.95
00702016	Classic Blues for Easy Guitar	$12.95
00702141	Classic Rock	$8.95
00702203	CMT's 100 Greatest Country Songs	$27.95
00702170	Contemporary Christian Christmas	$9.95
00702006	Contemporary Christian Favorites	$9.95
00702065	Contemporary Women of Country	$9.95
00702239	Country Classics for Easy Guitar	$19.99
00702282	Country Hits of 2009-2010	$14.99
00702240	Country Hits of 2007-2008	$12.95
00702225	Country Hits of '06-'07	$12.95
00702085	Disney Movie Hits	$12.95
00702257	Easy Acoustic Guitar Songs	$14.99
00702280	Easy Guitar Tab White Pages	$29.99
00702212	Essential Christmas	$9.95
00702041	Favorite Hymns for Easy Guitar	$9.95
00702281	4 Chord Rock	$9.99
00702286	Glee	$16.99
00702174	God Bless America® & Other Songs for a Better Nation	$8.95
00699374	Gospel Favorites	$14.95
00702160	The Great American Country Songbook	$14.95
00702050	Great Classical Themes for Easy Guitar	$6.95
00702131	Great Country Hits of the '90s	$8.95
00702116	Greatest Hymns for Guitar	$8.95
00702130	The Groovy Years	$9.95
00702184	Guitar Instrumentals	$9.95

00702231	High School Musical for Easy Guitar	$12.95
00702241	High School Musical 2	$12.95
00702046	Hits of the '70s for Easy Guitar	$8.95
00702032	International Songs for Easy Guitar	$12.95
00702275	Jazz Favorites for Easy Guitar	$14.99
00702051	Jock Rock for Easy Guitar	$9.95
00702162	Jumbo Easy Guitar Songbook	$19.95
00702112	Latin Favorites	$9.95
00702258	Legends of Rock	$14.99
00702138	Mellow Rock Hits	$10.95
00702261	Modern Worship Hits	$14.99
00702147	Motown's Greatest Hits	$9.95
00702189	MTV's 100 Greatest Pop Songs	$24.95
00702272	1950s Rock	$14.99
00702271	1960s Rock	$14.99
00702270	1970s Rock	$14.99
00702269	1980s Rock	$14.99
00702268	1990s Rock	$14.99
00702187	Selections from O Brother Where Art Thou?	$12.95
00702178	100 Songs for Kids	$12.95
00702125	Praise and Worship for Guitar	$9.95
00702155	Rock Hits for Guitar	$9.95
00702242	Rock Band	$19.95
00702256	Rock Band 2	$19.99
00702128	Rockin' Down the Highway	$9.95
00702110	The Sound of Music	$9.99
00702285	Southern Rock Hits	$12.99
00702124	Today's Christian Rock – 2nd Edition	$9.95
00702220	Today's Country Hits	$9.95
00702198	Today's Hits for Guitar	$9.95
00702217	Top Christian Hits	$12.95
00702235	Top Christian Hits of '07-'08	$14.95
00702284	Top Hits of 2010	$14.99
00702246	Top Hits of 2008	$12.95
00702206	Very Best of Rock	$9.95
00702255	VH1's 100 Greatest Hard Rock Songs	$27.99
00702175	VH1's 100 Greatest Songs of Rock and Roll	$24.95
00702253	Wicked	$12.99
00702192	Worship Favorites	$9.95

ARTIST COLLECTIONS

00702267	AC/DC for Easy Guitar	$14.99
00702001	Best of Aerosmith	$16.95
00702040	Best of the Allman Brothers	$14.99
00702169	Best of The Beach Boys	$10.95
00702201	The Essential Black Sabbath	$12.95
00702140	Best of Brooks & Dunn	$10.95
00702095	Best of Mariah Carey	$12.95
00702043	Best of Johnny Cash	$14.99
00702033	Best of Steven Curtis Chapman	$14.95
00702263	Best of Casting Crowns	$12.99
00702090	Eric Clapton's Best	$10.95
00702086	Eric Clapton – from the Album Unplugged	$10.95
00702202	The Essential Eric Clapton	$12.95
00702250	blink-182 – Greatest Hits	$12.99
00702053	Best of Patsy Cline	$10.95
00702229	The Very Best of Creedence Clearwater Revival	$12.95
00702145	Best of Jim Croce	$10.95
00702278	Crosby, Stills & Nash	$12.99
00702219	David Crowder*Band Collection	$12.95
00702122	The Doors for Easy Guitar	$12.99
00702276	Fleetwood Mac – Easy Guitar Collection	$12.99
00702099	Best of Amy Grant	$9.95
00702190	Best of Pat Green	$19.95
00702136	Best of Merle Haggard	$12.99
00702243	Hannah Montana	$14.95
00702244	Hannah Montana 2/Meet Miley Cyrus	$16.95
00702227	Jimi Hendrix – Smash Hits	$14.99
00702236	Best of Antonio Carlos Jobim	$12.95
00702087	Best of Billy Joel	$10.95
00702245	Elton John – Greatest Hits 1970-2002	$14.99
00702204	Robert Johnson	$9.95
00702277	Best of Jonas Brothers	$14.99
00702234	Selections from Toby Keith – 35 Biggest Hits	$12.95
00702003	Kiss	$9.95
00702193	Best of Jennifer Knapp	$12.95

00702097	John Lennon – Imagine	$9.95
00702216	Lynyrd Skynyrd	$15.99
00702182	The Essential Bob Marley	$12.95
00702248	Paul McCartney – All the Best	$14.99
00702129	Songs of Sarah McLachlan	$12.95
02501316	Metallica – Death Magnetic	$15.95
00702209	Steve Miller Band – Young Hearts (Greatest Hits)	$12.95
00702096	Best of Nirvana	$14.95
00702211	The Offspring – Greatest Hits	$12.95
00702030	Best of Roy Orbison	$12.95
00702144	Best of Ozzy Osbourne	$12.95
00702279	Tom Petty	$12.99
00702139	Elvis Country Favorites	$9.95
00699415	Best of Queen for Guitar	$14.99
00702208	Red Hot Chili Peppers – Greatest Hits	$12.95
00702093	Rolling Stones Collection	$17.95
00702092	Best of the Rolling Stones	$14.99
00702196	Best of Bob Seger	$12.95
00702252	Frank Sinatra – Nothing But the Best	$12.99
00702010	Best of Rod Stewart	$14.95
00702150	Best of Sting	$12.95
00702049	Best of George Strait	$12.95
00702259	Taylor Swift for Easy Guitar	$12.99
00702290	Taylor Swift – Speak Now	$12.99
00702223	Chris Tomlin – Arriving	$12.95
00702262	Chris Tomlin Collection	$14.99
00702226	Chris Tomlin – See the Morning	$12.95
00702132	Shania Twain – Greatest Hits	$10.95
00702108	Best of Stevie Ray Vaughan	$10.95
00702123	Best of Hank Williams	$12.99
00702111	Stevie Wonder – Guitar Collection	$9.95
00702228	Neil Young – Greatest Hits	$12.99
00702188	Essential ZZ Top	$10.95

0211

CONTEMPORARY CHRISTIAN

Guitar Recorded Versions® are note-for-note transcriptions of guitar music taken directly off recordings. Every book contains notes and tablature.

AUTHENTIC TRANSCRIPTIONS
WITH NOTES AND TABLATURE

FLYLEAF

Our matching folio to the debut release from this Christian alt rock/metal quintet hailing from Texas features notes and tab for all 11 tracks, including: Cassie • Fully Alive • I'm So Sick • I'm Sorry • Red Sam • So I Thought • There for You • and more.
00690870 . . . . $19.95

BEST OF PHIL KEAGGY

Multi-Dove winner and Grammy nominee Phil Keaggy is one of the world's finest guitarists. Here are transcriptions of 15 of his best in standard notation and tab: Arrow • Cajon Pass • County Down • Doin' Nothin' • Legacy • Metamorphosis • Nellie's Tune • Pilgrim's Flight • Salvation Army Band • What a Day • and more.
00690911 . . . . $24.99

KUTLESS – HEARTS OF THE INNOCENT

Note-for-note guitar transcriptions with tab for all 12 tracks off this alt-Christian rock band's fourth album: Beyond the Surface • Changing World • Hearts of the Innocent • Legacy • Promise of a Lifetime • Shut Me Out • Smile • and more.
00690861 . . . . $19.95

HAWK NELSON – LETTERS TO THE PRESIDENT

All 14 songs from the debut album by these Christian punk rockers. Includes: California • From Underneath • Letters to the President • Recess • Right Here • First Time • Like a Racecar • Long and Lonely Road • Take Me • and more.
00690778 . . . . $19.95

RELIENT K – FIVE SCORE AND SEVEN YEARS AGO

Hailed as "a masterpiece of punk-based power pop," this Christian band's fifth album features 14 songs, including: Bite My Tongue • Deathbed • Faking My Own Suicide • I Need You • Must Have Done Something Right • Up and Up • and more.
00690900 . . . . $19.95

RELIENT K – MMHMM

14 transcriptions from the latest release by these Christian punk rockers. Features: High of 75 • Let It All Out • Life After Death and Taxes (Failure II) • My Girl's Ex-Boyfriend • The One I'm Waiting For • When I Go Down • Which to Bury; Us or the Hatchet? • and more.
00690779 . . . . $19.95

RELIENT K – TWO LEFTS DON'T MAKE A RIGHT ... BUT THREE DO

14 tunes from the 2003 crossover release including their big hit "Chapstick, Chapped Lips and Things like Chemistry" and: College Kids • Falling Out • Forward Motion • Gibberish • Hoopes I Did It Again • I Am Understood • Jefferson Aero Plane • Mood Ring • Overthinking • Trademark • and more.
00690643 . . . . $19.95

SWITCHFOOT – THE BEAUTIFUL LETDOWN

All 11 songs from the 2003 release by these Dove Award-winning alt CCM rockers: Adding to the Noise • Ammunition • Beautiful Letdown • Dare You to Move • Gone • Meant to Live • More Than Fine • On Fire • Redemption • This Is Your Life • 24.
00690767 . . . . $19.95

Get Better at Guitar

...with these Great Guitar Instruction Books from Hal Leonard!

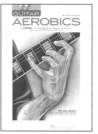

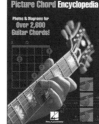

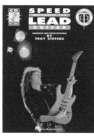
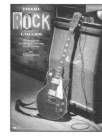